PITCHING AROUND FIDEL

PITCHING AROUND FIDEL

★

A Journey into the
Heart of Cuban Sports

S. L. Price

Photographs by Victor Baldizon

THE ECCO PRESS
An Imprint of HarperCollins*Publishers*

FIRST EDITION

Designed by William Ruoto

Printed on acid-free paper

Library of Congress Cataloging-in-Publication Data

Price, S. L. (Scott L.), 1962–
    Pitching around Fidel: a journey into the heart of Cuban sports / S. L. Price—1st ed.
      p. cm.
    ISBN 0–06–019660–2
      1. Sports—Cuba.   2. Sports and state—Cuba.   I. Title.

    GV592.C82 P75   2000
    796'.097291—dc21   00-020523

00 01 02 03 04 ❖/RRD 10 9 8 7 6 5 4 3 2 1

For Fran

PROLOGUE

The revolt never came. War never broke out. The dictator lives on, beard thin and gray, and his enemies have lost their country and grown rich and sit in exile, watching the time, fighting the exile's impotent war of words. There are no conventional battles, so there are no conventional victories. Winning comes in increments, over-hyped and vague: An air force pilot defects in a jet, returns to pick up his family on a quiet road, and escapes again. The American trade embargo is made even more severe. Rumors fly that the dictator is sick and will soon be dead, and that makes people feel good until he keeps breathing. A baseball player arrives in Miami.

This is March 17, 1998—St. Patrick's Day everywhere but the Bolero Room of Victor's Cafe, an exile haunt in Miami distinguished by its man-sized replica of the Statue of Liberty and the city's most relentless air-conditioning unit. The place is packed with bodies. Power cables writhe across the carpet. A side door opens every few seconds, revealing a parking lot jammed with humming television trucks and, in theory anyway, inviting in a punishing wave of late-afternoon humidity. But the temperature doesn't rise. The air-conditioning pumps so heroically that it blocks the outside air like an invisible wall, that people shiver, that you could easily imagine someone in charge equating the fact of controlled cold with the idea of success far more easily than, say, an abstraction like the Statue of Liberty, and decreeing that the thermostat will, come hell or Fidel Castro, never rise above sixty-five degrees.

This is a good day. In just a few minutes, there will be a press conference for Orlando "El Duque" Hernandez, the best pitcher in modern Cuban history or, to put a finer point on it, the best player at the most important position in Cuba's most beloved sport since the revolution swept Castro to power in 1959. Banned in his homeland, now Hernandez has come to Miami by way of Costa Rica by way of a small island in the Caribbean by way of a creaky twenty-foot motorboat that, on the day after Christmas, carried him and seven others from the coastal town of Caibarien. Now he has agreed to a four-year, $6.6 million contract with the New York Yankees, and on his way to signing it in Tampa he has stopped here to celebrate his new life. It is the right move. Unlike the "objective" Anglo media, Miami's Cuban press never apologizes for its role as exile mouthpiece, and today's event gives the first impression of a party. Smoke curls to the ceiling. Faces chatter and grin.

I am here for no good reason. The magazine I work for wants nothing about today's gathering. Yet I have come anyway out of curiosity, out of wanting to see a good story end, because in my earlier stints on the island I'd spoken often to El Duque—the Duke— and seen him go from a young star thrilled with his craft to a sour pitcher sucking a cigarette in a ratty Havana dugout, waiting for the rain and his growing desperation to pass. He hadn't been banned the last time we talked, but his younger half-brother, pitcher Livan Hernandez, had already bolted to the United States and a million-aire's life with the Florida Marlins. "I won't desert," El Duque kept insisting on a cool evening in the last days of 1995. All athletes in Cuba say this for public consumption, but he spoke then with an older man's candor, openly criticizing the regime yet discarding the option of leaving his wife and daughters. He'd had so many easy chances to defect—to walk into a waiting car like his brother did in Mexico, to slip out of a hotel in America—that his statement, "I play for love, not money," felt like the truth.

Yet now, at an age drifting somewhere between twenty-nine and thirty-four, El Duque had suddenly taken the Cuban's final gamble. He had walked into the sea. He had been driven from his life. I've come for that, too—the spectacle of a man pushed too far.

Soon after I arrive, I know I am wrong. There's something in the air beyond the usual exile elation, an undercurrent of fear that I can't quite figure until a cameraman takes me aside. Word has spread: Four more Cuban baseball players and a coach are feared lost at sea. It has been seven days since the men pushed off, and everyone here knows the odds. It's estimated that some 40 percent of all rafters—balseros—who leave Cuba are never heard from again, victims of a badgering sun, thirst, sharks, thirty-foot swells, and unpredictable tides. Their families have grown desperate with uncertainty, I'm told, and as the news hops from face to face here it leaves a residue of pain—no, a fear of pain, a dread of the coming hours that seem fated to end with bodies, debris, silence. Into this room now walks El Duque Hernandez with his agent, Joe Cubas; his new girlfriend; his uncle. They step to a microphone, showered by applause. Strobe lights blaze to life.

Duque begins to talk. He is wearing a white shirt, buttoned to the neck, and at first he can't stop crying. He rubs his palms on his pants; he has a brilliant smile, a charismatic gravity, and as he gathers himself together everyone leans forward. The room seems to shrink. He speaks of the liberty he has found here, of the nights he and the seven other rafters huddled together while stranded on Anguilla Cay, trying to stay warm, eating conch out of the shell, staving off panic. "The message to the Cuban athlete is: Try to learn about freedom, but don't take the risks I did," Duque says. Someone asks if he feels he is trading one dictator for another in his new boss, George Steinbrenner, and while Duque leans over to ask a friend, "Who's Steinbrenner?" Cubas steps up. "There is no comparison," he declares. "Steinbrenner is a businessman. Fidel is a traitor."

A TV reporter, face thickened with makeup, stands in the back of the room and begins shouting his report into the camera. People yell, "Sit down! Shut up!" but he doesn't stop. Duque goes on, speaking of the degraded condition of Cuban baseball, of how the national team had been supplied with just six bats and six gloves and no luggage. "Conditions are very bad," he says. A reporter asks if he knows about the five new rafters, and Duque stutters, "I'm just hearing of this for the first time . . ." when anarchy hits. The side door has burst open. Shouts fill the room, grow louder: It is his brother, Livan, pushing through the reporters and cables and chairs. The two men have not seen each other for two and a half years. Duque's mouth opens, but before he can speak Livan grabs him, takes his face in his hands, kisses his brother's bald head. He tells him, "Hold on, don't cry."

Duque rubs his face, sobbing, shaking as tears roll down his cheeks. "I can't help it," he says.

Livan looks sleek. There is a diamond the size of a pinkie nail in his left ear, a pair of tiny pink sunglasses on his face, a baggy black shirt on his back emblazoned with scarlet Japanese lettering. When he first came to the States in 1995, Livan unpacked a dancing fastball and a reputation as the cream of Cuba's next generation of pitchers. He was also little more than a child, a twenty-year-old, as Duque once said, mostly interested in "blond girls and lollipops." Isolated and surrounded by suspect characters, Livan foundered in the Marlins organization, drowning his loneliness in fast-food runs. His weight ballooned, adding more girth to a body already leaning toward Baby Huey proportions. But after a two-year stall, Livan finally took his career seriously, cut weight, and learned how to pitch. He won his first nine decisions in 1997, struck out fifteen Atlanta Braves in the signature game of the National League championship, won two World Series games, and was named Most Valuable Player. "I love you Miami!" Livan shouted after the seventh game, hoisting the trophy above his head. Now the man who taught him how to play, the last face he saw before defecting, stands beside him.

The two men share only a vague resemblance. Duque is rangier, leaner. He hangs his head like someone still trying to disappear. His eyes have gone glassy, wearied by two years of charting every angle of survival and escape, by a lack of sleep and nerves gone raw. Once Duque's brother defected, the Cuban government treated its most accomplished pitcher like a pariah. Duque was left off the 1996 Cuban Olympic team that won gold in Atlanta, and then, on October 29, 1996, found himself banned from baseball for life for consorting with convicted Cubas associate Juan Ignacio Hernandez Nodar. Barred even from practicing on an official ball field, Duke saw his monthly stipend slashed from 271 Cuban pesos—$9—to 148. His marriage of eleven years crumbled. He was allowed to work only at Havana's Psychiatric Hospital, where he'd mostly sit under a tree watching mental patients loll in the grass. Sometimes he passed out snacks.

"I'm 100 percent happy," Livan says to the crowd. "They did an injustice to him in Cuba, an injustice they would've done to me if I'd stayed. So my first advice is . . . Don't eat too much McDonald's!"

The audience buckles with laughter. A raucous vibe overtakes the room; it's as if everyone abruptly understands what they are seeing: Here, suddenly, are two of Castro's most valuable jewels, shining and free. When someone asks Duque what he thinks of Fidel, he says, "We're wasting our breath," and there is wild applause. Someone asks how he feels about seeing his brother, and he says, "Words

can't explain it. Only the heart can." The lost rafters have been forgotten; questions fly as reporters look to milk the moment dry. Why
not? This is the best kind of TV sports story, beyond fun-and-games
and driving the audience to an inescapably upbeat conclusion: Two
brothers are reunited, and this time they are rich. Distilled to its
essence, the modern.Cuban myth is the old American Dream—make
it to Miami, and you've got it made. There's little room in the long,
transnational saga for cynical tales about the dark side of success,
which is why all defector stories have the feel of the tawdry telenov-
elas that dominate Latin TV. It is why no one feels a pang of appre-
hension in the Bolero Room when Duque's emotion cedes ground
to a perfectly realized moment of postmodern plasticity, and he
announces with his final words, "If there's time on my vacation to
make a movie, I will."

But by then, I've already lost interest. By then, what was briefly a
Miami story of exile triumph has already begun to evolve into a New
York story, which means agents and networks and beeper numbers;
Steinbrenner, Yankee Stadium, rights fees and free agency and
money. It means an endless, sporty replay of political narrative at its
most black and white—Freedom defeats Repression!—and I've
known for a long time that nothing concerning Cuba is as simple as
that. Whatever drew me here today has little to do with where Livan
and Duque Hernandez go next.

No, I have come most of all because I am confused. I possess fair
intelligence and a judgmental bent, yet I spent the 1990s unable to
reconcile two strong and utterly opposed ideas. The first, never
more powerfully demonstrated than on this day, holds that the
great Cuban sports machine—instrument of totalitarian control
and propaganda—is rightfully cracking apart. The second holds
that Castro's regime not only has produced an unparalleled athletic
system, but has also fostered a sports purist's delight, an American

ideal, no less, for Cuba is one of the last places where athletes play for little more than love of the game. Mine is an unseemly standoff between head and heart, a logical mess: I applaud Duque's escape, but I'd rather see him pitch in Havana.

Knowing the regime's cruelties has done nothing to dampen my love for the sports scene Castro has created. On the contrary. Each defection has caused me to become only more mesmerized by the championships Cuba keeps winning, more thrilled to sit in shabby ballparks surrounded by rum-soaked fanatics, more intrigued by both the apolitical players who chase greatness while snarled in the system and the true believers who insist they will never leave. For Cuba is sport's ultimate high-wire act. No athlete in the world today plays in a more politically charged and pressurized atmosphere. None is asked to regularly negotiate a trail so scattered with social and financial obstacles. None is held to such a high standard of excellence while grappling with the issues of loyalty, family, patriotism, perhaps even life and death. Too, no athlete in the world lives in a place more dedicated to discovering, nurturing, and celebrating great athletes. If you are a dirt-poor, ten-year-old phenom buried somewhere in Cuba's deepest backwater, you will be found. You will win. You will be a national hero.

I know what everyone knows: Cuba is the worst place on the globe to be an athlete today. But I'm sure I know something even stranger. It is also the best.

Such a standoff cannot last. Watching El Duque and Livan, I know that the home they've left forever is unique and dying, and offering in its struggle a quality far more noble than mere contradiction. I know that somewhere between head and heart lies something approaching truth, and I'd better get there before it's too late.

Four days later, I am one of two passengers on a midnight plane. The engines scream as we land in the heart of the country.

PART ONE

CHAPTER 1

The Cadiz prefect informed me that at eight o'clock the follow-
ing morning I would be sent to Havana, for which, by happy
chance, a steamer was sailing that day.
  "Where?"
  "To Havana."
  "Ha-van-a?"
  "Havana."
  "I won't go voluntarily."

  —LEON TROTSKY, *My Life*

I am George Washington. I am Abe Lincoln and Alexander Hamil-
ton and Andrew Jackson and, if things work out perfectly, I just
might end up being Benjamin Franklin. I know: Little Daddy is trying to be nice. He laughs at my jokes and gets us beer and, yes, earlier we even had one of those serendipitous moments that can spark
a warm friendship. But I'm an American and Little Daddy needs
dollars like everyone else in Cuba, so in the moments when I look
away at some sixteen-year-old hooker or take a pull at my
Buchanero, I can feel him turn off the charm long enough to cut me
up into currency. Five dollars? Twenty dollars? Maybe I'm good for
more drinks, a shirt, a dinner, even straight cash. I try not to mind.
After all, we sit right at the heart of the Havana hustle, in a bar

called Castillo de Farnes that, at this time of night, serves as a hub for every kind of dealer, pimp, prostitute, gigolo, and beggar. And I am money.

Little Daddy is a baseball fanatic. Every day, with about a hundred other men, he makes his way to the shade of Havana's Parque Central to take part in La Pena, which is the semiofficial name for what was once called La Esquina Caliente—the Hot Corner—and what is no more than a bunch of red-faced aficionados standing in front of park benches for hours on end, yelling at one another about Cuban baseball, about who is great and who sucks, about those who left the country and those who stayed behind. Little Daddy keeps detailed statistics, watches games every night. But at forty-five he is also younger than most of the men at La Pena, with the face of a beefed-up Shaft, and he has six kids and no job. "My wife and I, we fuck, fuck, fuck," he says, defeated. "It's loco."

We sit at a table near the door, watching the parade of *jineteras*— literally, lady jockeys—clop by in chunky high heels and stunningly similar pink, lime, or orange Day-Glo spandex outfits. They are very thin or very fat. They walk slow to the bar and ask for water, rake the crowd with dead eyes, wait for someone to start talking.

"It's good for the heart."

I look over and Little Daddy is nodding, smiling, tapping his chest. First I think he's talking about sex, but after an instant I realize he means our little stroke of luck. Earlier in the day, we'd been to Havana's grand ballpark, Estadio Latinoamericano, to see Havana's Metropolitanos team play its final regular season doubleheader against Matanzas. The place held no more than three hundred people, and as the second game began we were heading for the street when I saw something I'd never seen before on a baseball field. A player rolled a bunt so gently, so perfectly down the third base line that no one could be sure it wouldn't go foul; and he was so fast that by the time the mesmerized fielders snapped to, he stood on second with a clean double.

"He's tied the record!" Little Daddy yelled then, grabbing my arm, and so it was: Seventeen-year-old center fielder Yasser Gomez, the youngest Cuban big leaguer since the great Omar Linares broke in as a sixteen-year-old in 1985, had tied the twenty-nine-year-old National Series record for hits by a rookie. My first ball game this year, and I stumble on gold. So Little Daddy spent the rest of the afternoon finding out where Gomez lives, and by 9:30 P.M. we were choking on fumes in the back of a '46 Dodge gypsy cab on the way to a small apartment on Calle Espada.

We knocked on the door, unexpected. Yasser was on the couch, watching TV with his attractively bored girlfriend; his shirtless, cannonball-gutted father strode about, beer in hand. A poster of then-Dodgers catcher Mike Piazza hung on the living room wall. I tried to apologize for the late hour, but Little Daddy and Yasser's mother, Lola, just gasped at each other, eyes wide. As a teenager, Little Daddy had dated Lola's sister, been close friends with Lola, and the two hadn't seen either since. We're in. The family would love to talk. We made plans and left.

"I knew her thirty years ago!" Little Daddy sighs now. "Can you believe it?" We shake our heads and drink in tandem, marveling at the idea of ever being teenagers. It's our one unique experience, wholly devoid of commerce, and I sense a breakthrough. I try to get crafty. Women flow around us like river around stones, so I say things seem worse since I was here two years ago: more hookers in the street. More in this room, notably.

For it was on the early morning of January 9, 1959, in the dim morning hours after rolling into Havana and giving his first major speech in the capital as Maximum Leader—a white dove landed on his shoulder then, sending an otherworldly shiver through millions—that a thirty-two-year-old Castro came to the Castillo de Farnes with his brother Raul and Che Guevara. He had eaten many meals here as a law student, no doubt haranguing his companeros about the Batista era's corruption and prostitution, vowing that things would be different if only he were in charge. And now he had won. A picture of the men on that triumphant morning hangs in a hallway here, but it has none of the calculated romance found in the work of revolutionary photographers Raul Corrales or Alberto Korda. No, this is a portrait of 4:45 A.M., of men gone pale and blasted by fatigue and looking as if they'd just begun to understand that killing a regime is nothing compared to building one.

I sagely tell Little Daddy that this epidemic of prostitution is bad for Cuba. He couldn't agree more.

"I have two daughters, ten and eight," he says. "I keep them very close, protect them. All these girls are smoking marijuana, doing cocaine. A friend of mine, his daughter's a *jinetera*." Little Daddy begins pulling imaginary dollars out of the sky. "He just tells her 'More money, more money, more money.'"

He points to a hatchet-faced man stopping tourists on the side-walk: "The husband of a *jinetera*." He tells me that most prostitutes in Havana come from the rural areas surrounding Santiago and Guantanamo, where living conditions are far worse than here, where blackouts shut down the city for hours, sometimes days, at a time. He stops one girl dressed in skin-tight black, her bulbous ass jutting like an open drawer.

"How old are you?"

"Eighteen."

"Where are you from?"

"Santiago."

Little Daddy gives me a glance. We sit in silence, sipping, watch-ing the parade in what I am sure is a shared state of enlightened despair. It is getting late. He asks me a question, but I can't hear it. Little Daddy leans over the table.

"You want a girl for $20?" he says.

The next morning, Wednesday, March 25, I go to the International Press Center in Vedado to pay $60 for a press card I'll never use. This is required each time I come to Cuba. But before I enter, two brothers stop me. They're both in their late twenties. One is holding a pair of hedge clippers, the other leans on a hand truck. "Where you from?" Hedge Clipper asks in broken English. I tell him Miami. I never get the chance to say another word.

"My father's in Miami. He's an *hijo de puta*. He left eighteen years ago during Mariel. He never writes. He never calls." Hedge Clipper draws a grimy finger across his throat. "It's like we're dead. Things are very bad here. Very hungry, no gas. Do you have a dollar?"

He nudges his brother, points to the broad back of a cop standing at the next corner. Both men hurry off in the opposite direction. They leave the clippers and the hand truck behind. But I am not alone.

Charles Hill says, "My daughter was seven when I left." Sunlight slices through the leaves above, dappling the sidewalk. "Man," he says. "Time flies."

It is my third day in Havana. I haven't seen Hill since a chance meeting three years before when, in a high-rise restaurant with a pleasant, hazy view of the Florida Straits, he admitted he was the same Charles Hill wanted in the United States, with two other men, for murdering a New Mexico state policeman and then hijacking a jet to Havana in November 1971. One of the men drowned years ago, but the other, Michael Finney, works in Havana for Radio Habanacuba. Though Finney is the prime suspect, neither has ever said publicly who pulled the trigger, and when I asked Charles pointblank in that restaurant over a plate of stringy chicken while a three-piece band ran through a bouncy rendition of "Love Is Here to Stay," Hill simply and imperviously repeated, "The guy got shot."

The last few years have been good to Hill. He's put on weight, started exercising, and shaved off his goatee because no one in Havana wears beards anymore; that look is long out of style. He scrambles for the essentials like everyone else, serving as fixer, guide, and translator for English-speaking *turistas*, but there is a quality in his gait that wasn't there the last time, that rolling, don't-fuck-with-me statement of urban cool that seems to have resurfaced with the least bit of prosperity. Hill has been in Cuba nearly thirty years, immersing himself so deeply into the Afro-Caribbean religion of Santeria that he sometimes calls himself a priest, a *babalao*. But he still walks like an American. And now, edging toward fifty, he's less strident than the last time I saw him. He speaks of how he misses his friends, American baseball games, speaking English, little things. "I miss graham crackers in milk," he says.

Hill comes inside, where my photo is snapped and I pay and pocket my press card. We skip down the stairs, round the corner, and head up a sloping street to a high-rise apartment two blocks away. Past the entrance of the Hotel Nacional, I realize this is the precise spot where I'd met Hill years before in my first vivid lesson in Cuban kismet. It was a similar morning, in those last sweet moments before the heat takes hold, and I had been out at Radio Habanacuba trying—and failing—to track down Finney for a possible story. As I was about to turn into the hotel, from across the street a black man called to me in American English; he'd seen the *International Herald-Tribune* under my arm. I told him where I'd been. He said, "I know Michael Finney. I came here with him." Who knows? Maybe Hill had been following me. But I prefer to consider our meeting just a bizarre coincidence, because I've since learned it was nothing rare. Despite its 2 million-plus population, Havana is the smallest big city in the world, a place where the usual six degrees of separation are halved and melodramatic collisions are as much a part of life as summer rain. Hill wasn't a bit surprised to bump into me like that. But then, he'd been here awhile.

We climb the steps to the high-rise, and it's instantly clear that something has changed. For the first time in years, the hand on one of my key Cuba barometers has begun to quiver. This is, after all, the apartment building of Ana Fidelia Quirot, Cuba's most famous tragedy and Castro's favorite athlete and the best eight-hundred-meter runner in the world, and in its unguarded lobby and eternally broken elevator I always took measure of the regime's health: If they couldn't spare Quirot an eleven-story climb, there's no telling how bad life was for the typical Cuban. But now the glass doors are locked; now a man is getting up from his checkers game to open them, and at the scabby blue elevator I get another shock. It works. We lurch slowly up the shaft and knock on her door. No one home. I leave a note.

We push a down button for the elevator and wait, and wait. A faint chorus of rattles and wheezes rises from below, and the light socket above is empty. A sea breeze whisks through the hallway, kicking up dust. We hit the stairs, winding down through the gloom, feeling for broken steps. On the walls I notice something curious: thousands of black slashes, many fresh, laid over thousands of others in what looks to be a flurry of scuffmarks from a thousand angry heels. But they're all at shoulder level, and I spend thirty seconds squinting like the first man to come upon a cave painting before it hits me. Lug a Chinese bicycle up three, six, ten flights in the dark, and you wouldn't care what the walls look like, either.

*   *   *

If you want to get Teofilo Stevenson, you must buy him a meal. This is what Olga tells me as we roll down to the Malecon in a mercurial Lada, and I have learned: Olga knows best. There are two kinds of interviews in Cuba. The first, reserved for old friends, dissidents, and ballplayers with a dangerous curiosity about America, entails showing up at someone's home at night and without government knowledge, introducing yourself, and asking questions. The second, reserved for bureaucrats and true believers, demands that you go through proper channels, which in Teofilo's case means Cubadeportes—the marketing arm of The National Institute of Sports, Physical Education, and Recreation (INDER), which serves as the ruling umbrella organization for all athletics in Cuba—and in my case means Olga.

For five years, Cubadeportes has been charged with using athletics to bring in cash—and if that means selling baseball cards, farming out more than 1,000 coaches and athletes to thirty-four countries and cadging 80 percent of their salaries, or charging whatever the market will bear to set up interviews, so be it. If, like the proverbial duck, this all smells, looks, and walks like creeping capitalism, communist Cuba doesn't care. As running legend Alberto Juantorena, now an INDER vice president, once told me, "We still control the athlete. We control the money." Besides, ever since he was twelve and personally wrote President Franklin Roosevelt to brazenly demand $10, Castro hasn't exactly been shy when it comes to cash. Consider it a trickle-down effect: One walk down a Havana sidewalk will tell you that, whether they're begging Soviet subsidies or renting out a room, Cubans are some of the most savage capitalists on the globe.

To me, though, Olga is worth every Yanqui dollar. I have seen her plead, threaten, cajole, and flirt reluctant subjects into talking, and her feel for the right approach is unerring. It doesn't hurt that, though she is fortyish, Olga's huge dark eyes and brilliant grin make her look a decade younger; men like her. Stevenson rarely grants American interviews. I will buy him lunch.

It is a small price. During the Cold War, heavyweight Teofilo Stevenson was Cuba's most renowned fighter, a three-time Olympic gold-medal winner who mastered opponents with a fierce jab and monstrous power. Standing six-foot-five, with his head held imperiously upright, Stevenson prowled the ring with casual menace; all over the island people would watch and shout, "Here comes the *patada de burro!*"—mulekick—as Stevenson's fist came hurtling down. His legend began when he knocked out American Duane Bobick and German Peter Hussing at the '72 Games in Munich, and further triumphs in '76 and '80 made him one of boxing's all-time mysteries. No one doubted his intelligence and strength, but Stevenson never stripped off the headgear. He was never measured against the era's best pro fighters. For years, promoters tried to set up a never-realized showdown with Muhammad Ali, even tried to entice him with a $2 million offer, and because of this—and the fact that Stevenson resembles Ali to the point of eeriness—he has been linked in the American mind more with Ali than with anyone he actually fought. Too, rumors about Stevenson's retirement years have not been kind. Murky reports of a fatal drunk-driving accident, a tumultuous first marriage, and mental decline have fixed him and the now-diminished Ali into a real-life extension of the odd, parallel course they followed when young. Twinned as champions, they now seem fated to crumble in the same time-honored and awful way.

I'd seen Stevenson in person twice. The first time was near midnight, an August Sunday, the final evening of Cuba's stunning triumph as hosts of the 1991 Pan Am Games. I was standing outside the lobby of the Habana Libre with a group of Americans, and word hopped from mouth to mouth like contagion: Soviet president

Mikhail Gorbachev had been jailed in an attempted coup by hard-line security forces. A reprieve for Castro? Cuba and the USSR back in business? A friend nudged me. There, coming out of the hotel's dollar store—then reserved only for foreigners, and hugely resented by the Cubans who couldn't get in—was Stevenson, his towering bulk crimped by the two depressing, lumpy plastic bags he carried. Not long before, he'd been a handy symbol of Cuba's outsized place in the superpower dynamic. No one else saw him now. Alone on Cuban sport's big night, he strolled out of the lobby light and into darkness.

The second time came in 1996, on the day of the Olympic boxing finals in Atlanta. Ali edged his way across the arena floor, and Stevenson left his seat to greet him. They spoke briefly. Stevenson smiled, Ali nodded. They looked good together.

The sea is choppy with whitecaps today, mean and gray. A bill-board at the start of the Malecon, Havana's famous seawall, declares, "We Have Confidence in Our Ideas." Olga says the first place to look for Stevenson is a bar near his house in Nautica, and when we pull up, he is, naturally, there. Olga knows best. She dodges the spotty traffic to cross the four o'clock street, talks a few minutes, waves me over. I introduce myself, shake hands. Olga tells Teofilo I'd like to buy him lunch and talk. He gives me a wary look. His bottom teeth have been ground to nubs, but at forty-six Steven-son is slim and retains his box-headed handsomeness. He wears a pair of slacks, a pullover shirt from the '96 Olympics. The sun beats on our faces. A cloud of liquor floats my way.

"No, no," he shouts at me in slightly slurred, broken, but quite understandable English. "I have nothing to do with Cuban sports."

"Nothing?" I say. "You *are* Cuban sports."

His eyebrows lift. "You think that? For how long you watch?"

I tell him I saw him fight in 1972, 1976, and 1980. "Okay," he says. "I am a little hungry." Regardless, we make the date for Friday, 1 P.M., El Alhibe restaurant. But now the conversation stops cold; Stevenson has drawn a creased personal calendar out of his pocket and is slowly thumbing through pages. He wants to write the appointment down. A carload of men drives by, shouting, "Ai, Teo!" He ignores them. Thirty seconds, a minute pass; no one says a word. We stand on the baking sidewalk as he tries to find the day. I look down and notice Stevenson is wearing a horrifically cheap pair of black shoes. Olga stops his hand: He's squinting, trying to write the appointment down on February 27. "It's confusing," he says. "February, March . . ."

Olga tells him to write the appointment down for March 27. "No," Stevenson says. "That will only confuse me." He scribbles something on February 27, pockets the calendar, and abruptly announces he'd rather go out alone with Olga. Teofilo bends to kiss her, wraps his long arms around her torso, and begins working his way from her cheeks to her mouth. Olga, simultaneously red-faced and bored, does the universal female maneuver of dip, squirm, and shove, and scampers back into the car before Stevenson can realize he's making out with air. She grins, and shakes a naughty-boy finger at him from the backseat. He turns to walk back to the bar. I get in and start to tease her and instantly realize my mistake. Olga's eyes are shining, and she isn't smiling now.

The new boyfriend sits and stares. There's a two-year-old screaming in the next room, but the man makes no move. It's not his baby, and this is his woman talking now and she's speaking of the first husband who's still famous and loved and he doesn't want to miss a word. His hands grip the armrests of the low, vinyl-covered chair, like someone taking a scary ride at a carnival. Norma Manso doesn't seem to notice. She sits across the table, voice steady and light, telling how the Cuban government ravaged her life. "What made him leave was the impossibility that he'd ever play baseball again," she says. "If they let him play, he would've never left Cuba."

The stink of jet fuel wafts through the room. We are in the spare living room of El Duque's house, or at least the house he lived in before splitting with his wife and defecting, and it is dark. A bulb-less light fixture dangles from the ceiling like a stripped cluster of grapes, leaving the chipped tan floors and the odd framed poster of NBA mediocrity Clarence Weatherspoon in shadow. It is late, 9 P.M. or so. Occasionally the conversation gets interrupted by the howling din of a 747. Through the hurricane fence in the backyard, I can see the Havanautos rent-a-car office and landing strips of Havana's Jose Marti International Airport. There's a hole in the kitchen wall the size of a small human head. The last time I was here, Duque spoke of how he'd often run outside with a bat to chase off thieves.

He and Norma have two beautiful daughters—Yahumara, eight years old and bearing her dad's high cheekbones, and two-year-old Steffi. Duque calls twice a week from America to talk to them. It is not enough. "For the oldest one it's really bad," Norma says. "She had been crying all night long. She's getting better, though. The last few nights she hasn't cried."

It has been just three months since Duque left. But for the family, things began to crack fifteen months earlier, in October 1996, when, the morning after Duque testified in the five-hour trial of Juan Ignacio Hernandez Nodar, he woke up at 7:15 to hear on the radio that he, as well as shortstop German Mesa and catcher Alberto Hernandez, had been banned for life from Cuban baseball— the first players sanctioned for contact with a sports agent. Hernandez Nodar, a cousin of Miami agent Joe Cubas, was sentenced to fifteen years for trying to lure ballplayers to defect. Though the players weren't on trial, the fact that Hernandez Nodar had their names on transit visas—and Duque had received him in his house and taken money from him sent by Livan—was enough to make them all guilty. But the biggest strike against Duque, of course, was the fact that his half-brother had already hopped to America. His career in Cuba died the minute Livan decided to go.

"We knew Duque was going to leave," Manuel Zayas, a Cubadeportes media officer, told me with a smile a few days earlier. "We just didn't want to pay for his plane ticket."

His exit was disaster for the regime. No modern Cuban baseball player can compare to Duque in both lineage and accomplishment. His father, the original El Duque, starred in the National Series as a pitcher and infielder in the seventies, and his only full brother, Arnaldo, played first base for Metropolitanos until April 1994, when he collapsed and died at the age of twenty-nine from a ruptured brain aneurysm. The loss of his closest brother shattered Duque, and that, along with a gap-toothed charm, frightening intensity, and stylish results made him a national hero. For eight years, hiding a multitude of dancing curveballs behind a chin-brushing kick imitated on every dusty street, he dueled with superstar pitcher Lazaro Valle, a teammate on Industriales, for the best career record in modern Cuban history. When Valle began to struggle with arm problems three years ago, Duque kept winning, and his 129–46 record now reigns supreme. Despite that, the regime never granted him the favors they bestowed on Valle; Duque's house was always a wreck. He kept hearing promises about a car, but never got one. The endless schedule then—after two split seasons totaling 110 games, players like Duque filled out the rest of the year with the national team's extensive tours—left him exhausted.

"The country doesn't see us as human beings," he told me once. "They treat us like machines."

He complained about the car, his house. He didn't shy from criticizing the Cuban politicians and fans. But Duque also spoke then of how many chances he'd had to defect and how he turned them all down. He ripped the players who'd left for forgetting their families. "We play for the love," he said. "They play for other things: money. They're not interested in what country they're in." He said that no matter how bad life got in Cuba, he would not go.

Then, eleven months later, came the news of his banning over the radio. Duque hurled himself out of bed, began yelling and cursing and hopping into his clothes. He went to the INDER offices, but no one would see him. He was told to return later that afternoon, when he was informed that he could never again set foot in a Cuban baseball stadium or on a practice field. He was banned from studying at university. "He felt betrayed," Norma says. "Everything changed for him. Emotionally it turned him upside down. It hurt us. He was in the streets a lot."

Duque could work only at the Havana Psychiatric Hospital as an aide, moving mental patients from place to place, relegated to spending most of his days talking nonsense. Norma, who also worked there, would see her husband shepherding the patients outside, his face tight and drawn. "It was so depressing I can't even talk about it," she says.

Four months later, the marriage was over. Norma smashed his trophies in a rage. Duque didn't forget his daughters. He came to the house daily, brought shoes, clothing, even a bit of money when he could get some. When they were sick, he would take them to the hospital. When, in December, he didn't come by for a stretch of days, Norma began to wonder. Then she heard the news on Radio Marti that he had gone. Yahumara told her mother, "He didn't take me with him. I'm going to get him for that." So far he has sent $350. Norma is sure he will send more because, she says, she knows

Duque. He is not, she says, like other athletes who've left children behind, not like New York Mets shortstop Rey Ordoñez, the majors' most gifted fielder and another exile icon.

"We were just talking today about how Ordoñez got married in the States and forgot his wife and children," Norma says. "They weren't even separated. His baby was just a few months old when he left."

She has Steffi in her lap now. A voice cuts in: the metallic announcement of flights to Madrid and Brussels. Norma smiles sweetly. She is thirty but looks no older than twenty-two, and in the half-light her creamy, unlined face looks so untroubled that it'd be easy to believe she'd grown up rich. I begin gathering myself to leave, but something makes me stop. I ask Norma if she knew Duque's new girlfriend. For the first time all night, she doesn't chatter out an answer; she nods and emits a raspy assent from the back of her throat. I ask if the woman lived nearby and Norma barely nods again but says nothing, eyes wide. Her boyfriend watches from his vinyl chair. I babble my goodbyes, but they aren't listening anymore.

I get back to my room at the Hotel Inglaterra and decide to check out in the morning. My first few nights here, I had no hot water; tonight, I have no water at all. Pity. The Inglaterra is the oldest hotel in Havana. Winston Churchill stayed here a century ago, and with its closet-sized rooms and colonial ambiance it is one of those delightful places that history has parked smack at the intersection of past and future. My room opens over Parque Central, a leafy oasis now framed by construction cranes. At least five new hotels are being built in Old Havana alone, and here, for the first time in Cuba, I heard a car alarm whoop-and-buzz just outside the lobby door. Another day I was awakened with a furious headache at dawn by the sound of someone pounding a drum and chanting like some Caribbean muezzin. You can't beat the place for cheap atmosphere. But I need a shower.

I cross the park, blow past Hemingway's Floridita, so packed with tourists now that old Papa would surely have steered clear, and order a beer at the bar in Castillo de Farnes. The place is packed. I settle in at a table by a window. Within seconds a girl looking about seventeen asks if she can sit down, changes her mind, and moves on. A rosy-cheeked American deb hears my voice and comes over, says her name is Sally. She lives on Grand Cayman, came to Cuba for a five-day jaunt—"It's so safe," she says—and wonders if there's a base-ball game to see in Havana the next few days. I tell her the playoffs will begin soon.

A slack-faced man in a ponytail leans over from the next table. "Go to a game," he commands. "I went to one in Pinar Del Rio and it was the most emotional thing I've ever seen." He tells us he's from Victoria, Canada; he looks about thirty-eight, with the smeary smile and vaporous attention span of a serious pothead. "I've been here six months," he says. "I used to be fat." Sally scrapes her chair back and is soon swallowed by the crowd. Another American walks up, this time a blond, fortyish man in a $50 T-shirt. He shakes hands with Mr. Victoria, shakes my hand and squints in distaste. He says he's from Aspen. He's got a big stogie in his chest pocket and talks with a sneer. I ask him how he's liking Cuba.

"I came here the first time a year and a half ago and I'm liking it less and less," he says wearily. "It's getting to be like Disneyland. Soon it'll be like everyplace else. Time to move on."

"To the next place?"

"There is no next place."

Victoria cuts in. "Go to Holguin. Get out to the provinces." But Aspen shrugs, shakes hands again, and walks away.

Ten minutes later, I see Victoria nuzzling a girl no older than sixteen, wearing flowered hot pants and beige heels. The *jinetera* differs from her American counterpart because upfront cash is hardly required; often a good meal or a clean bed or the promise of a week spent with some free-spending *turista* is enough to seal matters, so blurring the exchange that a john can spend his entire visit happily deluded. Every day, men fly out of Havana certain that they just had the infatuation of a lifetime. Now Victoria is on his way: She's sitting in his lap and he's stroking her thighs. She stands, turns, and bends over; he mushes his face into her ass with a look of unalloyed bliss. Finally he stands and says to me, "Good luck," throws his arm around her shoulders, and announces, "I'm thinking another two or three months."

The two of them lurch outside and pass my window, Victoria's shirt gaping to reveal a sickly white belly. They pass a pneumatic nymphet in a hot pink ballroom gown. A tubby guy in a white beard materializes by her side, whispers, and the two scoot off. I have seen these men all my life. At home they squat on barstools, eyeing the waitresses and always saying the wrong thing; bartenders chuckle politely and run them a tab. But tonight is different. Tonight is a bonanza. They are the kings of sex.

CHAPTER 2

I felt as if I sailed with Long John Silver and first gazed on Treasure Island. Here was a place where anything might happen. Here was a place where something would certainly happen. Here I might leave my bones.

—WINSTON CHURCHILL,
upon first sighting Havana, 1895

Fidel sat watching. High in an arena, surrounded by 10,000 faithful. The massive dreamy face of Che Guevara glared down from one wall. Fidel was not the show, not today. No, this day there was a boxing ring down on the floor, and he watched intently while his boys kept winning. One after another, the boxers would duck under the ropes and destroy their opponents, and with each raised hand and flag and the first tinny notes of the national anthem, the celebratory din expanded, multiplied, raced from mouth to mouth in a fevered contagion. "Cu-BA!" It was just before 4 p.m. Now the great Cuban heavyweight Felix Savon was in the ring, now he was clubbing the American with a sledgehammer right hand. The American dropped dazed to the canvas, flat on his ass. Men danced. The wave began, everyone standing and throwing arms to the sky and sitting again, now a human tide circling toward the dictator, screams growing more hysterical the closer it got. Would he stand? Would he join them?

Fidel stood. Over and over, he fluttered his hands above his head. Here he was, the man who embarrassed John F. Kennedy, who has ruled longer than any leader alive, who is both Miami monster and Latin American hero, acting like some boozy yahoo in the cheap seats. The crowd's cheering grew more frenzied. "Fee-DEL!" they chanted. It was the summer of 1991 and this was the final day of my first trip to Cuba and now I simply sat, openmouthed, as the surreal pageant reached its climax. Castro's country was devastated. He did not care. The crowd did not care. On this Sunday, eleven of his boxers had won gold medals, embarrassing the United States and making his latest gamble a triumph. Over the public address system came the news: For the first time in the forty-year history of the Pan American Games, the United States had been beaten in the gold medal count. Cu-BA!

That's when it hit me hardest. For three weeks, I'd heard stories of how these Pan Am Games had been cobbled together, how Castro had insisted on putting them on despite the crippling loss of his vital trading partners in the Soviet bloc, of how champion boxers, baseball players, and gymnasts had helped construct the stadiums, stacking cinder blocks, shoveling dirt. But now I'd seen Cubans otherwise furious about the lack of soap and toilet paper during what Fidel called the "Special Period" chant his name because some boxers had won a fight, and I understood. Sports here had power unlike anywhere else on the planet. I have dodged flying bricks in a World Cup soccer riot, I've sensed blossoming pride in American downtowns rebuilt around ballparks, I've seen college boosters bribe and cheat and destroy their own good names for the sake of winning a football game. But nothing approaches the passion for athletics, the total investment by government and fan, that I've seen in Cuba then and since.

In 1959, the same year he took power, Castro declared that "after many years under a tyranny when sports had grown rotten, a new era in Cuban baseball has begun under a clean sky, in a free country." He soon expanded his scope to all sports, acting to replace the corruption of professional boxing, horse racing, and gambling with amateurism, opening the exclusive sporting clubs and facilities to the masses, creating an extensive nationwide program of recreation and training. Within four years, pro sports had been outlawed and Castro had taken to using his sporting system as a moral cudgel on his neighbor to the north: "Our people have got a conviction that amateur sports are worth 1,000 times more than professional sports," Castro said in 1963. "Many times we've seen the Americans come over here to play and they didn't even slide on the bases. They would come here to rest. To see our guys now, the way they slide on the bases, playing with barbarian courage—in all sports, in boxing too. . . . It's a great lesson, because it shows that sports is stronger than money. The love of oneself, the honor of the athlete, is the obligation he has toward the fan. That's what makes him do things that the professional athlete will never do. . . ."

Decades later, high in the arena that day in 1991, Fidel's painted words still shone like some gospel truth: "Sport Is the Right of the People." The regime had reason to strut. Its embrace of amateurism had been a smash success. Out of a population of just 11 million, Cuba not only kept producing the world's best boxers and amateur baseball players, but had expanded beyond its traditional sports base to churn out the world's best women volleyball players and some of its most vivid and durable track stars, including future world champs in the high jump, long jump, eight hundred meters, and triple jump. And Cuba's sports prowess had practical uses beyond providing a vehicle for national pride. In the midst of a crisis more acute than America's Great Depression, it had become Castro's almighty glue.

For thirty years, the regime had used as justification the success of its three social pillars—health care, education, and athletics. But as a Cuban official would tell me years later, "Medicine and education have really been damaged by the lack of money, but sports has never been affected. Sports has been the most solid and consistent achievement of the revolution." And it's true: As the tourist trade began elevating waiters and cabbies over doctors and professors in the savage scramble for dollars, the tiny Cuban sports machine chugged on. In the post-Soviet era, it was Castro's last symbol of excellence. When that celebratory wave rolled his way, he had no choice. Fidel had nothing else to stand for.

The comparisons have always been wrong. To his enemies, Castro is another Hitler, another Stalin, another power-mad Mussolini. But Castro is not like them; in Cuba, nothing, much less the trains, runs on time. More to the point, Castro is that rarest of twentieth-century leaders—a true leftist tyrant. He befuddles because, compared to the fascists and especially compared to the pocket-lining excesses of his Cuban predecessors, he actually conspired to better the lives of the lower classes. That he trampled freedoms and destroyed dissent, executed enemies, cozied up to the Soviets, and brooked no opposition is, of course, abhorrent. But in truth, his spellbinding demagoguery and social triumphs—with a 94.5 percent literacy rate, there is no better-educated populace in Latin America—make him resemble no one so much as Depression-era governor Huey Long, who vastly upgraded the lives of his subjects while ruling Louisiana like a czar. And as T. Harry Williams's definitive biography makes comically clear, Long was acutely aware of the power of sports. He immersed himself in the Louisiana State football team, suggesting plays, giving half-time speeches, putting up injured players at his mansion, running up and down the sideline following the action. "He was thinking of the future in all this," said one former LSU player in Williams's biography. "He was getting people who would be for him when he'd follow the ball up and down the field and wave to students."

Cuba's Kingfish can be just as shameless. Huge pictures of Fidel in boxing gloves, in baseball flannels, grinning next to any Cuban athlete of note, cover walls in gyms across the country. During the '91 Pan Am Games, Castro cavorted from one venue to another, showing up unexpectedly to award medals and get himself seen. Not since the revolution had he KO'd the Yanquis so cleanly—and it had been a long time coming. From the beginning, Castro has wrapped his athletes in the communist banner and used them as tools in his fight against capitalism. The national boxing championships held each January are called, simply, Playa Giron after the Cuban military's 1961 victory over United States–backed invaders at the Bay of Pigs. The most distinctive feature about the Interior Ministry's infamous Villa Marista prison in Havana—first stop for enemies of the revolution—is its well-tended baseball field, complete with Bunyanesque rifle towering over center field. Athletes are not entertainers in Cuba. Athletes march in lockstep with soldiers, party members, students, and informers to the paranoid rhythm of Castro's big idea.

"For the people who said that sports would fail in Cuba without professionalism, in Puerto Rico we had the answer," Castro said after Cuba won the baseball and dominated the boxing competitions at the '66 Central American and Caribbean Games in Puerto Rico. "It was a moral victory for the highest principles in our sports. It was shown that professionalism is a conspiracy against sports. Professional athletes are the antithesis of sport, a cultural instrument to ruin sports, and only our revolutionary concept of sport will be an instrument to educate our culture, an instrument of well-being. . . ."

Since the 1970s, when Cuba produced its first two international superstars in Teofilo Stevenson and runner Alberto Juantorena, Castro has used sport to show that his regime still has muscle. But once Soviet aid dried up and military adventures like Angola and Grenada became too costly, athletics became his most prominent battlefield. "Sport is the outcome of the revolution," Castro told a Cuban delegation of athletes in 1995. "Look at what's going on in many other places, where sport is corrupted and being destroyed. No one will be able to destroy the accomplishments we have made in sport."

But even by 1991, the destruction had begun. Just days before the Pan Am Games were to open in Havana, a Cuban pitcher named Rene Arocha became the first player from the mighty national baseball team to defect. When he later signed with the St. Louis Cardinals, the plug popped out of the dike. Over the next seven years, more than one hundred athletes—more than thirty of them baseball players—streamed out of the country, each heaping abuse on Fidel the moment he could touch them no more. Even as Cuba continued to excel—winning more medals per capita than any country at the '92 Olympics in Barcelona, dominating boxing and baseball at the '96 Atlanta games, winning four gold medals at the '97 World Track and Field championships in Athens—the strain began to show. Once content to dismiss the defectors as unwanted cowards, Castro's rhetoric escalated as the exodus began sucking away the regime's best. When Rolando Arrojo, the nation's most gifted pitcher, bolted in Georgia just prior to the Atlanta games, Cuba's lead atheist called him "a Judas" who sold out his country "for twelve gold coins." When El Duque left, Castro called him "a sports mercenary" who "betrayed his country."

But now, this second boatload of baseball rafters has obviously raised temperatures even higher. Nothing, it seems, could be more embarrassing to Castro than a steady flow of his baseball players wading into the sea, for when I pick up the communist daily *Granma* Thursday morning, there, next to an article about the end of the regular season, is yet another nervous broadside. "We will always have deserters, people of weak character who have been deceived by the illusion of material goods," Carlos Lage, Cuba's vice president and economic czar, told a meeting of officials from INDER the day before. Lage went on to praise the examples set by Ana Quirot, Linares, and Stevenson, and railed against the "tentacles of professionalism" that had grabbed hold of Cuban baseball. He ended by calling sports "not only the fruit, but also the symbol of our Socialist revolution."

Ninety miles away, the United States endures its golden age. American sports at century's end is a landscape of astonishing richness. The old superstars have just about completed their retirement fade, but that does nothing to eclipse the fact that the current era rivals the legendary 1920s and 1950s in duration and quality. Channel-surf your TV in 1998, and you could still witness the greatest basketball player (Michael Jordan), hockey player (Wayne Gretzky), passer (Dan Marino), wide receiver (Jerry Rice) and, arguably, tennis player (Pete Sampras) of all time; you could see one of baseball's greatest sluggers (Mark McGwire) and great surprises (Sammy Sosa) assaulting one of American sport's most revered records; you could watch one of the best right-handed pitchers in baseball history (Greg Maddux) and a parade of young talents like Ken Griffey Jr., Ivan Rodriguez, Alex Rodriguez, and Juan Gonzalez march toward the Hall of Fame.

Expansion and age have undoubtedly dragged the level of American competition, particularly in the NBA, down from its early-nineties apex. But the fact that today's athletic talent pool includes an unprecedented flood of European and Latino faces, not to mention the dominant black athlete, lays a far more durable question mark on the whitewashed glory days of Ruth and Mantle than on the achievements of today. To concentrate on such barroom quibbling, however, is to ignore the larger reality. The explosion of cable and pay-per-view TV has made any game, any team, any player available to more fans than at any time in sports history. We've literally never had it so good.

Not that anyone is celebrating. To many aficionados today, comparing eras has become a useless exercise in the face of a far more insidious force—one that has transformed what should be a glorious sporting scene into a Hieronymus Bosch mural of knaves, fools, suckers, and thieves. For as sports have grown ever more accessible and more dominant a part of American culture—and more valuable a sales vehicle—the same market mentality that has dumbed down moviemaking, destroyed corporate loyalty to employee or community, and now edges its way into health care and public education has eroded the bond between fan and team. It's not that athletes make too much money. Athletes have been "overpaid" since the era of Babe Ruth, who, after getting a raise that paid him more than the U.S. president, correctly explained: "I had a better year." The problem is a widespread perception that, in American sports, dollars now define the game.

A fan will forgive—and pay—most anything if his loyalty is reciprocated, if certain basics stand: The sport can't shut down, the team can't move, the players must emotionally invest at least as much into the game as the man cheering in his living room. But by the late nineties, the American sports fan had been hammered with so many body blows—the labor lockout that destroyed the 1994 baseball season and canceled the World Series, the move of the avidly supported

Cleveland Browns to Baltimore in 1995, a free agency so fluid that no player could expect to stay a lifetime with one team, repeated threats to relocate teams if resource-strapped cities don't pony up new facilities, the 1998 NBA lockout—that all illusions drained away. This is why a win-now attitude prevails in every sport, in every city; there is no fan patience because the old emotional ties have been severed. The owners have cornered themselves. The fans have adopted market mentality. Only an NBA championship, a Super Bowl, a World Series satisfies—and not for long.

I live in Miami, where in 1997 all the elements of cashbox sports came crashing to a horrendous crescendo. After spending $89 million on free agents, Florida Marlins owner H. Wayne Huizenga, the bottom-line builder of trash, video, and car empires who once described a fly ball as a "transaction," began making noise about a new stadium and threatened to sell if fans didn't support his cash cow. They didn't. As the Marlins made their improbable run through the end of the regular season and the 1997 playoffs, demand for tickets remained tepid. The World Series sold out, but it was too late; when presented with the World Series trophy Huizenga announced, in the stilted cadence of an automaton, "This is for you, South Florida . . . ," and no one believed him. By the break of spring training, the team was gutted, a championship flung overboard like so much chum. Never had a winner been bought and sold so mercilessly. All that remained was Livan Hernandez, pitching to empty seats.

Miami radio shows and bars have since been filled with bilious nattering about how Marlins fans—after devoting five whole years to the team—had their hearts ripped out, but such knee-jerk venting only speaks of a deeper hunger. South Florida is a fractured, rootless, corrupt community, but for ten days during the '97 World Series there was something to cheer, and a gorgeous mirage of unity. At its core, the fan mentality isn't comfortable with the market;

more than winning, it seeks connection, a way for the individual to plug in. That's why the current "good ol' days" trend in stadium-building—a marketing ploy to make one forget the market—currently holds sway nationwide, why books about the Brooklyn Dodgers and postwar baseball still command a large audience; for middle-class whites, especially, "Dem Bums" evoke a time when ballplayers took the subway and lived where people knew one another by name. Even those addicted to the action of sports resent today's mercenary feel. Everyone knows the nostalgia trip is over. Only a fool goes to a ballpark looking for a way back to the past.

But now I am there. Now I'm in a place where free agency is unknown, where agents are a mystery, where no one gets traded and teams never move. Now I'm in a place where, during the playoffs, a foreigner can walk up to the ticket window and get three seats for 9 Cuban pesos, about 50 cents, and watch some of the finest baseball in the world. Now it is 4 P.M. on a March afternoon, and I'm standing in front of the family apartment of rookie center fielder Yasser Gomez, waiting. He is late for our appointment, but just as I begin to boil I notice a boy in a baseball uniform at the far end of Calle Espada. He is walking between his parents. They stop every few steps for a backslapping group of mechanics or the random passerby, all yelling, "Congratulations, Yasser!" Everybody already knows: He went two-for-two today to finish the season at .359—the fifth-best batting average in Cuba. Here he comes, the league's most sensational rookie on the season's final day, as he has come after every game at Latinoamericano: through the Havana streets, equipment bag over one shoulder, a half-hour walk all the way home.

"I'm very happy," Yasser says. "Guys come from around the neighborhood and people stop me on the street and ask for autographs. A guy at the stadium the other day made me sign his overalls. A grown man."

His story is typical. His father is a produce inspector. Yasser grew up loving baseball like every other Cuban boy, playing the street game of *tacos*—a plastic bottlecap for a ball, a branch or sawed-off broomstick for a bat—then in more organized youth leagues at the local park. When he was twelve years old, "inspectors" for the local EIDE—a nationwide chain of sports boarding schools, the first stop in the Cuban sports system—spotted him. At thirteen, he moved into a bunk at the Cotorro EIDE named for the Martyrs of Barbados—those seventy-three people, including twenty-four members of Cuba's national fencing team, killed in the October 6, 1976, crash of a Cubana jetliner that was orchestrated by anti-Castro exiles. In the morning Yasser went to classes; in the afternoon he drilled and practiced and played baseball. "When you go there you're *capturado*"—captured—Yasser says. "You're put in that sport and you play the sport you're captured for. Baseball is the only sport I've ever played."

At sixteen, Yasser advanced to the local ESPA—an advanced sports academy—played in the national developmental league—the Liga de Desarrollo, a step below the Cuban majors—and was named to the junior national team. One morning in the fall of 1997, in a moment comparable to being discovered on a stool at Schwab's drugstore, the seventeen-year-old Yasser was sitting high in the stands watching Metropolitanos run through a practice game. It was the final day of cuts. The score was tied 3–3 in the seventh inning when the manager, Guillermo Carmona, who knew of Yasser but had never seen him play, sent a man into the stands to get him. There was a runner on second. The manager told Yasser to put on his spikes, grab a bat, and "win this game for me." Yasser nods at the obvious: "A once-in-a-lifetime opportunity," he says. So he cracked a fastball into left field for an RBI double, muttering to himself, "I did what I had to do," as he stood breathing hard at second base. Fans laughed and jumped from their seats, shouting "Do it, kid!" After the game, Carmona announced that Yasser had made the team.

Not since Linares, the greatest all-around player in modern Cuban history and once the most coveted by American teams, has a player broken in so young and so well. No one puts Yasser on the same level as the thirty-year-old El Nino, but his great speed and preternatural maturity have impressed everyone. "He's just so loose," La Habana pitcher Jose Ibar, who'd gone an unprecedented 20–2 during the 1997–98 season, told me a few days later, after Yasser had gone two-for–two off him in a playoff game. "He plays like an old man. He doesn't get nervous. He's going to be huge in baseball."

But today, two hours after he's come home, Yasser looks anything but. He sports a wispy mustache, and in his dirty uniform looks precisely his age. He speaks in a soft, even tone, punctuating his thoughts by sucking back a squawking ball of phlegm. "The first time I played against Pinar Del Rio, I laid a bunt down third base and Linares took off after it," Yasser says. "It rolled right over the bag. By the time he pulled up to throw I was already on first. He just looked at me and laughed."

I change the subject. On Sunday, the four players and coach who followed El Duque's lead and took to the sea in a raft were found. For ten days, they'd hidden out on the island and spent just one day at sea before being picked up and taken to an immigration center in the Bahamas, where they now sit behind a fence waiting for any country to take them as refugees. The biggest prize for the major leagues is former national team first baseman Jorge Luis Toca, but Yasser played on the junior national team with seventeen-year-old Maikel Jova—a talented outfielder, son of banned manager Pedro Jova, the baby on the boat. "It was stupid," Yasser says. "There are sharks . . ."

Yasser's mother, Lola, breaks in, her voice beginning to rise. A science teacher, she carries herself with the thin and imposing direct- ness of someone used to riding herd on teenage bullshit, and the kind of tough beauty that even the slightest anger transforms into ugliness. "I'd be really disappointed if my son did that," she says. "He was trained in Cuba and made a player here. What he was, is, and will be was created here in Cuba, under a Cuban flag."

A man sticks his head in the front door, still open to the street. "Congratulations, rookie!" Yasser nods.

Lola travels to every one of her son's games, no matter where in the country, no matter how circuitous the bus trip. Every home game, they all walk home together. She shows off his trophies. Their bathroom is the size of a broom closet; the toilet doesn't flush. The place is spotless. Sometimes, they will watch a tape on the VCR Yasser brought home from his one trip to America. "I'm so proud," Lola says.

Maybe they are lying. This is always a possibility in Cuba: Maybe one day, after a lifetime of vowing fealty to the regime, the whole family will walk down to some quiet shore and cast their lives and hopes into the water, gambling that Yasser will make it to Dodger Stadium. But as I say goodbye, I find myself nurturing a notion I cannot defend. I have heard about the political prisoners locked up in Combinado Del Este and shock treatments in the Havana Psy- chiatric Hospital and the dissidents beaten in the streets. I know Cubans fear to speak freely because of who might be listening, and I know the lives of this family would be instantly better in Miami or New Jersey. But I don't want them to go.

Back at my hotel, I find a message waiting from Ana Quirot, so I stop by her apartment to say hello. She can't talk. She is wearing a black pants suit, perfect makeup. Her long braids trip down her back like vines. I tell her she looks well and she giggles, dipping her head into her shoulder. I ask where she is going, so late at night. "Oh," she says. "A reception with El Comandante." Minutes later, her dark blue Mercedes passes me standing on a streetcorner. She waves from the backseat.

The next morning I wake up to a totalitarian cliché, the tyrant dream. The last thing I see as I break into wakefulness is Fidel, fading but unmistakably there, scurrying around my skull. I've been on the island four nights. What can sleep be for those who've lived here forty years? For those who left? How many phantoms float nightly over Cuba, drift through kitchens, negotiate their way past mumble and snore? How many people, exactly, open their eyes to the memory of that ubiquitous face?

CHAPTER 3

It was a city to visit, not a city to live in . . .

—GRAHAM GREENE, *Our Man in Havana*

I am still fighting myself here. By the fourth or fifth day, usually, the battle is over; I've given in completely to what the island does to people like me and get lost. But this time I'm determined to ride out the romance, the dizzying feel of being in a movie populated by overactors and second-rate clichés. There's a scene in *Lawrence of Arabia* where King Feisal sizes up Lawrence and, recognizing his dangerous naivete, calls him "one of those desert-loving English." Exiles despise my type: the Cuba-loving Anglo, the foreigner jazzed by the old cars and crumbling buildings, the communist rhetoric and dissident struggle, the thrill of skirting a thirty-seven-year trade embargo and tasting the denied. Much of their disgust rises from fear that my cash keeps Castro alive, but more unsettling is that fact that I have nothing at stake, no memories of home and childhood taken. For too many people like me, down at the bone Cuba is neither war nor depression nor a place where liberty and repression wrestle every day. It's a safe trip to crisis, a story to tell. It is a place where you can get out clean.

This is, I think, despicable. I know better. I have seen too many friends here living on the margin; I've heard too many stories of people passing bloated bodies in the surf. Photographers adore Cuba because of the buttery light and antique air, but I know that every picturesque jalopy is cursed daily by its owner because it is hell to keep running, I know the nutritional bankruptcy doled out by the weekly ration book. Hepatitis, AIDS, pneumonia, the proportion of underweight babies—all are on the rise in Cuba. Castro has locked up at least 381 political prisoners. The suicide rate is the highest in the Western Hemisphere. What writer Andrei Codrescu says is true: Cuban faces have that gaunt El Greco beauty, the eyes so luminous and alluring, because everyone is slowly dying. American sports fans scoffed at Livan Hernandez's McDonald's habit, but it is fact that every ballplayer who jumps to the States instantly gains fifteen pounds. They aren't fat. This is what they should've weighed all along.

Yet it is precisely such desperation that draws me to Cuba. I am not used to a world where people grapple with issues huge and real and simple: life, death, freedom, love, country, escape. I come from a place where health, liberty, and the future of the republic are taken for granted, and at times such comfort can leave an abiding emptiness. Riding a bus into Havana from Varadero last weekend, I sat in front of a thirtyish Brit making his third trip here in three years. He spoke of this girl he'd met once on the bus to Santiago, how her family welcomed him and his buddies to their farm. One Sunday, not knowing it was their only day to use the local tractor, he brought a bottle of scotch: Everybody stopped working and, under the blazing sun, got beautifully drunk. The story, of course, had no point beyond that—which was precisely his point. As he spoke of that, or of the many times the old taxi broke down and everyone had to pile out and push to get it started, his face assumed this expression of mystified joy because he was sure he'd broken through and caught a glimpse of the authentic. Never before, he said, would he have dreamed of wasting his vacation on the same place twice. This time, he left his buddies behind.

I have acquaintances back in the States, middle-class white boys like me, and every time I hear of their latest sex tour in Havana, their cool little week of cocktail culture, I'm overtaken by a spasm of dismay. But I understand them, too, and hate that understanding, because I know we share the same dirty fear that Fidel will fall and it will all be gone. Cuba will have Starbucks and answering machines in every house; Cuba will be like anywhere. Never mind that every Cuban wants change, *now*. For us, Cuba has been merely an exotic outlet for terror and lust: Our grandparents' generation honeymooned, gambled, and gazed in awe at the Superman sex shows, our parents saw it as the fulcrum of near-nuclear war. For us it is a cage containing the brutalized remains of a discredited faith. When I first moved to Miami, a landlady told of how, as a nurse, she'd once treated the exiled Fulgencio Batista and found herself mesmerized by the huge black revolver he kept on a night table. I had to go to Cuba then. I had to see that gun.

The writer wants a story. In Cuba stories pile up like pesos on a dresser. One thick spring night in 1995, after a day spent probing Castro's beloved sports system, a photographer brought me to a towering dark house to see Natalia Revuelta. I'd never heard of her. He provided a sketch: Naty came of age rich under Batista's regime and threw it all away. She fell in love with Fidel, left her husband, raised money for the revolution, and bore Castro a daughter. Castro left her. The door opened to reveal a Latina version of Dickens's Miss Havisham. We sat, we talked. With knuckles purpled, Naty's ancient mother negotiated a walker around a faded and torn living room set. A television flickered, cutting the gloom with a dancing murmur of light. "I can say anything because here if you do something wrong they put you under house arrest," Naty said. "But I've been under house arrest for twenty years."

Naty's daughter, Alina, had defected and made a new life denouncing her father the dictator. Naty said she didn't miss Alina nearly as much as she missed Alina's baby girl. Inevitably, all eyes fell on the face on the wall—a stunning oil portrait of Naty herself when she was young, supremely beautiful, dark and cruel like Vivien Leigh. It was like seeing before-and-after pictures: the thing he loved, the wreckage he left behind. Naty asked if we had any aspirin. As we trooped down the high stairs, a man doing nothing stood across the street. He glared at us, arms crossed, and didn't avert his eyes until we drove out of sight.

A few nights later, a group of us—the photographer, an editor, an assistant—bought Naty drinks at the rooftop bar of the Nacional. We were the only patrons there, staring out at a city gone quiet and black save for the oil refinery smokestack spewing over Regla. We could see the giant flame licking the sky. "It never goes out," she said. The bombastic rhythm of the hotel's salsa band had followed us up the stairs, making it difficult to hear. I had never seen anyone smoke with a cigarette holder before. Naty looked wonderful. Finally, I had to ask about Fidel. How would he handle the continuing crisis?

"Everything will change now, but what he says won't change," she said. "He'll act as if nothing has happened." I asked if she thought Fidel was dishonest. She shrugged and said, "He's a great politician."

I asked for the check. I'd gotten what I came for, and I was happy to pay for it.

On Friday morning, March 27, I move across the park to my new hotel, the Plaza—cheaper, roomier, and flush with running water. I pick up *Granma* on my way out of the Inglaterra, and wend my way through the cacophonous bustle of car gears grinding, hustlers bumping too close, past the jackhammers slicing through pavement. The newest luxury hotel is rising right across the street and, as I will soon find, construction goes on seven days a week. I stop by a travel office to book a plane ticket. "Cuba had been asleep, but now it has woken up to tourism," says the agent, Raysa Cabrera. Raysa? "It's Russian. We used to have close relations with Russia."

I stop into Castillo de Farnes for a cup of coffee. It is empty. The spare tracings of a single acoustic guitar fills the air, and I recognize the tune: "Another Day in Paradise." I try to ignore it but can't, and I am again hammered by a moment of irony that, in a film, would be dismissed as heavy-handed. What was, in the hands of singer Phil Collins, a soupy, inane dirge now comes off as profoundly sad. I open *Granma*. On the back page is the kind of story that always delights the regime: "Violence Hits Arkansas Again." Two schoolchildren have killed five classmates and a teacher in Jonesboro, Arkansas, and any news about the diseased American soul gets big play. I turn the page. The baseball playoffs haven't begun yet, but there's an off-day story by Sigfredo Barros, *Granma*'s longtime baseball writer, about which players had the best regular season. I skim it. Five paragraphs down, I stop short.

There, after a sentence about baseball's shortstops, is this: "Speaking of shortstops, German Mesa and Eduardo Paret have had their bans lifted, as have Osmany Garcia and the coaches Pedro Jova and Luis E. Gonzales."

That's it. The next sentence goes on to talk about Omar Linares's injuries. This is a stunning reversal. Mesa had been banned for life with El Duque in 1996, and the other two players and two coaches had been banned in July 1997 along with Toca and the rest of the rafters just picked up in the Bahamas for "communication with traitors to Cuban baseball." Pedro Jova, the father of seventeen-year-old rafter Maikel Jova and widely considered the nation's best manager, had been charged specifically with talking on the phone with Tampa Bay's Rolando Arrojo, one of his former pitchers. Paret and Mesa are major league–quality players. All had been disgraced. All, suddenly, have been forgiven.

Why?

Teofilo is late. We have been outside El Alhibe a half-hour now, watching the tour buses spit out their red-faced, blinking herds. Three steps, and they all begin digging into fannypacks for money—as appropriate an instinct, under the circumstances, as recoiling at the sight of a viper. It's not just that El Alhibe is overpriced. To drive out here to Miramar from central Havana is a sudden glide into a honeyed past: The vast, palm-brushed houses once claimed by the island's pale elite need paint, but there remains a faint charge of grandness in the wide lawns and coral paths, an echo of useless laughter. It is cooler here, leafy and quiet. Diplomats and party officials and heroes like high-jumper Javier Sotomayor live in Miramar, but all has changed, and changed again. A few years ago, I came to one mansion by the sea with an exile returning for the first time; he'd grown up in America haunted for decades by the memory of its turquoise pool. When we arrived, a passel of families lived upstairs, his grandfather's private bar had been converted to a local tavern, the pool was empty—a perfect vision of the proletariat claiming its due. Today, across the street from El Alhibe, I can see a new eyeglass store where they peddle Ralph Lauren frames for $200.

It is about now that Charles Hill says, quite casually, that my time with him could be seen as aiding and abetting by the U.S. government. My stomach hops. This, I had not considered. As a writer, I'd only seen Hill as a perfect guide, someone who could provide a Cuban perspective from an American point of view, just one more odd twist in the weird dance between the two countries. I'd bought him meals and drinks and cab rides, and for the first time it hits me that maybe I was wrong. Maybe nothing in Cuba stays clean for long, including me.

Olga and Stevenson pull up, an hour late now, and park. Teofilo unfolds himself slowly from the car; later, Olga will tell me that she'd woken him up. He shakes my hand and vaguely apologizes. A man came by just as he was about to leave, he says—Enrique Figuerola, the hundred-meter runner who won Cuba's first-ever Olympic track medal, a silver, in 1964. Teofilo is wearing a yellow guayabera, gray slacks, the same black shoes. His deep voice is steadier today. People wave as he strides to the table; four men stand to hug him. "That's the bad thing about being famous. Everybody wants to say hello, shake your hand," he says. Then, as if realizing that he has made it to his table faster than usual, he says, "I've never seen this place so quiet."

He's right. The restaurant, renowned for its succulent chicken dishes, is usually packed. But today there are a dozen empty tables; if not for the tourists it would be dead. A waiter comes; we order the chicken. Teofilo ask for a glass of white rum. I have gotten him at a good time. This is his first meal of the day.

Still, I don't know what to expect. I start with the basics, and Teofilo reels them off. He was born in the small maritime city of Puerto Padre in 1952, far from the capital in Cuba's dusty eastern flank. His father, Teofilo, came to Cuba in 1923 on a boat from the island of St. Vincent. He was poor, working odd jobs as a mechanic at the U.S. base at Guantanamo, as a stevedore, as an English teacher. He boxed professionally for a short time, and spent much of his later years giving his world champion son tips and demanding to know why he couldn't speak English like Alberto Juantorena. His boy fought 340 times, losing nineteen. In 1986, at the age of thirty-four, Teofilo won his final world championship. He retired in 1988. Of all the sports he played as a kid, he liked boxing least.

"I never thought about becoming a boxer," Teofilo says. "I said, 'Let some other sucker put on the gloves. I wasn't made to be hit.' But when I was twelve I started boxing with some kid. I said to him, 'Don't hit me hard. If you do I'll pick up a stick and we'll really fight.' I acted like I knew what I was doing. My father had given me a comic book in English so I could learn it but I just looked at the pictures of boxing. The next year, I started for real. The first time, I started fighting this guy and I hit him once and he went down. When he got up he really wanted to start boxing; he looked like a mad lion. I said, 'No more, that's it, I'm taking the gloves off.'

"Of the first ten fights I had, I lost six. If it'd been the other way around and I had won six, I probably wouldn't have kept at it. But I didn't like to lose."

He goes on about his career, who he fought and when, and stops to brag. "A book just came out about the best boxers of all time—Ali, Joe Louis, Frazier, Kid Gavilan, Kid Chocolate—and the only amateur in there is me."

The mention of Gavilan, a superb postwar Cuban welterweight who, in the early 1990s, was found half-blind and mush-mouthed in a two-room Miami flat, makes me realize that some of the rumors about Teofilo's fogginess were wrong. When I spoke to Gavilan, he was your classic Mayor of Queer Street—brain stolen by punches decades old, trophies stolen by kids, rambling and sad. Teofilo is nothing like that. He remembers dates, he asks questions, he has wit. He speaks of his decade spent as a representative of the National Assembly, his current position as vice president of Cuba's boxing federation, his twenty-day trip across America with Ali in

1995. "He was a great boxer, and he's a better person than I ever thought," Stevenson says. "A better man than he ever was a boxer. That's saying a lot."

As for Ali's current bout with Parkinson's syndrome, Teofilo thinks much of it is an act. "He thinks, he knows," Teofilo says. "He's sharp and he expresses himself. I asked him, 'Ali, why don't you speak in public?' He says he doesn't want to. Sometimes he'll talk with people very normally, have conversations no problem. His tongue is a bit loose, but he understands everything perfectly." Asked if he thinks boxing brought on Ali's sickness, Stevenson smiles. "Why does the Pope have Parkinson's then?"

The waiter brings Teofilo another shot of rum. Before the man can turn away, Teofilo knocks it back and hands him the glass. "Take this," he says. "Bring me a double. I don't drink singles."

We dig into the chicken and a massive amount of rice, all of it drenched in an addictive gravy. A skinny gray cat sets up camp at Teofilo's feet, and he begins to gently pass a pile of bones under the table. He speaks again about Ali, about his magic tricks, his traveling. "You have to keep living life, you know," Teofilo says. I figure this is as good a time as any. I ask him about his car accident.

"I wasn't hurt," he says. "That was in 1987. It was just a normal accident like happens with cars in Cuba . . . Yes, the guy was on a motorcycle. . . . Yes, somebody was killed. And if you're a human being you feel it."

I ask if it was hard to put the thought of killing a man behind him, and Stevenson stares at his plate. He doesn't like this line of questioning. He begins tapping on an empty plastic water bottle with a stirrer, and after a moment he mentions again how his father worked the docks at Puerto Padre. "Everything is easy," Teofilo says finally. "Nothing is hard."

The water bottle topples over, and Stevenson's mouth twists in annoyance. He grabs the bottle and places it upright, studying its contours as if he'd never seen a bottle like this before. I switch gears, wonder how often people tell him he looks like Ali.

"They've asked me in the States if I'm his brother," he says. "They've even come up and asked me if I'm Ali. . . . But I don't see it. I've got a videotape from my trip and I see Ali and me and I keep looking and I don't see it."

His drinks keep coming, three, four, five, six of them—but Stevenson doesn't seem at all affected. In fact, as he talks about how Cuba remains strong in sport, his voice booms and picks up speed.

"We're a third-world country," he says. "We're a poor country. We don't have the resources other countries have, we don't have developed industry, we don't have a lot of natural resources. So you work together, and you work to weariness because you don't know how things are going to work out. And aside from the natural enemies of an economy, there are also unnatural enemies like the blockade. It's been there for years. The U.S. government doesn't want relations with Cuba and they are trying to stop other countries from having relations. They don't want to allow food or medicine, they negate visas and a series of ridiculous things. It makes it a lot more difficult. It could've been a lot easier.

"We work hard. We say in Cuba that we prepare the athlete, but we don't. We prepare the individual."

Defectors? "They were given schooling, training—everything to make them what they are now. Everybody in life should be grateful for what they've been taught and been given. Ask most of them, what was your family like before the revolution? Ask them who they were before they started playing sports. Without the revolution, practically being born would've been impossible. Ask them if they thought about all that before they left."

He takes a deep breath, turns to Olga.

"How'd I do?" he says. She pats his hand like a mother.

It's as if a switch has been flipped; suddenly we're all great friends, laughing, joking. Teofilo invites us to his house on Sunday. It will be his birthday, and he wants us there. He makes a mock lunge at Olga, shouts, "Come on, or I'll tell my wife you're flirting with me!"

"No," Olga says. "You're a bad man. My husband is a cop with a gun. . . ."

"He doesn't have as many guns as me!"

Teofilo turns to me, says in English, "Hey, when I want to fuck, I say to my wife, 'Olga was with me. . . .' She gets mad, and it's good!"

I pay the bill. We step out into the late-afternoon light, say good-bye, promise to show up Sunday. On the way back into town, rolling along Calle Reina y Aguila, I am again struck by the slow pace here, by the feel of a metropolis moving at the speed of 1930. No one drives fast in Havana; the streets are pocked by massive craters, and a broken axle can spell a family's economic disaster. We pass a small crowd gathered in the middle of the street. A bicycle is lying pinned under the wheel of a fallen motorcycle. There are no bodies.

"Not one day goes by that I don't see that four or five times," Olga says.

Back at the hotel, my wife calls. She tells me that the *Miami Herald* has reported today not only that the bans have been lifted on the three players and two coaches, but that Cuba has also decided to reverse its three-year-old policy of farming out more than seventy-five retired players to leagues in Japan, Colombia, Ecuador, El Salvador, and Nicaragua. The report, which came directly from baseball commissioner Carlos Rodriguez through the official Cuban press agency, gives me firsthand experience in the typical Cuban's struggle to decode the regime's cryptic statements. The boys at La Pena, and all over the country, have been complaining about the decline of the Cuban national team since it lost four straight games to the United States in a 1995 exhibition series—"Like an atomic bomb dropping," said pitcher Lazaro Valle—and then had all fears confirmed when Japan snapped Cuba's ten-year, 152-game winning streak in official competition with a humiliating 11–2 beating in the final of the 1997 Intercontinental Cup. Maybe this is Castro's response. Maybe it isn't. Who can say?

I scan *Granma* again: There's only that one short paragraph about lifting the bans buried in an unrelated story. Why isn't there any mention of the players coming home? Why is there far more explanation—quotes from Rodriguez about bringing back the thirteen players, who had departed just last week, once their Japanese season ends—in Miami than in Havana? While the reinstatement of the banned players seems to signal a more flexible line than the one toed by El Duque, the end of overseas jobs will do more than cut off a nice source of income for INDER. It will shut down Cuban baseball's only safety valve. Legends like the thirty-five-year-old Valle, who turned down offer after offer to defect to America, played semi-pro ball for Japan's Mitsubishi team in 1997; though 80 percent of his salary went to INDER, he still cleared $5,000—a massive amount compared to his usual $10 monthly stipend. Going to Japan was the one way for a ballplayer to be rewarded, the only alternative to defection. Now that alternative is gone.

I put the paper aside, and make my guesses. What I do know, through talks with officials and players, is that the overseas experiment ravaged morale. In an attempt to harness capitalism, even in so slight a manner, Cuban officials learned too late that the market can never be controlled: Players who should've been playing on the national team retired early so they could make money overseas, the players left behind resented the good life of the ones who left, the national team began to fray. I'm sure these new measures will do little to lift any player's spirits. I also remember a conversation earlier in the week with Valle's wife, and I fear the implications. "There's a difference in the generations," said Margarita Vazquez Verde, sitting in the house she shares with Valle in Playa Guanabo. "There's going to be more defections: These younger guys are going to go and not come back. We're living in different times. You need TVs, you need shoes, people need dollars. Everybody is after the dollars. The state is still teaching the same principles, but it's what these guys are seeing: the changes in society, the tourist shops, the two kinds of money—one good and one no good. They say, 'Wow. That other player is not as good as I am and he's making more money. I've got to go.'"

I asked her then if she thought El Duque and these recent copycat rafters were the first signs of a baseball flotilla. "That's what I'm afraid of," she said. Margarita had been to the airport to meet the team plane too many times when other women's husbands didn't return, felt Rene Arocha's wife sag against her and weep so deeply that the shudders coursed into her own body. But then, at least, the women knew their men were safe.

"They're on the edge of an abyss," she said. "People are saying, 'If he made it, I can make it.' They're young, overanxious. But they're all on the edge and somebody's going to fall in. There's going to be some tragedy."

Fights tonight. I cross the park and walk two blocks to the absolute best boxing venue I've ever seen, Havana's Kid Chocolate Boxing Hall. Built in 1991 for the Pan Am Games in the shell of an ornate colonial structure opposite the Capitolio, the Kid's cramped, dingy, un-air-conditioned confines lend it the tawdry patina of the fistic palaces once found in every major American city. Even when they build something new, the Cubans can't help but make it a throwback. Though tonight's action is an hour away and merely an exhibition, there's a nice crowd milling outside when I arrive, fighters and kids and wives easing past each other, nobody tense.

A gigantic plastic face of Kid Chocolate, one of Cuba's great pros from the 1930s, hangs smiling over the doorway. I've never understood why the place is named for him; Castro banned professional sports in 1961 because of their exploitative nature, and Kid Chocolate ended his days a rheumy mess. Ask a Cuban boxer about fighting professionally and, publicly anyway, he'll always recite the party line about that game's parade of broken victims. The regime has never bothered to square that noble stance with the fact that using athletes as political tools—or selling their talents to the Japanese—is merely exploitation by another name, but I've come to consider the Kid's eternally laughing face the most honest commentary on the matter. No matter how you dress it up, boxing always ends up a mean joke.

That doesn't mean I don't love it. At the '96 Olympics in Atlanta, the Cubans dominated the boxing competition as usual but still provided foils for two of the games' most dramatic scenes. The first came in the quarterfinals, when six-foot-six superheavyweight Alexis Rubalcaba, with a body carved out of obsidian and the psychic heft provided by Cuba's unequaled place as the sport's lone superpower, faced off against an obscure building-with-feet from Tonga named Paea Wolfgramm. The bell rang, Wolfgramm fell upon Rubalcaba and pounded at his startled face, and the audience wound itself into a frenzy of happy surprise as Cuba suffered its first-ever superheavyweight loss in Olympic competition. Then, in the finals, American light middleweight David Reid, trailing 15-5 in the final round, uncorked a desperate right hand into the face of world number one Alfredo Duvergel and left him flat on his chest, winning the USA's only gold medal. I can't remember the last time a sports event filled me with such amazement.

Tonight promises nothing of the kind. After an undercard featuring a series of matches between some Cuban and French juniors, both Rubalcaba and light middleweight Juan Hernandez, two of the nine Cubans named number one in their weight classes by the world rankings published yesterday in *Granma*, will face off against lesser Cuban opponents. No one expects them to lose, but with Rubalcaba you never know. Not that it matters much. To me, it's enough that the grime on the floorboards is now fingernail thick, Kool and the Gang is being piped through the speakers; an antique, three-sided scoreboard dangles from the ceiling over the ring. I look over to a table where three scorers sit idly. Alcides Sagarra, the legendary and autocratic head coach of the national team, stands chatting. He is wearing a billowy pink-and-gray-striped shirt, pulled free and hanging over his gut like a tablecloth.

Now sixty-two, Sagarra has been with the national team as fighter, assistant coach, and czar since 1964, and he's considered the infallible architect of its current success. His brilliant career stems from ultimate control and a subtle command of the international rules; all boxers love a knockout, but a Sagarra fighter is a smart fighter—content to bore the crowd and charm the scorers with perfectly placed smacks, building a nice lead and then spending the last rounds dancing out of reach. What made Duvergel's loss so stupefying was not so much Reid's punch, but the fact that Duvergel forgot he was Cuban. He ignored the score, got macho, and waded in looking for the KO, defying everything Sagarra teaches. Winning, not manhood, always matters most.

His only dream, Sagarra once told me, was to win all twelve gold medals at an Olympic games. He wields his authority like a billy-club, tolerates no opposition, and can be heartlessly arbitrary. Once, Olga spent months negotiating a session at La Finca for some foreign photographers. Sagarra agreed, but when the day finally came and Olga showed up with the crew, he reversed himself, grew furious, and, in front of fighters and press, shouted that no boxer would be going anywhere with her. She could do nothing but stand there silently and take it, eyes welling with tears.

Sagarra isn't smiling now, and it strikes me that I've never seen him smile at all. Interviews with American journalists are always terse, officious exchanges; when we sat down for a chat earlier tonight, he pulled out a stubby pencil and a folded piece of paper and then, finally settled, barked, "First question!" He gives nothing away, admits no emotion, numbingly spouts the party line: Sagarra comes across, in fact, as more rigid a true believer than even Fidel himself. He carefully copied down every question he was asked. Whether this makes him smart or merely terrified is unclear, of course, but it's a distinction Sagarra would never publicly consider. All I know is that he's a rock I have wearied of butting my head against, and I have other appointments to keep.

The crowd files in, the air thickens with smoke. I climb the cement stairs of the grandstand to talk with the toughest man in the world.

No one but me calls Felix Savon that. In fact, no one calls any heavyweight that anymore. Pro boxing's big boys have distinguished themselves most famously by biting (Mike Tyson), weeping (Oliver McCall), doddering (Larry Holmes), or kidnapping (Riddick Bowe), and the division has entered yet another period of popular eclipse. Meanwhile, since 1986 no boxer, pro or amateur, has reigned as regally as Savon, the six-foot-four-inch tower of power who has won an unprecedented six world and two Olympic heavyweight championships. Critics rightly snipe that Savon's amateur status will forever make him a pugilistic mystery, but he has been well-served by avoiding the Don King circus. Unlike even the brave Evander Holyfield, Savon hops into any ring shrouded in the same mythic dominance of a Marciano or a young Tyson. Even his own teammates fear him: The Cubans often spar regardless of weight class and Savon never shows mercy. Middleweight Ariel Hernandez, who was, until 1997, for many the best pound-for-pound amateur boxer in the world, has often finished such sessions a bloody mess. "What can I do? I defend myself," Hernandez told me once. "Whoever enters the ring with him is taking his life into his hands."

Each Savon bout is a simple dance: His opponent dodges, feints, works desperately to avoid his heavy right hand, and Savon pursues, arm eternally cocked, seeking the chance to unload. It's never interesting, but always compelling. With his unvaried A-bomb approach—always looking to end things with one blow—Savon will never be the stylish boxer Stevenson was, but at thirty there's little doubt he has now edged into Teofilo's class. He cruised through the field in Atlanta in '96, demolishing Canadian David Defiagbon, 20–2, in the Olympic final. And he's determined to win two more gold medals to break his idol's Olympic record.

"I'm not even worried about 2000," Savon says now of the Sydney games. "I'm thinking about Athens in 2004."

We are sitting in a room marked "Protocol," behind the stands. Between matches, eleven-year-olds from the boroughs of Boyeros and Cerro snap on the gear and flail quite impressively on each other; their hands are quick and their fundamentals solid, and the room is a well of encouragement. The standing-room-only crowd roars and giggles at the endless flurry of blows. After the first round of the first fight, Savon had strolled into the place, his place, in a short-sleeved green striped shirt and green pants. His grotesque, grapefruit biceps strained under the fabric. He smiled easily at the people stepping up to say hello. I'd never seen him so relaxed. When we start talking, he is loose, laughing.

This is odd. Savon is usually chilly with foreign writers. He is considered something of a simpleton—one baseball player referred to him as "a Cro-Magnon"—and his tongue crashes against his teeth as he speaks, so I had always attributed his distance in earlier meetings to shyness or shame. He has a handsome, mocha-skinned face that, when he scowls, looks more perplexed than menacing, and I had good reason to expect a full dose of that tonight. Recently, Savon has begun to show his first signs of vulnerability. In February 1997, he lost to fellow Cuban Juan Carlos Delis on a technical knockout— his first loss since 1994—and then in October he lost again at the World Championships in Budapest to Uzbekistan boxer Ruslan Chagayev, 14–4. But Savon isn't concerned. In July, Savon predicts, Chagayev will be stripped of the title because he'd boxed professionally. He seems almost lightened by the setbacks, as if some great pressure had finally eased.

"I couldn't concentrate," Savon says of the Delis loss. "I was listening to all the noise. I lost my natural fighting rhythm. I wasn't my normal self. He punched me, I charged him, and he hit me again on the back of the neck. The force of it sent me down on the mat; it wasn't a good mat, very hard. He pulled me down and I fell on my head. . . .

"You have to know how to win and lose. I wasn't concentrating and I took him lightly. I was embarrassed. I felt bad. Everybody has asked me what was wrong, and tried to give me advice and support. But I was just beat. That can happen to anyone. I know I can dominate any boxer with my left hand. Sometimes I get overanxious in the ring, but you can't be a tough guy. You have to be intelligent. That's what Stevenson told me."

Savon grew up in Guantanamo, in the shadow of the U.S. naval base, the son of a bricklayer and one of five kids. He wasn't a prodigy; three times he applied to the Gitmo EIDE and was turned down. The way he tells it, only some intense campaigning by his sister convinced the coaches there to take one last look at the skinny kid, and he floundered about in track and basketball and rowing before finding himself, at thirteen, in boxing. His father, Felix, harped on only one thing: No matter the opponent, make sure you knock him out. "So," Savon says. "If my dad or mom gets in the ring with me, they lose."

Another round begins. The noise of the crowd rises, crests, and crashes like a wave, a muffled roar crashing against the curtained window behind Savon's head.

The door opens, and three boys come in, led by a woman. "They're in the boxing academy," she says. "It was their dream to meet you." Savon smiles gently, and invites them all closer. The biggest, a fourteen-year-old, takes Savon's right hand, the deadly one with the thick hump rising off its back like a second row of knuckles. Months later, when I ask Savon's first coach, Hugo Fernandez, what caused the deformity, he would say, "Savon is very strong—so strong that when he hits, it's too much for his bones to take. That's why he has that ridge: Every time, it's like a bicycle hitting a truck."

The woman keeps talking, but the boy doesn't hear. He stares, mouth slightly ajar. He's holding Savon's right hand in both hands like a gift. Savon speaks of his own development, how he gained weight at the EIDE by constantly dipping into a barrel of molasses, how he moved on to the ESPA, the region's advanced school for sports training. When Stevenson retired in 1988, Savon took his place as the nation's premiere giant; the men he regularly beat, like the now-dead '92 Olympic champ Roberto Balado, were forced to move up a class to superheavy in order to keep fighting.

Savon is told the fourteen-year-old is now at Cuba's top boxing academy at La Finca, the farm outside Havana where the Cuban national team lives and trains.

"I wish I could inject you with my blood," he tells the fourteen-year-old. "So you could be like me."

The boys leave. Savon begins talking about the loss in Budapest, says it was obvious that the referee and judges were "favoring the Europeans," he says. "It's happened other times. At almost all the competitions in Europe we've had to put up with that. We're Cubans. They try to make Cubans lose as much as they can. They can't believe such a small country could be the best in the world."

He says he would knock out Tyson or any other heavyweight the Americans throw at him. He feels no void because he hasn't fought professionally, has no interest. His hands are full enough as it is. The door opens again; a man rushes in to tell Savon that his son has a fever. He must go. Savon nods. We stand up and say goodbye, but Savon keeps talking. He wants to emphasize: His confidence is the same. He hasn't lost a thing.

"I try to learn from all my opponents," he says, grinning, wiggling his fist. "And I try to be gentle with them. But if they get naughty with me, I put the whammy on them."

CHAPTER 4

*I am so angry with that infernal little Cuban republic that I
would like to wipe its people off the face of the earth. All we
have wanted from them is that they would behave themselves
and be prosperous and happy so that we would not have to
interfere. And now, lo and behold, they have started an utterly
unjustifiable and pointless revolution and may get things into
such a snarl that we have no alternative. . . .*

—THEODORE ROOSEVELT, **September 1906**

Here is a dangerous man. I know this, because Humberto
Rodriguez has no doubt. Because he stares unflinchingly and tries
to convince me of nothing. Because if I don't agree at once with his
logic, too bad. Because he does not, like every other Cuban communist I've interviewed, try to soften his criticism of the USA with the
usual line about having no quarrel with the American people.
Because he doesn't try to reel me in with earthy palaver as if to say,
"We're men after all, and, yes, we're on opposite sides, but in the end
all we really want is to get laid." Because this is not a conversation.
This is a diatribe. Humberto Rodriguez is the president of INDER,
the island's recently minted sports czar, and he is young and intense
and deadly serious.

I have been waiting for him a long time. I have been waiting, antennae out, for years now, waiting for Rodriguez's type to reveal himself to me because I am sure he will be the defining factor on this island, the enemy of easy solutions, the reason life may never change no matter when Fidel breathes his last. Castro is seventy-one, and his cadre of revolutionaries has been dying for years. It is assumed in Miami that when he goes, the regime goes, but I'm not so sure. Fidel has anointed his less popular but equally ruthless brother Raul his *relevo*—relief pitcher—and there are thousands of functionaries, not to mention the entrenched young troika of vice president Carlos Lage, foreign minister Roberto Robaina, and National Assembly chief Ricardo Alarcon, who've invested their lives in communism's survival. Ever since the Cuban air force blithely blasted two unarmed, leaflet-laden American Cessnas out of the sky on February 24, 1996—with one anonymous MiG-29 pilot screaming, "We took out his balls!" and the other one declaring "Fatherland or death!"—it has been easy to imagine that Fidel isn't the only one in this for keeps. The shootdown pushed President Clinton to sign the Helms-Burton Act, tightening the embargo and penalizing other countries who invest in Cuba, but the fevered edginess—the feeling five years ago that, given just one proper trigger, Havana could ignite in riotous violence—hasn't resurfaced. And in the fading whine of jet engines, you could almost hear the sounds of a tiny new generation clawing out of its eggshell.

"Sports here is an actual part of life," Rodriguez continues. "It is a symbol of our revolution and constitutes a paradigm of our national identity, its human sentiments, its patriotic feelings.

"This one-sided conflict . . . our sports are affected by it. We will continue to defend the security of our national athletics, sanely and clearly and humanely. We will continue our conquest within that paradigm. . . ."

I look up at the wall. There's a framed collage of Teofilo, Juantorena, Sotomayor, and a quote from Fidel: "You contributed not only to the glory of sports, but also to the patriotic glory of our country." The air is thick with ideology. It's like chatting with a doughier, Latino Lenin.

"Lifting the bans was purely educational," Rodriguez says of yesterday's announcement restoring the careers to the three ballplayers and two coaches. "We spoke with them, and they had good attitudes; therefore our objective with that punishment was realized. Our revolution never condemns unjustly, nor do we condemn men. We condemn their errors.

"Our sports is not an individual thing. It's not a matter of winning medals. We defend values—patriotic, human. Errors of this type are subject to reeducation. Everyone who was banned decided to continue with us. They stayed with us. They showed total agreement with us and they recognized the errors they committed. Now it's all forgotten."

I ask if El Duque would've had his ban revoked too, had he stayed. "Yes, if his attitude had been like German Mesa's, his sanction would've been lifted," he says. "We weren't looking to condemn anyone. I talked personally to each man. I couldn't talk to Duque because he was already gone."

Rodriguez is thirty-eight, a communist wunderkind who served six years as mayor of Santa Clara before a three-year stint as governor of the province of Villa Clara. He has been in this office since October 31, 1997, when the previous INDER administration under Reynaldo Gonzalez, which had collected more than $40 million since it began selling equipment, expertise, and athletes overseas in 1992, was sacked after the regime's accounting commission found "gross irregularities" in the management of both INDER and Cubadeportes and seized control of the books. In his October 17 comments on the matter, Carlos Lage sparked speculation that the INDER scandal was rooted in personal corruption when he recommended further inquiry and declared in *Granma*: "There are signs of grave and apparent errors that don't come from mere ignorance or a mismanagement of accounts."

But now, Rodriguez says, the investigation is finished. All irregularities, he insists, were merely accounting errors and managerial ineptitude and a lack of accountability, solved by a new system of regularly scheduled audits and a total revamp of business methods. "There has been no corruption of INDER," he says. "In not one case did any person take things they shouldn't. I personally understand how hard it is to struggle to develop sports under such difficult conditions. We maintained our sports system. Nobody did anything wrong. There was no personal greed."

In fact, he says, INDER and the role of sports in Cuban society is destined to grow larger. Last night's fights were just a hint; the plan now is to nationally televise boxing, swimming, and track and field on a regular basis for the first time. More important, the regime is intent on producing more talent to fill the gaps left by defections. Once content to have its farm system stop at the municipal level, INDER is now working with the local Committees for the Defense of the Revolution (CDR)—which have long served as the regime's most effective weapons at weeding out dissent—to unearth the nation's best athletes, no matter how young, with block-by-block thoroughness.

"We are at a very interesting moment in the history of our sports," Rodriguez says. "We are returning to the most important aspect of revolutionary sports—mass participation. Everyone takes part. We want all to practice sports—old, young, women, students, the fat and the thin. We are now evaluating new technical concepts, new applications of sports science that will allow us to guarantee continuity in our athletics.

"We will go to Sydney and continue to defend our eternal position. You ask how we'll be able to do it with all these limitations? We'll have to export more technology and perfect INDER's administration and find a way to rebuild our sports facilities, equipment, and uniforms, and get higher performances from our coaches. We'll improve our system of sports science. We already have our Olympic champions for 2008. They're in our EIDEs. It's up to us to prepare them, develop them, and create mass involvement. The numbers show that with more participation in neighborhoods, more athletes will end up in an EIDE or ESPA and the more champions we'll have."

I walk out of the office spent. The monotonous momentum of Rodriguez's rhetoric has left my fingers cramped and my brain fogged. 2008? I can muster only one prediction about 2008. Promoted, fired, exiled or dead, in a decade this man will still have an answer for everything.

It is a government plot. I am hearing this more and more. All those millions being thrown at El Duque, Livan, Arrojo? All the intrigues by agent Joe Cubas, the boats, the airplanes taken to scour the Florida Straits for rafters? None of it has anything to do with baseball, or owners looking to fill seats or win a pennant. Something else is going on. It's the Cuban-American National Foundation, the State Department, the CIA. "Behind Joe Cubas, there is a political motive to destroy sports here," says Alberto Juantorena. "It's a blow against our social system, our pride."

Juantorena drove up in front of the arena just as we were leaving. Could we talk? "Now, now, now," he said, racing to a chair. We sit now in the lobby, near the broad, black-and-white mural of Teofilo hammering Bobick, and soon Juantorena casts his usual spell. He leans forward just inches from my face, he smacks my knee to make his points, he waves his hands, he smiles, he laughs, he bounces his own leg like a restless adolescent. At forty-eight, Juantorena has more force and fire than anyone I know. He is one of the few people I've ever met for whom it's appropriate to employ the overused label of "charismatic." It doesn't matter what he says, how dogmatic he gets, how serious or absurd. You can't take your eyes off him. The thinking of athletes can be fairly predictable, but fielding Juantorena's choppy, colorful English is conversational poker; you never know what you're going to get. "Bad po-ta-toes! Out of the sack!" he once yelled at me when I mentioned defectors. "Pigeons who fly . . . awaaay!"

After that meeting with Rodriguez, such cartoon passion is exactly what I need. Juantorena is one of track's enduring legends. At six-foot-three he is taller and broader than most speedsters, more line-backer than runner, yet at the Montreal Olympics of 1976 he pulled off an astounding double by winning both the four-hundred- and eight-hundred-meter races. Twenty years later, everyone raved about Michael Johnson's Olympic gold in the two hundred and four hundred, but Juantorena's feat was more remarkable. Johnson was the acknowledged master at both distances in 1996, and his two wins left a distinct aftertaste of relief: He didn't blow it. But before Montreal, Juantorena had run the eight hundred only three times in his life. A four-hundred specialist, he had never even run both events at one meet. The two races demand different tactics, psychology, training; before Juantorena, no modern Olympic runner ever had the gall to think he could win both—least of all Juantorena himself. But just a month before the '76 Olympics, Juantorena was altitude-training in Mexico City when his Polish coach, Zigmunt Zabierzowski, looked up from a sheet of paper and announced he would go for the double. "I was very afraid," Juantorena says.

He fought with Zabierzowski long and hard, but the coach won. The eight hundred came first, and the strategy was simple and unheard of: Take huge, nine-foot strides, don't pace yourself, run balls-out from the start. No one expected Juantorena to win. I remember watching the race from the comfort of an American adolescence, half-bored, hardly expecting a track meet to provide me with either a thrill or a mystery. Then he took off, mouth agape, afro bouncing side-to-side. Halfway through, Juantorena had passed everybody. India's Sriram Singh, American Richard Wohlhuter, and Belgian Ivo Van Damme tried to challenge, but Juantorena never let up, pushing himself like a soul escaping hell. It was a vision of power and need from the most unexpected place—who is that?—and I found myself transfixed; the first Cuban hook had lodged under my skin. "With those long strides I'm like a car; it's difficult to pass me on a curve," Juantorena says. As for Van Damme, the silver medalist? "Barbudo was running right behind me, but he blew up," Juantorena says, laughing. "That car had no fuel." Juantorena's mark of 1:43.50 set a world record, and he went on to run a personal-best 44.26 to easily win the four hundred. He lost eleven pounds running in Montreal. In Cuba he was dubbed, like Fidel, El Caballo—the horse. Others called him the Man in Seven-League Boots.

His eyes glow with the memory. Juantorena loves that it hasn't happened since. "Things are too specialized," he says. "You'd need two athletes—Wilson Kipketer and Michael Johnson. It'd be very difficult to do that now. In my opinion, impossible."

I'd always considered Juantorena a natural to climb the communist ladder—a popular hero with magnetism and true-believer rage, eloquent and smart. The son of a carpenter from

Santiago, he long ago made the transition from jock to administra-
tor, and as vice president of Cuba's Olympic Committee and
INDER, he had earned the ultimate badge recently when, for the
third time, the United States denied him a visa for a conference at
Berkeley. "They say now I am a politician," he says with a shrug. In
this, the United States is correct. Why Juantorena wasn't made the
next president of INDER is beyond me, because the regime has no
more visceral defender. Every turn in the conversation eventually
leads to the same place. Cuba will keep winning. Cuba must.

"It's important because we represent society, the country, the philosophy of sports," Juantorena says. "We educate people, and we
don't practice sport to make money. It's about more than money. I
am standing on the corner talking to the boss and kids are yelling,
'Hey Juantorena.' You can see their eyes shining: 'I want to be like
you.'

"We don't sell athletes. We don't sell souls. We can earn lots of
money, we can have a big budget. But we put all the money together
and decide: Maybe we send it to archery, to water polo, to buy medicine, food. . . . Of course we've made mistakes. We did not use our
resources. We are human. We are not perfect. But if you have a system—surrounded by the United States, surrounded by Helms-
Burton—that produces forty-two Olympic champions, you're doing
something right. Something's going on, my friend.

"The majority—and listen carefully—the main people in Cuban
sports live here. Only people without vision run after money. They
believe they can go to the U.S. to become millionaires, but inside
they are empty. They are merchandise. We prefer to stay and fight
and support our system. We prefer to die here."

Enough. He picks up his keys, rattles them like dice. He bounds
up the stairs, two steps at a time.

*   *   *

Noon. Charles Hill is taking me to a paladar. We walk down the tree-roofed calm of Paseo del Prado. We pass three boys playing baseball with a stick, a group of a hundred adults clustered around watching something with blank faces. I crane my neck: In the center of the crowd five ten-year-old girls perform their act, lip-synching perfectly the MTV moves of the Spice Girls as a song booms out of a tape deck. We pass down a side street, step inside an unmarked door, climb two flights in the dark. Hill knocks, announces himself, and an apartment door swings open to reveal a light, cozy cafe and bar. Semilegalized in 1995, paladares are private restaurants set up in individual homes, and in theory serve only chicken or pork. This place, though, serves fresh vegetables and lobster and shrimp. We sit.

The place is empty. Bob Marley's "Three Little Birds" burbles through the air, a perfect oasis soundtrack. Every little thing . . . is gonna be alright . . . I scan today's Granma: A short item about Humberto Rodriguez's meeting with the president of the Iranian Olympic Committee and their new sports cooperation pact, another about how 40.3 percent of all Hispanic children in the United States live in poverty. I hand the paper to Hill and look around. Across the street, a white-haired, hawk-beaked man is hanging his dripping laundry. He sucks his gums, chest collapsing on itself; he looks like Samuel Beckett. The sound of a game of tacos—bottlecap baseball—rises from the sun-blasted street below. I go look in the bar. The wall is filled with graffiti from all over the world—the usual drunken salutations and romantic vows: "Cuba Libre—Sergio '96." A fan wobbles overhead.

A door opens in the ceiling and a boy in long underwear walks downstairs into the restaurant. Our waitress's son, I think. Plastic deer heads hang on the walls. I sit back down. A weird chill runs over my skin: Now Bob Marley is singing "I Shot the Sheriff." I look over at Hill, but he doesn't notice. He's reading the paper.

I ask him what it has been like, an American living here for thirty years. "When I first came, I was just like you; I was real inquisitive," he says. "But after a while, you just learn: Don't ask why. Just put down your head like a Brahma bull and go." He had to make it work because there was no going back: "This was it. This was it forever." He has always felt like an outsider.

"People think that I'm Cuban because of the clothing I wear, because they're all wearing it now. But I say, 'Don't you remember the seventies and eighties, when you had to have a very good reason to wear blue jeans and sneakers?' It was considered almost ideological diversionism to wear that stuff. You had to have a very good reason to have a VCR and a color TV. 'Don't you remember?'"

He shakes his head. His face goes slack, his eyes drift around the room. It is hot for March. ". . . these songs of freedom are all I ever had . . . redemption songs, redemption songs." He says he listens to WIOD from Miami all day long, ball games, news. When talk turns to the future, he says, "It's going to be really sticky here the next seven, eight years. It may be that the dollar goes wild, it may not. But you may find me off somewhere in the countryside, gone. . . .

"I think I'm going to have to move. I'm a bit scared—not of the U.S. government, but bounty hunters. I've still got a $30,000 reward on my head in New Mexico."

The food comes, one heaping plate after another. I have never been hungrier. We eat. It is one of the best meals I've ever had.

There is no residential telephone book. There is no directory assistance. If you want to find somebody in Cuba, you simply ask and ask and ask, from house to house to the man walking down the street. It rarely fails. No one can hide for long here; sooner or later you must borrow cooking grease or ask a neighbor to stand in line or have him watch your kids while you stand in line. The walls are thin. Everybody knows everybody.

I am looking for the wife of New York Mets shortstop Rey Ordoñez. I have been wondering about her for more than a week, ever since a photographer I know told me a story. In 1997, Victor Baldizon traveled to Monterrey, Mexico, to shoot an exhibition game between the Mets and Padres. He told the twenty-seven-year-old Ordoñez that he'd be going to Cuba soon and, as is customary, asked if Ordoñez wanted to send any money, supplies, medicine along to his wife and young son. "Fuck all those people," Ordoñez replied. "As far as I'm concerned, the whole island can sink. My family is here."

Hill doesn't think she should be difficult to find. The boys at La Pena say Ordoñez came from Cerro, so we start there, driving slow, nudging the ubiquitous baseball game of four shirtless boys onto the crumbling sidewalk. Dust cakes the tires, our foreheads, throats; there is nothing hotter than rambling in an old Lada in the Havana afternoon. We park. A boy retakes the imaginary pitcher's mound in the street, wiggles his hips, and interrupts his windup to dance to the beat of salsa pounding out of some window. Pow! The boy with a bat made of a single narrow slice of wood sends the ball hopping far down the street. Someone sends us to Calle Zequiera, someone there sends us to a restaurant nearby where the woman who helped raise Ordoñez after his mother died supposedly works, someone at the restaurant tells us she won't be back until morning.

This is great progress, considering. When he emerges from the restaurant, Hill points a finger, grabs his wrist, and cocks and fires an invisible gun at my chest. I never think to ask him why.

* * *

I'm drinking a beer at Castillo de Farnes, thick Saturday night crowd. Mr. Aspen walks in with a teenage girl barely dressed. I smirk: So he has found his next thing.

I walk back to my room, switch on the Guantanamo-Santiago game live from Guillermon Moncada Stadium. It is the first night of baseball playoffs. In dead center field, a giant picture of Che's face gazes over the proceedings. Santiago wins, 8–6.

CHAPTER 5

There is no country in the world . . . where economic coloniza-
tion, humiliation and exploitation were worse than in Cuba, in
part owing to my country's policies during the Batista regime. I
believe that we created, built and manufactured the Castro
movement out of whole cloth and without realizing it.

I have understood the Cubans. I approved the proclamation
which Fidel Castro made in the Sierra Maestra. . . . I will go
even further: To some extent it is as though Batista was the
incarnation of a number of sins on the part of the United
States. Now we shall have to pay for those sins.

—JOHN F. KENNEDY, October 24, 1963

She expected weakness. He is a man easily led. She expected stu-
pidity. He is not very smart. But Hilda Maria Fiallo never thought
her husband capable of this. When his son, Reynaldo, was born in
1993, Rey Ordoñez was a picture of devotion. "He loved his son. He
was obsessed with him," Hilda says. "It was a Cesarean birth; I was
in the hospital five days and they didn't allow men in there. But Rey
hid and slept under the bed for two nights. It's incredible that someone could change so much. It's like he's bewitched."

It is 9:30 Sunday morning. I am a stranger, I have come unan-
nounced, it is the worst possible time. When I knocked, I was told to

wait; minutes passed and I knew that no one had yet gotten out of bedclothes. But as is typical in Cuba, Hilda answered with her son by her side, smiled, and held open the door. Not once, in all my visits, has anyone ever told me to come back later. She offered coffee. The first thing Little Rey said when he heard I am from America is, "I have a video of my father." He has bright brown eyes, an open and innocent face, his father's Italianate features. Hilda has dark cropped hair, a quick and warm smile. She is twenty-two. Everything she hoped for in life is gone.

"I'm not embarrassed to talk about it," she says. "Everything was great, everything was fine, the love from his letters was wonderful. He called every day. The whole thing started because of the damned money."

Rey Ordoñez is the most dazzling shortstop baseball has produced since Ozzie Smith. In 1997, he won the National League Gold Glove as the best at his position, but his play goes far beyond dependable. With his slick acrobatics and dramatic flair—in his first major league game he took a relay from the outfield and threw out a runner at home, all on his knees—he makes the routine spectacular and the difficult a sideshow. If his escape from Cuba depended on his bat, Ordoñez would still be bailing water in the Straits, but his fielding is so sublime that he has single-handedly revived a stereotype long thought dead—the light-hitting shortstop. New Yorkers love him for his style and heroic story: He is the Mets' answer to El Duque, and he plays every day.

In July 1993, Ordoñez hopped a fence at the stadium in Buffalo, New York, where the Cuban team was playing in the World University Games. Exiles automatically lauded him as the latest freedom-seeker, but Ordoñez's motives were more prosaic. As a member of Cuba's junior team, he knew it would be years before he'd even have a shot at replacing entrenched shortstop German Mesa. Still, his was a brave step; Ordoñez ran across a street and into a waiting car, one of the first Cuban ballplayers to follow Rene Arocha's lead and head into the unknown. Four months later, forty Cuban athletes bolted in a wholesale breakout during the Central American and Caribbean Games in Ponce, Puerto Rico. Ordoñez was one of the pioneers. And the whole affair was choreographed by Hilda. "It was me," she says. "He never even thought about staying outside the country."

"Can I have my milk?" Little Rey asks. Hilda hands him a cup. He wanders out of the room.

Hilda's father, Arnaldo Fiallo, left for Miami in 1980 in the notorious Mariel boatlift. He made a career for himself as a contractor in Hialeah, and when Hilda became pregnant with Little Rey early in 1992, she and Rey began cooking up a plan to get the entire family to the States. In no place is the American Dream healthier than in the streets of Havana. At first, Hilda was to leave with Little Rey, with Rey following eventually, but Ordoñez could not stand the thought of being separated indefinitely from his son. So a second plan evolved: The two divorced to lift suspicion from Hilda, and Fiallo hired a man to spirit Rey out of Buffalo, bought Rey's plane ticket to Miami. The final step was for Hilda to get a visa to Nicaragua and a Cuban exit visa known as a tarjeta blanca—white card—for both herself and Little Rey. On December 1, 1994, all her paperwork came through. Yet she is still here. When I begin to ask why, Hilda cuts in.

"My father," she says. "The worst thing I ever did was hand Rey to my father. Rey's a man. Rey could've done anything. But my father cheated me."

A light wind passes through open windows. Dustballs tumble across the living room's sea-green tile. Against one wall, a shelf holds a Goldstar TV, a Sony stereo with megabass speakers and

equalizer, and a Hitachi videotape machine. It is a basic two-bedroom apartment, clean and spacious. She digs out a baseball card of
Ordoñez from his stint with the Mets' Florida League team in Port
St. Lucie. "He shaved a year off his birthdate," she says. "He was
born in 1971." Out on the sun-washed balcony, a caged green parrot
squawks monotonously: "Hilda! Hilda! Hilda!"

Knowing no one when he came to Miami, Rey moved in with
Hilda's father. "When Rey first got there, my father kept saying he
had nothing, he had no contract, and he was uneducated, he swore
a lot," Hilda says. "But once he signed a contract, he didn't bother
my father anymore. Suddenly, he became blond-haired and blue-
eyed."

I laugh despite myself and apologize, but Hilda just smiles. "You
haven't heard anything yet," she says.

Her father had remarried in America, raising two stepchildren, a
boy and a girl. At first, Rey lived at the house with the teenage step-
daughter, Gloryanne, and Hilda's father and new wife. The first
year, Rey called Hilda every day. He would tell Hilda, "The ring we
married with in Cuba, we will marry with again in America." The
two would open to the same ad in a magazine they'd each gotten
hold of, and dream together about decorating their new bedroom
the same way. He sent money, some $400.

But by July 1994, Rey had begun to complain: Gloryanne kept
calling him in Port St. Lucie, asking him to take her for rides in his
car. It made him uncomfortable. The winter before, he had moved
out of Gloryanne's house, spending the '93 off-season at the Miami
home of fellow defector Osvaldo Fernandez. Hilda told him not to
worry. We're all family, she said.

Once in a while, Gloryanne would get on the phone with Hilda,
"Women are chasing Rey, but don't worry. We're waiting for you."

Hilda believed it. Then Rey called less and less. In September

1994, she had her last good conversation with Rey. He called once more in October, but she wasn't home. She began to worry. In December, her tarjeta blanca came through; she now had everything she needed to fly to America. Even her flight was paid for. The next day, she called the house of her father. Her stepmother, Nery, answered, and Hilda told her the good news. "I don't know what Rey's going to do with you," Nery said. "He got married to Gloryanne."

Hilda hung up. She thought it was a joke. Her stepsister? Five minutes later, she called back and asked for her father. He wasn't there. For a week she called, two or three times a day. Neither Rey nor her father would speak to her. "He didn't have the guts to say it to me," Hilda says of Rey. "And since December 2, 1994, I haven't spoken to my father. If my father was honest, he would've called and said, 'I can't control Rey's pants; what can I do?' But he never did."

A month later, the mother-in-law of Osvaldo Fernandez, who now pitches with the San Francisco Giants, came to Hilda with some clothing from Rey and the whole story. Her father and stepmother had been encouraging Gloryanne and Rey all along. Rey is so sorry, the woman told Hilda; he still loves you and Little Rey.

In February 1995 Rey heard a rumor that Hilda had remarried. He called, she answered, and he accused her of betraying him, called her a whore and a bitch. She told him she didn't even have a boyfriend. They screamed at each other. The two met when she was sixteen. She went to see him play every day in Havana. Rey was her first and only love. "You've destroyed my life with all these lies," she told him.

Since then, Hilda says, Rey has sent no money, medicine, nothing. She pulls out a pile of tattered magazine stories about him. "He always talks about how he loves his kid, how he talks to him all the time, how he sends money," she says. "It's all a lie."

I have reason to be skeptical. Any marriage is difficult to plumb, much less a marriage in Cuba, where the divorce rate hovers at 50 percent and adultery is common. But a marriage involving rich Cuban exiles is a minefield of politics and betrayal, feelings of escape, liberation, renewal. Miami is filled with men who've left families behind. But two things convince me Hilda tells what she believes is true. First, it does her no good in Cuba to openly admit planning the defection of one of the nation's top baseball players— and it does her no good in America, if she is receiving money from Ordoñez, to trash him and say she isn't. Also, if she and Rey weren't planning to reunite in the United States, then why would he be living at her father's house? Later, I find out that at the exact moment I am talking with Hilda, readers in New York are opening to a *Daily News* story on Ordoñez that confirms the basic facts: her father's role in the defection, Rey's immaturity, Rey's new marriage to Hilda's stepsister and their three-year-old daughter.

When I speak, months later, with Gus Dominguez, Ordoñez's agent until 1996, he tells me that, yes, Rey and Hilda divorced only "to relieve pressure on her once he defected." When I repeat Ordoñez's disdainful comments about his family in Cuba, Dominguez says, "That doesn't sound like the Rey I know. He used to call his ex-wife all the time. If you're asking me whether he would say that? Not when he was with us. But could he say it now? I'd say, yeah, he could. He has an explosive personality. He doesn't like to be asked too many questions." When I contacted Rey's agent, Andy Mota, to tell him I wanted to speak about the defection and, if Rey wished, about Hilda, he called back later in the day. "I have Rey right here," Mota said. "He says he'll be glad to talk right now . . ." A voice spoke in the background. ". . . but only if his ex-wife isn't mentioned in anything you write." Fiallo, too, refused my request for an interview.

Hilda shrugs. Yes, she says, her life is like some bad soap opera. Rey's father and siblings live just down the street here in Cerro; she sees them now and then. She has a few pictures of Rey in his new life, posing with Gloryanne. "I wish I did have another man," Hilda says.

Little Rey is five. "He knows his father is far away," she says. "He always says, 'Why doesn't my father call me?' It's incredible that Rey is so famous and great a baseball player and such a bad father. No. He's not even a bad father; he's no father. Even a bad father recognizes his children."

Little Rey is skinny and eager, his hair cut in a soft brown burr. He studies his father's pictures, watches him play on videotape. He speaks of how he throws a baseball like Rey Ordoñez, plays like Rey Ordoñez. "I'm just like my dad," he says. "I'm a Power Ranger." Hilda tries not to badmouth Rey in front of their son. She tells Little Rey he doesn't call because he is far away, and working.

"His father is his idol," she says. "Let him keep thinking it."

"Cuban Baseball in Recovery" declares today's *Juventud Rebelde*, a weekly newspaper that, like every other, is published by the government. So here it is. Two days after the announcement was made in the United States, baseball commissioner Carlos Rodriguez finally says publicly that Cuba will no longer send players to Japan. "Retirement can never be a pretext for our players to wear uniforms of a friendly nation," he says. "Retirement will simply be the consequence of age, a decline in quality or the presence of younger players." He also speaks of the fact that the Cuban junior team has won the last two world championships; says Cuban baseball is "on the road to recuperation"; mentions the importance of mass participation—the renewed buzzword: Masividad—and, lastly, gives the first public reasoning for lifting sanctions on five players and coaches. "They have had a very positive attitude," he says.

Translation: We blew it. We gave our players a whiff of money, and it wounded our game. We have regained control; these younger players aren't going anywhere. And you older guys? Don't be like Duque. Don't embarrass us by getting in a raft. Nothing is forever, even when we say it is. Just sing the party song and all will be forgiven. Now get out there and play ball.

The cab pulls up in front of Teofilo's four-bedroom house in Nautica, a quiet residential area for favored Cubans and foreigners. His forty-sixth birthday party is in full swing—friends spilling onto the front porch, friends stuffed into every available chair, friends wandering around the pool out back. Teofilo isn't here. He's gone to get rum and supplies, and the result is a wedding without the bride; all through the house some two dozen people are talking quietly, thumbing through books, waiting. The house is breezy but worn, the expected athletic shrine. On one wall is the usual huge black-and-white shot of Stevenson smacking around Bobick, plus a vivid color shot of Fidel, cigar in teeth, holding up Teofilo's arm in victory. It was 1977, Fidel in olive fatigues, Teo in a bloodred tank top. They both look unbeatable.

Teofilo's second wife, a tiny grinning attorney half his age named Fraymaris, apologizes, puts down her three-year-old son David, and leads me into the bright terrace. Out the window, I can see the pool's brown water, the islands of algae, its crumbling staircase. Fraymaris hands me the Ali scrapbook. In November 1995, Stevenson went to see Ali at his ranch in Berrien Springs, Michigan, then traveled with him all over America—San Francisco, Los Angeles, Atlanta, Gettysburg, Ali's boyhood home in Louisville, Kentucky. I turn the pages: photos of Ali and Stevenson gazing out at the ranch, mock-sparring (Stevenson's reach a good six inches longer than Ali's), watching an interview of Fidel on CNN, standing before a statue of Abraham Lincoln.

I open another book, an Ali biography inscribed in his cribbed, childlike scrawl. "Love always," Ali wrote. Next to that is a carefully drawn picture of a black heart, dripping blood.

In January 1996, the two men switched roles. Ali visited Havana. In town at the time was New Mexico Congressman Bill Richardson, who had his lifetime hope of meeting Teofilo preempted by Ali. Richardson settled for a meeting with Castro. They talked about Teofilo.

"You know, Fidel," Richardson said then. "One of the great tragedies is that because of your system the world will never know if Stevenson was one of the best of all time."

"Listen," Fidel replied. "The judge of that is one man. The judge is Stevenson. It was Stevenson who never wanted to change, and that's why he's a hero of the revolution."

No sign of Teofilo. I flip through his 1980 official biography, written by Manolo Cabale Ruiz. In the chapter, "Fidel Talks About Stevenson," Castro says, "This poor humble guy says he would not give up his country for all the money in the world. It's refreshing to see the education of the new generation has paid off."

About the win over Bobick and the gold medal, Castro addressed a large crowd at the Plaza of the Revolution on the anniversary of the CDR: "From mercantile capitalism, they brought their great white hope to beat Stevenson, but this guy from a poor family beat him with his body and soul.

"He gave a good example of what Cuba is. Against millions of dollars.

"Men's sacred values are beyond gold and money. It's impossible to understand this, when you live in a world where everything is bought and sold and gotten through gold."

The walls need paint. A man amuses himself by running along the pool deck, trying to flush out a turtle seen swimming among the muck. Out past the pool, I see the white-lipped waves of the Florida Straits rolling into shore. I tell Fraymaris I have an appointment and will come back later; I am going to see Ana Quirot. Her eyes brighten. Bring her back with you, Fraymaris says. Tell her I said hello.

Ana Quirot is screaming. She stands in her living room, scars shining in the March light, and her words come loud, fast and furious, for she is speaking about the choice one makes in Cuba now, the justification any true believer must swallow to carry on, and the mere voicing of it has made her angry. I listen carefully. I've pushed her to this point by mentioning that every defector tells of the regime's repression, of how even the slightest deviation from the party line provokes the crushing weight of state security and CDR informers, but I expected the usual answer: They lie, we are free, we say what we like. I am wrong. No one in favor says what Ana is saying now. No one admits, in effect, that a deal has been struck by those who follow Castro's communist dream: We surrender freedom so we don't have to be scared.

"I'd prefer to have a son here in Cuba safe, than going to a school and getting shot by some kid with a gun," she says. "They say they're so free there in the U.S. But they live with too much tension. Too much tension. . . . Guard bars for my son or daughter, my sister, my grandmother . . . taking your kid to school with a bodyguard—do you call that liberty? Here, if your kid goes down the street to the park, you know he's coming back. Not in the United States. Do you call that liberty?

"I'd rather have the CDR watching me so that my children grow up healthy mentally and physically, so I can sleep well. You can have a lot of money there, but you can be blackmailed. Life is healthy here. I'd rather have the CDR watching me all day long than live in a society like that."

I am looking at the face of Cuba. Ana Fidelia Quirot, born in the revolution in Fidel's home province of Oriente, skin ravaged and melted by a stovetop inferno just as her nation suffered its most severe period of economic crisis, battling back to win two world championships and a 1996 Olympic silver medal in the eight hundred meters while her homeland shows its first signs of recovery, is the fierce embodiment of Cuban endurance and will. Her middle name is a mother's tribute to Fidel, and now Castro lauds her as the nation's prime example of how to overcome hard times. "It's like looking in a mirror," Juantorena said about watching Quirot run again. "And we're reflected."

I'm willing to accept this conceit, because Quirot's triumph transcends anything she or the regime says about it. I accept it because the pain she endured was so harrowing that it claims even the respect of her enemies. I accept it knowing there are other mirrors, other symbols that the regime fed and trained to be its most famous defenders.

But then Livan defected, and Duque, as he put it, "wasn't a devoted saint. I spoke out, and I spoke the truth."

But then Joel Casamayor, the bantamweight Olympic champion at the 1992 Barcelona Games who bolted on the eve of the '96 games, refused to join the Union of Communist Youth.

But then Rene Arocha, the first Cuban national baseball team member to defect in 1991, couldn't take the hypocrisy. Left off the team in 1982 because the CDR had denounced him, Arocha couldn't believe what happened when he returned to Cuba in 1988 after helping beat the United States at the World Championships in Italy. "The leaders of the revolution were waiting for us," Arocha said. "And they said: 'For beating the Americans, we're going to give you your Communist Youth party card.' I didn't ask for that. In their eyes, beating the Americans made me a communist."

But then Euclides Rojas, Cuba's all-time save leader and the only national team player brave enough to pick up Arocha's luggage when it returned to Havana without him, found himself interrogated three times by state security in a building at the athletes' village during the '91 Pan Am Games, and harassed further when the regime found he had joined a dissident group called Democratic Solidarity. "I figured: Fifteen miles in a little boat or fifteen years in jail," Rojas said.

But then some 25,000 Cubans took to the sea, and by the late winter of 1995 the U.S. base at Guantanamo had become a refugee camp with its own small complement of boxers, baseball players, athletes. "If everything is so good there, why are all these people in Guantanamo?" Rojas asked after he'd made it to the United States. "The champions from here don't go elsewhere looking for liberty. Why did we risk our lives? Why did we risk the lives of our families?"

I remember the dust of Guantanamo. I remember the blinding heat and palms and saguarro cactus, packs of massive, ratlike nutrias rustling in the brush, the quiet tents of Camp Echo and an absence of shade, the minefields where occasionally someone maddened by captivity would hop the fence and blow himself up trying to get back home. I remember Arocha and Rojas talking in the dark in a new home on the edge of the Florida Everglades, their voices tinged by bitterness that will never die. I remember Casamayor's triumph in Barcelona, and the fact that he was forced to sell the cheap bicycle he got as his only reward. I remember all this as I sit in Quirot's spacious apartment and take the glass of fresh-squeezed orange juice that sits in her dark hand like some phosphorescent nectar. And I know that one person's necessity is another's abstraction, something to be dismissed if you're one of the select and have been handed a life that—food lines and *jineteras* and all—is far from awful.

Cuba's track athletes are the elite of the elite. They have it both ways. Because their sport is all but ignored in the United States until the Olympics, Quirot and others like Javier Sotomayor, the world-record holder in the high jump, 1997 world champion long-jumper Ivan Pedroso and 1997 world champion triple-jumper Yoelbi Quesada spend months at a time competing in Europe's Grand Prix circuit, making hard cash while bypassing any need to flirt with America. More than a dozen Cuban athletes spent the past winter based in Guadalajara, Spain, wearing the logos of the capitalists at adidas on their shirts. The regime takes much of their money, but allows them to keep any Mercedes-Benzes they win, plus their substantial stipends and cash payments. Nobody tries to entice them into defecting. There is no need. Boxers and baseball players go to the United States because that's where the money is. But for the regime, which is selling off Cuban hotel rights to Spain's Sol Melia SA chain at a feverish pace, Europe is the destination of choice. For track stars like Ana Quirot, who never needed to consider the option, getting in a raft is incomprehensible.

"It's madness," she says, voice still snapping like a whip. "If you go after the money and don't make it, what's your economy then? Death? Those guys are ungrateful. Who made you an athlete? They leave their families and friends, and the anxiety of not having family and friends can kill you.

"Say I was in the United States after my accident. I may have recuperated, but how much would it have cost? All the psychological work they did with me? Would I have had the money to be in the hospital for a year and a half? My mother was at the hospital with me every day; she had a bed beside me. That's two beds in a hospital, double the expense. Here, the support of the people is what got me back on my feet."

On the evening of January 22, 1993, Quirot fell to the floor of her kitchen, on fire. The kerosene cooker on the stove had exploded, flames leaping onto her sweater, clawing across her torso and up to her eyes, consuming hair, skin, nerves. Nearly 40 percent of her body had been ravaged by third-degree burns when they rolled her into Havana's Hermanos Ameijeiras Hospital; the nurse who saw her then was sure she would die. Castro was one of the first to see her. He came just hours after she was admitted, his black Mercedes-Benz whisking through Havana's quiet midnight streets, and he wore sterilized scrubs and a mask over his mouth. Quirot was in shock, her mind drifting in and out. He asked her how she felt, what happened, if her mother knew.

Quirot told Fidel she was going to run again. He nodded, didn't say anything; he could see her horrible form. Neither of them knew the worst. Six months earlier, she had won a bronze medal at the '92 Olympics in Barcelona while unknowingly pregnant. Now, under her bandages, in her womb, the baby turned. She was twenty-nine. In ten days, the baby would be dead.

In her prime, I'd never seen an athlete so magnificent. I covered Michael Jordan as he emerged into stardom as a college sophomore, witnessed Tyson at his monstrous best. But two years earlier at the '91 Pan Am Games, the sight of Quirot running the four hundred and eight hundred had been a revelation. Echoing Juantorena, she took off fast and never let up, and with those thick churning thighs, snarled mouth, long braids flowing behind her, she created something beyond dominance: a portrait of beautiful female power. There are few moments in life, much less in sport, when mere excellence somehow generates a deep emotional vibration, but to watch Ana Quirot run was like watching a matador defy death with sad-

dening grace; you want to laugh and cry and shout all at once. The
Spanish call this quality *duende*—that rare, semimystical combination of charisma, will, cultural expression, and physical honesty
that is impossible to describe but instantly recognized: You know it
when you see it. I saw it once. I saw Ana Quirot at Pan American Stadium, running through the afternoon as 25,000 voices filled the air,
"A-na! A-na Fi-DEL-ia!"

Now she was ugly. Ana Fidelia had grown up chubby in Palma
Soriano, outside Santiago, and Cubans aren't shy about labeling
people by age, skin color, or heft. They called her Gorda—Fatty—and
even after she carved away the pounds to reveal her striking form,
the name stuck. She was flirtatious, giggly, vain, and like all vain
people Quirot at core believed there was something wrong with her
appearance. "Your nose is too wide. Your lips aren't quite right."
. . . After the accident, it all came true: Her skin was scalloped by
wave after chocolate wave of ridges and swirls, a paralyzed surface of
thickened skin. She could not close her hands; she couldn't raise her
arms high enough to comb her hair. The first time she looked at
herself in the mirror, she forgot her promise to return to the track.
She wanted to hide.

Doctors reassured her: Given time and therapy and many operations, she could be well again. Sometimes Ana Fidelia would listen.
Other times, she would catch a glimpse of her face—"I looked horrible"—and tears would stream over the stiff plastic smoothness of
her chin. She was sure the doctors were lying. She screamed at them
all to leave her alone. Her spirit withered and crumbled like ash. She
told her mother they should have let her die.

Too, she heard all the rumors, better than any script from a
telenovela: The explosion wasn't an accident. She'd tried to com-
mit suicide after a fight with her famous and married lover,
Sotomayor. She'd wanted to name the child after him, he refused

and broke off the affair. She doused herself with kerosene and struck a match.

Quirot denies all that, except the part about Sotomayor being the father. The night of her accident, she says, she'd merely gone to light her cooker, a kerosene contraption used all over Cuba and a frequent cause of fire. Shortages of bleach and soap throughout the nineties have forced Cubans to wash their clothes on the stove, in a heated mixture of isopropyl alcohol and water. Ana Fidelia thought the cooker was off. She poured in the alcohol and it flowed down over the lip of the pot, into the fire. "And the flames came up," she says. Either way it is tragic. Even Quirot's less dramatic explanation uncoils a rich irony: No shortages, no fire. Castro's pride, the woman who took one Pan Am gold medal and placed it around Fidel's neck, had been literally eaten alive by Castro's tottering economy.

But she had neither the time nor the inclination to blame. Quirot began to train. Her legs had been unaffected, and by March she was doing light cardiovascular exercises. By April she was running up and down the hospital stairs. It usually takes six or seven months to recover from such burns, but Quirot's genes were impatient. She healed quickly. Bandages were removed after two months. After three, she was released. Before four months had passed, she walked out on the track at Havana's Juan Abrantes Stadium. It was near 8 P.M., because her healing skin still couldn't be exposed to strong sunlight. She ran for eight minutes and forty seconds, five laps. Her first words to the four journalists watching: "I'm overweight by seven kilos."

In November, Ana Fidelia ran her first race at the Central American and Caribbean Games in Ponce, Puerto Rico. The United States was peppered by news reports of the forty athletes defecting day after day from ball fields and hotels, but in Cuba the official news could only rejoice. Her arms and neck constricted by scar tissue, Quirot finished second in the eight hundred with a time of 2:05.22. "The greatest feeling I've ever had," she says. When the athletes returned home, Fidel declared her achievement, "one of the most impressive things we've ever seen in our lives. She won a silver medal, and the gold medal for bravery." He hugged Ana Fidelia, blinked away tears. Officially, no one talked about the defectors much.

"Thousands of people are born every day," she says. "A person like Fidel is an historic figure that comes along once a century. When he uses me as a heroine, the best I can do is try to live up to that and get better."

She did. The far corner of Quirot's living room holds the trophy shelf of everything that has come in the five years since: Cups, medals, the certificate from her 1997 world championship win over world number one Maria Mutola in Athens, a small figurine of Che Guevara, an autographed picture from Castro. Her running style changed after the burning, becoming more contained, considered; she hung back behind the leader now, saving energy, waiting to make her move. But if the accident robbed her of precious time, it wasn't much—her personal bests before and after were separated by less than 4/10ths of a second—and her biggest wins all came in a rush at the late age of thirty-three.

"After the burning I got stronger," she says. "I did more weights, I was more durable. I kept asking myself, 'How is this possible? I'm stronger than ever, and running just as fast as before. . . .'"

Her wins at the 1995 world championship in Goteburg, Sweden, and her '96 Olympic silver medal in Atlanta have became the stuff of comeback legend, but by then Quirot had already weathered the worst of her recovery. Forget running; when she stepped into the blocks in Ponce in 1993, what frightened her most were the eyes of thousands, tracing disapproval up and down her bare arms and face. People had told her coach, Leandro Civil, that she shouldn't even try to race again. "I knew they were all looking at me, but I didn't listen to the gossip," she says. "I didn't listen to what people said about how I looked and that gave me confidence. The scars weren't important. The most important thing was to live."

Then people began to change. Ana Fidelia walked into a store in Atlanta, and people began to follow her, stopped her to whisper thankful words. People kept giving her gold: A bracelet that said "Vaya con Dios," another that said "I love you." Over and over, women would approach, eyes thick with tears. Even now, when Ana Fidelia spirals down her dark staircase at 6 A.M. for a morning run along the Malecon (when I hear this I try to imagine it: Michael Jordan taking his daily workout in Central Park), dreamers halt their gaze at the sea, lovers uncouple: They stop her while waves pound the seawall, and touch her shoulders and start to cry.

Men have come and gone. She and Sotomayor see each other almost daily, but all the emotion has drained off. "You get used to everything," she says. She has had plenty of lovers and, yes, the first time after the burning she worried mightily that he wouldn't find her attractive. He did. Hundreds of sessions with state-provided psychologists gave her the strength to lead men to bed when they might hesitate. She soon learned how to weed out the men interested in her fame or privilege, and if one dwelled too long on her scars, Ana Fidelia would sit him down and state the rules: If you can't get past how I look, then you must go.

She has been seeing a man seriously for five months now. She is happy, feels confident that it can work, knows that he doesn't find her repulsive. "I took the mentality that this man is on my side," she says. "I am positive he doesn't feel that way. He looks at me for what I am. He may find someone with a perfect body, with no flaws, but I tell him: She won't love you like I do."

Ana Fidelia laughs from the back of her throat. No, she says almost daintily, she doesn't worry about being ugly anymore. "I've had special care," she says. "I have these marks on myself, but they're soft—not hard. I'm like a baby girl now."

She's right. After eight operations, her skin has been planed down to a rich smoothness, her disfigurement now a matter of discolorment, not landscape. There's a wash of brown across her neck, a shadow along her right jawbone, a goatee dyed dark around her chin by the strength of the sun. Only the backs of her hands still resemble gnarled wood. She'll have some more minor operations, but feels almost as if she'd been born with the scars. She goes to the beach in a bikini, and walks with her head high and proud. "Because they're a part of me, I know how to live with them," she says. "If I didn't, I'd die. I love life, and I want to live forever."

Quirot has nothing left to prove. Last year, in August, she ran her fastest time—1:54.82—since the burning, faster than her world championship and Olympic runs, faster than anyone had run the event in eight years. She is thirty-five. She wants to try to conceive another baby before it is too late, and bear and raise it with every bit of strength she has. When 1998 ends, so does her career. She will coach, maybe.

Ana Fidelia sits forward in her couch, one leg folded beneath, and tugs loose a narrow braid from her head. She unravels it and begins to braid again. She's the face of Cuba, I am told, and she looks better than she has in years. I say she is invited to come over to Teofilo's birthday party, but Ana Fidelia just giggles. "I'm not going to Stevenson's," she says. "I'm scared of that guy."

The last thing I see on the way out of her apartment is the wall decorated with nineteen pictures: Ana Fidelia with Fidel on a plane, Ana Fidelia with Fidel at a reception, Ana Fidelia with Fidel at a function. "Fidel says he and I are *tocayos*," she says. Namesakes.

Both are smiling broadly. She wears her scars and medals, and he wears his uniform.

A late-afternoon light cracks across the waves off the Malecon, burnishing the surface into something frozen and endless, a metallic immensity: It looks like God's silver platter. It is 4:26 P.M., and when my taxi pulls up at Teofilo's house he calls me into the kitchen. The table is a small skyline of rum bottles. He is dropping large fistfuls of onions into a steaming pot, fiercely guarding the makings of his birthday *caldosa*, or stew. Every year Stevenson does this, mixing mojo and garlic and pork and squid into a wondrous concoction anticipated by friends and family with a ravenous awe. Someone walks in and lifts a glass. "Peace and love," Teofilo says. Trumpets, drums, maracas, song: The stereo blasts.

A bird cage hangs near the kitchen table, and the green, red-necked parrot, a dead ringer for the bird I saw this morning at Hilda's, is now crawling out the door and onto the roof. Stevenson rushes over, finger extended, but the bird is too fast for him. It scrambles onto the floor in a flurry, and now Teofilo is bent over, knocking aside chairs, giving chase. "Co-ti! Co-ti!" he shouts in the now-familiar bass. Finally his big bulk rises, coming up with Coti perched on a finger. He shoves the bird back in the cage.

Stevenson is wearing a Cuba boxing shirt, a pair of blue shorts, a pair of adidas flip-flops. I'm not sure if I'm here for work or play, so I try to ask him about the Russian. Igor Vysotsky was the only boxer to dominate Stevenson, beating him in Santiago in 1973 and Minsk in 1976; the second time, Vysotsky hammered him so badly the ref stopped the contest. "I had the same problems with him as everyone else," Stevenson mutters. "But today is my birthday."

I begin talking with his sister, Nancy, one of six Stevenson kids.

She speaks happily of their father, of the boxing lessons he tried to give his son, and when I ask Teofilo about this he is walking out of the kitchen carrying his pot of caldosa.

"I don't remember a thing," he says. "It's my birthday!"

At least I have one answer: I'm here strictly for play. Also at the table is Enrique Regueiferos, a skinny, road map–faced black man who won Cuba's first boxing medal, a silver, as a light-welterweight at the 1968 Olympic Games in Mexico City. Enrique grew up in the days before EIDEs and ESPAs and time at La Finca, and got hooked on the sport after watching newsreels of Joe Louis and Sugar Ray Robinson. The son of a Santiago baker and destitute, Enrique says, "I had nothing to lose." He made the Cuban national team at the age of fourteen, and became almost as celebrated for his closely contested losses as he did for his wins. "In many cases, the judges at those games were Yanquis—and not just Yanquis, but CIA agents," Castro said after Enrique failed to win at the '66 Central American Games. "Only a CIA agent, only a pirate, only a mercenary will challenge public opinion the way these people did. They challenged the most fundamental rules, taking away one of the most brilliant moments in boxing the world has ever seen. They were not committed to good judging but to arbitrariness against our athletes in numerous events. They took away our gold medal in Chocolatico Perez against the Venezuelan. They also took away the triumph of our magnificent boxer: Reguiferos of Santiago. . . ."

Enrique lost a 3-2 decision in the '68 Olympic final to Polish policeman Jerzy Kulej, and came home a hero.

Stevenson hurries back in with his pot, sets it on the stove, and leaves. When he returns some guests are poking their noses under the lid. "What the hell!" he says. "Everybody's fucking with my caldosa!"

Enrique regales me with the usual story about boxing before the revolution, yet another of those sexy cautionary tales told by Cubans like ghost stories before bed. "Douglas Vaillant: He hung himself in the States," Enrique says, nodding. "When he got there, he fought a little. They caught him with some drugs in his car—like a lot of professionals he was broke. My family lived right in front of his house in Santiago. We got word from the United States."

Coti has scaled back on top of the cage. Teofilo is standing in the center of the living room, happily singing along with the sad tune, "Lupe, I'll never forget you . . . if you go away I'll never forget you . . ." His bullhorn voice echoes through the house. He rushes out to the pool and picks up a long broken branch the width of his arm. Next to it, there's a sizzling aluminum pot the size of a witch's cauldron squatting over two cinder blocks, and Teofilo rams the branch into the fire. This is the mother pot, home of all the ingredients he has been mixing in the kitchen. He peers down into the cauldron, blackened and battered, dips a spoon to take a taste. It has been cooking for four hours. Three of his friends back up. "Stop fucking with my caldosa!" he says: Not ready yet. A white rooster prances slowly across the backyard.

I go back to the living room. It is 5:49. Enrique, wearing a mesh jersey over a boxing tank top, is dancing in the living room with a lovely lady in black. "Guantanamera," the Cuban classic, comes on, and now everybody is dancing, Fraymaris, Teofilo, three other couples, all moving light and easy with none of that Anglo self-consciousness, and now it's Benny Moré, the Barbarian of Rhythm long dead and gone, but Teofilo's bellowing has made him live: "We'll be happy! We're going to party! We'll always have life!" He has a cigarette in one hand, a cup of rum in the other, shuffling his feet in time.

The kitchen is packed, and one of Teofilo's nieces, Lois, is watching him dance through the door. "He's just a big naughty boy," she says.

Everyone is getting hungry. Teofilo bulls toward the stove. "Get out of my kitchen!" he says. No one moves. I tell Teofilo it's time to go, but he pulls me outside, back toward the cauldron. "Not until you eat some caldosa," he says. He bends over, begins dishing the melange into a pot. His cigarette drops out of his mouth and lands in the stew; he casually reaches down and fishes it out, takes a drag. I follow him back to the kitchen, where he ladles out a cupful and hands it to me. I take a bite. "It's delicious," I say.

"What? You want more?" he yells. "Out of my way!" Stevenson grabs the pot, wheels out of the kitchen through the dancing, to the backyard. I finish off my cup with a slurp.

It's 6:33, darkness dropping, and as I step outside I see that the party has broken into silent clusters, groups of five and six sitting or milling about with cups in hand, munching. Teofilo shakes my hand. "When you coming back?" he says. "You come back, my house is your house, anytime, day or night, okay?" I thank him, and mean it. How often do you get a chance to wish the prince a happy birthday?

The TV in my hotel room is showing the Sunday night game, Ciego de Avila versus Camaguey. The stands are packed. One of Cuba's best pitchers, Omar Luis, stands stone-faced on the mound for Camaguey, firing strikeout after strikeout. The Ciego team wears elegant powder-blue uniforms with pineapple patches on the left shoulder. Between innings, a nifty graphic pops on the screen: "37th National Baseball Series," followed by a message from the electric company about conservation, followed by a dated highlights package of the Big Red Machine, Cuba's formidable national team, beating up as usual on the Americans.

I'm restless, so I take the elevator up to the roof of the Plaza and walk around in the dim light. The city isn't as dark as it was three years ago. No big city is quieter than Havana at midnight, but it's busier than it was, less desolate, as if some sort of armistice had been declared. From one corner I can see the tops of the trees of Parque Central, from the other the lighthouse at El Morro making its blinding orbit—and from both I can smell the sea. Across the street, there's a great concrete husk that will be a hotel someday. I walk around back, and behind the Plaza I notice the old Bacardi building with its intricate art deco tiling and central tower thrusting like a toast into the air. Scaffolding surrounds the place, the dust and plywood signaling a massive renovation. In an apartment in the building next door, I can hear the Eagles singing "Hotel California." A rocking chair tips back and forth, framed by a bare window, empty.

From up here I can see the Floridita, where the daiquiri was born and Hemingway began to die, and beyond that a fringe of light leaking out of Castillo de Farnes. A young couple is walking alone down the street, very close and slow. At first I dismiss them as just another tourist-hooker combo, but before I can look away I'm suddenly afflicted by this desperate wish to believe they are Cuban, mad and devoted, maybe even in love. I squint, follow their progress, and wait for some kind of sign, but they walk into shadow. From here it is impossible to tell.

CHAPTER 6

One night I sat in the restaurant next to the hotel eating a bowl of soup. And I stirred the soup and a cockroach came up out of it. I threw up everything I had in me all over the counter.

—BROOKLYN DODGERS PITCHER DON NEWCOMBE
on Havana, 1947

This is not a country for walking proud. It is Monday, my first free morning, and as I head toward the Malecon it becomes clear why no Cubans stride about with head high and shoulders back: To do so would be a suicide of dignity. The sidewalks lining Calle Agramonte are a moonscape of jutting water pipes, foot-deep holes, and toe-jarring concrete slabs. You must watch your step. I allow the gentle slope to carry me past the fierce-looking guards in scarlet berets around the exhibit of the *Granma*, the plastic-encased fishing boat that carried Fidel and eighty-two rebels from Mexico to Oriente in 1956, past the Museum of the Revolution, past a park where two boys toss a baseball. I hit the base of the Malecon, with its grimy plaque commemorating its construction by American governor-general Leonard Wood in 1901, swing my legs over to face the water, and wait for the parade to begin. The Malecon is the crossroads of Havana, a concrete paseo where young and old come to stare, walk, make love, and rage. Pull out a notebook or wallet, and it is only a matter of time before you are besieged.

I pull out a notebook. To my right is El Morro, silver-crowned and stone-bodied and spiked by a flapping Cuban flag; to my left the crumbling, gap-toothed array of colonial facades daubed with pastels. Behind me the sidewalk, before me—past a jumbled outcropping of barnacled foundation stones—spreading to the horizon, colliding with the pale sky, lie the Florida Straits, presenting a blank-faced invitation to salvation or death.

"What are you writing?"

A boy and a girl dressed in the kid-communist uniform of the Young Pioneers, bandannas about the neck, crawl up beside me. I show the scribbles in my notebook. Just below us a flight of stairs descends from street level to the water's edge; a tubby man navigates the pebbled steps, submerges his hands and splashes his face, then trudges back up the stairs. I hear a noise: Behind me, two mule-drawn cabs have silently pulled up, waiting. The boy asks where I'm from, and when I say the United States his eyes go wide. The water is calmer today, pouring between the foundation stones in a lazy rush of eddies and crosstides. One hundred yards out some kind of line is crossed, and the sea's vivid emerald hue deepens to pine. Sunlight careens off the surface, blinding. The effect is that of a tossed-off perfection, a beauty so casual it is almost painful.

A man in an odd straw baseball hat fills his beer can at the foot of a small pool randomly formed by the stones, climbs back up, and pours salt water on his mother's neck. He repeats this five times, then takes off his ragged T-shirt and, with black boots and olive pants still on, dives in. The waves flood in, but he somehow avoids being tossed against the rough walls.

"He's crazy," says the boy, a nine-year-old named Yoel. "I would never do that. I don't want to die."

But the man knows what he is doing. He clambers out over and over, reads the rhythm of the water, and waits for the moment of deepest recession, then jumps. When one wave rolls in over his head, he slaps at it and curses, insulted. "Crazy," Yoel says.

Out on the farthest outcrop, I see a snorkel, a hand, a fin: A man climbs out of the water with a curved, wooden stick with a long blade on its end. "*Pescador*," Yoel says. Fisherman. Yoel begins to unbutton his shirt.

A man in his twenties stops and leans against the wall behind us. He is wearing high-top Converse All-Stars. Within thirty seconds, he tells me his mother left during Mariel and now lives in Nebraska. "Fuck this place," he says in English. "I hate it. What am I going to do. I want to die. Better to kill me. Tourists come, I say buy cigars, they say no like. . . . What do I do? I am young but I am old. I am nothing. I am a dog. The government say wait, wait, wait. Wait for what? Nothing."

I nod. Before I can say a word he picks up and leaves.

Yoel scampers down to the pool. Out on the farthest outcropping, where I saw the fisherman, a beautiful girl in a magenta one-piece gingerly steps closer toward the edge. She is like some weird vision from a TV beer ad: raven hair, long tan legs, huge breasts. She stands poised, hands up, calf muscles dancing. She turns and smiles at someone, then dives, her feet falling in an awkward tumble over her butt. A red-and-white tanker, flying the flag of Nevis, chugs head-on into the Straits, smudging the silent sky with black puffs. The girl surfaces, clambers up onto her perch.

I find myself tempted. Something about the scene seems perfect for a writer seeking the pure moment, and maybe it is. If you come to an island looking to chart its athletic soul, what could be better than a turn back to basics, to an anonymous beauty risking tides and rocks for one glorious moment in the sun? Now she stands out there, hair falling in soaked tendrils halfway down her back, feet planted on the stone as the water shoots around her ankles, up to her knees, tries to knock her down. "Now that is crazy," Yoel says. She wobbles, she doesn't fall. She turns and grins again. Some twenty people are standing and watching her now, and if you wanted it could be taken as some kind of victory. She refuses to give in.

Yoel comes back, wet. A black, barefoot woman in red jeans steps down the stone staircase, carrying a sheet cake covered in white icing. I try reading the blue script on top, but the cake has collapsed on itself so completely that it's illegible. She walks out to the edge of the rocks, sets the cake down, and pulls out a pair of powder-blue maracas, then stops. She picks up the cake and walks farther down the beach, looking for a better spot. I look at Yoel quizzically. "*Santera,*" he says.

The girl in the magenta suit comes dripping up the stairs, happy to be the center of attention. She has a row of silver bracelets on her right arm, a stylish mole over her lip. Far off, I see the Santera—a devotee of the Santeria religion—has again set down the cake, and is shaking the maracas and chanting to Yemaya, the goddess of the sea. Waves wash over the icing, draw back. Within seconds the entire cake is gone. The Santera walks toward the stairs. It is 11:50 A.M. The girl in the magenta suit stops and lies down on the wall next to me. She tells me her name is Carine, and she is sixteen. She has a dazzling smile, a little belly. In fifteen years, she will be fat.

Carine tells me she lives nearby, in a flat off the Malecon with her mother, two brothers, and a sister. Her father is dead. She asks me where I am staying. She asks me if I'm traveling with a woman. No, I say in mock-sadness, I am a man alone. She looks me dead in the eye. *No tienes chica, no eres hombre,* she says. If you don't have a girl, you're not a man.

* * *

Back at the hotel, this morning's CNN broadcast is dominated by the killings in Jonesboro and the eerie execution in Florida of "Black Widow" Judy Buenoano, whose leg began spewing smoke after 5,500 volts of electricity shot through her dying body. *Trabajadores* has a story on last night's first-round playoff games, a pair of showcases for Cuban pitching. Omar Luis struck out eleven and walked none to beat Ciego De Avila, and La Habana's Jose Ibar, who this year became the first twenty-game winner in the history of the National Series—Cuba's name for its premiere league season—struck out a dozen to beat Metropolitanos, 3-0. I cross the street and head to Parque Central. Only the boys at La Pena can help me with this question.

I find Little Daddy standing under the trees, and ask: Who's the best pitcher in Cuba? He can't say. Ibar, the right-hander who finished the regular season with a 1.51 ERA, has a sneaky-quick fastball, full command of his curveball and slider, and broke out this year with the season of his life. Luis, who notched a 13-5 record, with a 1.77 ERA, can throw his dancing fastball as hard as ninety-eight miles per hour, and in last night's ninth inning he was still lighting up radar guns at ninety-two. Pinar Del Rio's Pedro Luis Lazo battled injuries this year but has the nastiest breaking ball and a ninety-mile-per-hour fastball that rises and dips at will. The next great gun may well be Ciego's Ariel Martinez, twenty-three, who went 11-4 with a 1.84 ERA in 1998 and throws a ninety-four-mile-per-hour fastball, or Pinar Del Rio's Jose Contreras, a big-game talent with an 8-3 record and a 1.61 ERA. Little Daddy shrugs, delighted to have such a quandary.

"If Duque was still in Cuba, he would've been in big trouble," he says. "These kids now are throwing harder than Duque or Valle ever did."

* * *

The toothless man has all the marks: flat ears, swollen knuckles, mashed face, slurred words—yes, he insists, he used to be a boxer. "My name is Alexander Rubalcaba," he says in English. "Alexis is my cousin. Can I have your shirt?"

It is close to midnight. I've had my beer at Castillo de Farnes, where a thin man named Abraham told me about his mother gone to America, and now, just a block from the hotel, I'm being stopped by this rum-drenched punchy. I tell him why I'm here, but my heart isn't in it. I'm tired. I know what's next: a bid for money, a meal. I don't want to hear anymore. I try edging away, when the old man points to a fresh-faced, gold-toothed muscular man standing in the doorway. "This is a great boxer!" he says. "The best in Cuba!"

The muscular man squints at me silently. I take my shot. "Hector Vinent?" I ask.

His eyebrows rise. I tell him I'm from the United States. He asks if I know Casamayor and Garbey, the two national team stars who defected on the eve of the '96 Olympics. Of course, I say, I know who they are. He relaxes, nods, and smiles.

"Hector Vinent," he says.

We go inside, order a plate of greasy fried chicken. This is strange. It is past midnight now, and the man who says he is Vinent says he has to be at La Finca at 5 A.M. for training. But he seems in no hurry. He tells me he has won two Olympic gold medals and two world championships, then turns to Rubalcaba and whispers, "Do you think he can buy me a soda?"

A crowd mills out on the sidewalk where we first met: guitar players, taxihawks, *jineteras*, ex-boxers. Every few minutes, Vinent gets up to talk to a girl outside. He is smiling, friendly, but also distracted. I wonder what's worrying him. Before I can ask for an interview, he suddenly says he wants to talk more and invites me to his house tomorrow. He writes down his address on a piece of paper. I pay for the chicken, shake his hand. I cannot believe my luck.

The next morning, after breakfast, I go to the newsstand on the roof of the Plaza. There they sell a beautiful, $20 book of photographs by Raul Corrales, a man revered by photographers worldwide who now lives in a dingy house in Cojimar, selling prints and depending on foreign friends to keep him stocked with supplies. Corrales still believes mightily in the revolution, and I suppose it's all a matter of what you choose to see. It's clear that he saw power and romance in 1959, an unstoppable tide of human longing realized through Fidel Castro, and the force of that vision remains in every shot despite the failure that followed.

My favorite is a photo from that year that Corrales titled "The Dream," though I can't decide whether it's the shot or the story behind it that captivates me. "The Dream" is a black-and-white piece of history, perfectly framed: An exhausted black Cuban soldier sleeps, in uniform, on a cot in a bright room. His hat sits atop his crotch. Three feet above his head, a machine gun lies forgotten on a polished dresser; six feet above, an oil painting of a bare-breasted white woman stares seductively into the camera. It is a picture of peace in war, of base hopes beneath lofty rhetoric, of the corruption that awaits to tempt any winner. A few years ago, Corrales told me it was taken the same month Castro took Havana, when Fidel and a cadre of revolutionaries flew to Caracas, Venezuela, to thank the ruling junta for its support during the revolt. He and another photographer—maybe Korda, maybe Osvaldo Salas—had gone along on the trip, and they'd been walking down the hotel hallway when they both glanced through an open door to see the soldier asleep. The other photographer kept going. Corrales stopped, pivoted, and snapped his shutter.

Years later, after the photo had become an emblem of the revolution, the other shooter finally broke down and asked Corrales to
make him a print. Corrales obliged, but not before indulging himself: Great photographers all share the same streak of outsized, joy-
ous, competitive cruelty, and Corrales was not about to let the
moment pass. "I fucked you," he wrote to his colleague. "I saw it,
and you didn't."

I get lost whenever I thumb through Corrales's work, even standing in an empty newsstand, so it takes a few moments before I realize that I'm hearing someone singing in English. A woman's voice
keeps repeating, "I want to be in Am-er-i-ca! I want to be in Am-er-i-
ca!," and it strikes me that, since seeing *West Side Story* in my youth,
I've never heard that song anywhere but here.

It's 11 A.M., the last day of March. I buy a paper and head for the
elevator, passing a table of German men and a young, black *jinetera*.
They'd been guzzling beer and shouting an hour earlier, but now
the night has come to an end. One of the Germans is gone, another
stares at the wall, and the third is passed out, facedown, on the
table. Only the girl isn't finished. She has carefully built a pile on
the unconscious man's head: A banana peel, an eggshell, sugar
packets, food scraps, and is now working her hands through the
muck and jamming it into his scalp. The man doesn't move. She
catches me staring and laughs.

I bring up the defectors. The baseball commissioner leans forward
over his desk. "We're not impressed by that decision at all," says Carlos Rodriguez. "What impresses us is the more than seven hundred
players who play in the developmental league and the National
Series. The best, the most talented, the stars—they never left the
country. They represent their province and Cuba, despite offers of

millions. Linares, Kindelan, Pacheco, Pedro Luis Lazo: It's an infinite number."

I try, and fail, to hide my shock. I expected propaganda, but this is silly. Surely, I say, some thirty defections, including the major league pitching rotation of Arocha, El Duque, Livan, and Arrojo, has affected the quality of Cuban baseball? But Rodriguez deflects the very thought.

"No, in reality, the Cuban athlete and the Cuban people know that behind all that there's a well-orchestrated plan. They sign an athlete like Duque for $6.6 million? That's laughable. We know he's not worth all that money. Duque pitched for the national team, but he always pitched against a team like the Italians. He never pitched against high-quality players. This has been done to entice other athletes."

It is mid-afternoon. We are sitting in Rodriguez's office, recently redecorated, under the stands at Estadio Latinoamericano. He waits calmly behind his desk. I can barely contain myself. Wait, I sputter, but Duque still owns the best career record of any Cuban pitcher . . . and he did this day-in and day-out against the best Cuban hitters, including Linares, Orestes Kindelan, Antonio Pacheco, and all-time hit king Victor Mesa. Rodriguez shrugs. He is a short, bright-eyed man, his face a mask of cheeriness. He wears a white golf shirt with "Tigers" stitched over the heart. "Pitchers have good years and bad years," he says. "Some win games with a lot of unearned runs. You have to look at who they pitch against. A lot of pitchers win in the National Series, but when they get to the playoffs they don't win. That was El Duque. He never could get past the real tough teams."

Rodriguez, forty-five, has been in office since June 1997, when the crisis enveloping Cuban baseball forced the regime to make sweeping changes. Out went longtime commissioner Domingo Zabala, national team general manager Miguel Valdes, and national team manager Jorge Fuentes. In came a directorate that, I now see, is determined to take reactionary measures to stop seven years of bleeding. Rodriguez is not a former player or coach; his background lies solely in administration, most recently as the head of INDER in Pinar Del Rio. "They've brought in someone who's not a baseball guy; he's *partido*," says one of Cuba's baseball stars. "And he's bringing something into the game that wasn't there before—tension, insecurity. People don't trust each other. Before if you had a problem, you'd go to Zabala and he was a baseball man and he'd understand what you needed. For him it was about winning baseball games, so he'd try to work things out for everybody. This guy doesn't care about making guys comfortable. I fear for the future of Cuban baseball."

Some 140,000 boys and men play organized baseball in Cuba—and an estimated 1.2 million more play in the streets and vacant fields—all of them under the aegis of the Cuban Baseball Commission, and the whole system is designed to funnel talent to the national team. The spree of sanctions, the jailing of the agent Hernandez Nodar, the decision to reverse the three-year experiment of farming players overseas—all are signs that a commission long-paralyzed in the face of defections has finally decided to go on the offensive. But nothing speaks more eloquently of the bitterness coursing through the Cuban baseball establishment today than Rodriguez's words about El Duque. I'd often heard Cuban officials trash the character of defectors, but not their accomplishments; many, in fact, took quiet pride in producing players so coveted by the major leagues. It was as if talent itself was beyond ideology, unassailable. Not anymore. This is war.

"We have a right to protect our athletes," Rodriguez says. "You train an athlete since he was a child, since he was young, and then he gets to the point where he's producing important results . . . Cuban sports has a major investment in that athlete . . . and you're going to come and take him away? Nobody has that right. It's not morally correct or ethically correct, and we're right to take the necessary measures to protect ourselves from such piracy."

Yes, players must produce on the field. But, more than ever, Rodriguez says, they will be monitored for their thinking. "An athlete is selected to defend our country, all of our nationality," he says. "If he doesn't have an attitude where we—the people who created him—can have confidence in him, then he will never have the right to represent Cuba in an international event. He not only must be physically prepared, but on top of everything he must be patriotic, dignified, and participate like the athlete he is."

The reason sanctions were lifted on German Mesa and the rest, he says, has nothing to do with a fear of more rafters or a softening of the regime's stance toward those who flirt with American agents. On the contrary. If Duque had stayed in Cuba, the ban on him would never have been lifted. "No," Rodriguez says. "Duque didn't maintain the attitude held by the other athletes we lifted the sanctions on."

To be sure, the regime has taken other steps to shore up the franchise. The 11-2 loss to Japan in the 1997 Intercontinental Cup final, which ended Cuba's decade-long winning streak of 152 games, left everyone shaken. Players were exhausted, fans disgusted. Something had to give. For years players had complained about a schedule that had them playing nearly nonstop: First the sixty-plus-game regular season known as the National Series, followed by a forty-plus game season for the best players from each region called the Selective Series, followed by, for the best players, selection to the national team and a full summer's slate of travel and exhibitions and international competitions. But for 1998, the National Series and Selective seasons were streamlined into one ninety-game

National Series, followed by a nineteen-game playoff contested by the eight best teams.

Meanwhile, the practice of renting players to semipro teams overseas had become a nightmare. Not only did still-capable players retire prematurely to try and cash in, but the game's superstars resented that they played for a pittance while some over-the-hill inferiors got paid well playing for corporations thousands of miles away. Left behind by both defectors and expatriates, communism's great champions were thinking mostly about money. Morale plummeted. "Everyone agreed that what we'd been doing was wrong, and that way baseball had lost something," Rodriguez says. "The important job now is reorganizing and fortifying our baseball from within.

"All this is needed to break the ice. There's been a revival of Cuban baseball, but we're not satisfied. There's a lot of work to do, but we have the will. We're convinced we're on the right road. We're at a moment of reflowering, replanting, new seeds, new ideas."

He is smiling. Just talking about rejuvenation has made Rodriguez bubbly with satisfaction, but I'm not convinced. The closing of the overseas option can only further frustrate the younger players stacked up behind the national team's notoriously static lineup. I fear more rafts. Rodriguez professes not to care. He predicts that Cuba will again win Olympic gold in Sydney. "And without professionalism!" he declares. "We will win the battle!"

The address scribbled by Hector Vinent isn't clear. I'm late for our appointment, but it seems he could live in two completely different neighborhoods. My driver meanders across town from one to the other, and for three frantic hours we drive through the afternoon's sticky dust knocking on doors, stopping the people who pass. Neither address seems to exist. No one has heard of a boxer named Hector Vinent living nearby. Did I somehow get the wrong address? Have I been conned? Something has gone awry. I have no idea what it could be.

The wind rushes in through the windows at forty miles per hour, but it brings no cool. We pass a weary billboard that says, "We'll Always Have Socialism," pass the Pan American—now Olympic—Stadium with its giant photo of Che, pass no other cars at all. We are on the Via Monumental heading east out of Havana, but because no one rushes and gas is gold there's no rush hour in Cuba. The highway is ours. Tonight is game two between Metropolitanos and La Habana, the ball club that represents the province outside Havana city and plays its home games forty-five minutes away in San Jose de las Lajas. We have a little time.

Charles Hill is in the backseat, speaking about his life in exile. He has already told of moments when he considered suicide, of the three different stints he's spent in Cuban jails—the last a fourteen-month sentence for possession of a joint. He has told how he has never spoken to the son he left behind. He has just finished speaking about the night Officer Robert Rosenbloom died of a gunshot wound on a New Mexico highway. So I ask the obvious question about regrets.

"Yeah," Hill says. "I regret he was a stupid-ass racist. It's his fucking fault. All the papers said, 'Gunned Down' . . . He wasn't 'gunned down.' He didn't get the gun out of the holster, and the reason he didn't is because I had my hand on his gun hand. But that's another story. No, I don't have any regrets."

He stares out the window. No one in Cuba needs Fidel Castro to stay in power more than Hill. Cuba is his jail and his salvation, the place that for twenty-seven years has sheltered him from charges of kidnapping, murder, and air piracy and a long-awaited appointment with the electric chair. The United States has made the extradition of some eighty-four American fugitives a condition of any normalization of relations, and when then-Congressman Bill Richardson met with Castro on January 17, 1996, at a time when U.S.-Cuban relations seemed to be thawing, he specifically brought up the case of Finney and Hill. Castro told him he'd consider it. Five weeks later, the Cuban Air Force shot down the two unarmed Cessnas, Congress voted the restrictive Helms-Burton Act into law, and all thought of rapprochement faded.

"I'll never go back," Hill says. "Now if I go back, they'll fry me."

Hill was born in Olney, Illinois, on December 15, 1948, a stonemason's son who'd grown up hearing tales of a great-grandfather who'd escaped slavery and lived in the mountains with an Indian tribe. When his parents' marriage broke up, he moved to Oakland to live with an uncle and played some football at Castlemont High before fathering a daughter and dropping out to join the army. In October 1968, he says, he went to Vietnam as an infantryman in the 101st Airborne. After a few months of combat, he deserted in Hue, got court-martialed, served six months in the brig. After refusing to return to combat, he went AWOL again and spent forty-five more days in confinement. He was discharged, returned to the United States with a heroin addiction, and within two years had fallen in with the Republic of New Afrika, a militant offshoot of the black-power movement that called for the establishment of a black homeland in the deep South.

In November 1971, Hill says, "everything went down." He'd been with the Republic six months, and after a police raid on an RNA chapter in Jackson, Mississippi, left one officer dead and eleven RNA members charged with murder, he, Michael Finney, and another RNA member named Ralph Goodwin stole a rented 1972 Ford Galaxie and embarked, as Hill says, "on a mission to Mississippi." The bottom of the trunk, Hill says, contained two hundred pounds of dynamite and a cache of M–1 carbines and Garand rifles; officers who later found the car catalogued three military rifles, a twelve-gauge shotgun, bomb-making materials, hundreds of rounds of ammunition, and revolutionary literature. On November 8, Officer Rosenbloom, twenty-eight years old with two young children, pulled up next to the Galaxie. It was 10:41 P.M. when he radioed the dispatcher to request a check on the Galaxie's California license plates.

"He was by himself," Hill says. "He was about to pass us, but he saw three black dudes with afro hairdos and he searched us—up to a point. He looked at a number of suitcases in the trunk, but we wouldn't let him get all the way to the bottom. I said, 'That's enough. It's an illegal search.'

"He told two of us to get into the police car and told the other one to follow us in. He got suspicious, and he was getting into a ready position to go for his gun. He was told not to move, he went for his gun and was shot one time in his throat with a .45. In other words, we were defending ourselves. If he had anything but a John Wayne mentality, he would've gotten into his car, set up a roadblock, and stopped us. He went for his gun. It's that fucking simple."

The first officer on the scene found Rosenbloom lying facedown, a flashlight in one hand and his unfired gun in the other. His hat had rolled down an embankment. The killing set off a massive manhunt, with the three men eluding capture for nineteen days. They spent the night of November 26 camouflaged in the desert sands outside Albuquerque. The next day, Hill, Finney and Goodwin hijacked a tow truck at gunpoint and forced the driver to take them to the airport. They rode out on the runway, then bulled their way aboard a TWA 727 bound for Chicago. The plane stopped in Tampa to refuel, where all forty-three passengers were released, then took off for Havana. When it landed at Jose Marti, the men asked for political exile and were whisked off to State Security for six weeks of light incarceration: books, chess sets, a patio in the sun. Then they were turned over to a halfway house filled with foreigners, including some thirty Americans.

"I knew kids who came here because they had nothing else to do," Hill says. "People who hijacked because they were mentally ill and just wanted to get famous. People who didn't have any political ideology. It was like . . . fashion. It was a madhouse."

He cut sugarcane, worked construction for Fidel's brother Ramon, took history classes at the University of Havana. It was no paradise. Hill read once that Lenin equated exile with having one step in the grave, and the thought never left him. Just sixteen months after they arrived, Goodwin drowned. After an eleven-year lapse, Hill called his brother in June 1982 and was told that both his parents had died. The next few years were his worst. Hill was arrested twice for carrying dollars. In 1983, he and Finney made one final attempt to get out of Cuba and go to Africa, but without passports they got no farther than Jamaica. From then on, Hill figured, Cuba was home. "Yeah," he says. "I thought about killing myself. I'd asked too many 'whys' and didn't get an answer."

In the lean days of the early 1990s, with the peso near worthless and food scarce, Hill wasn't sure the regime would survive. Soap, new clothing, and food were as precious as diamonds, and rice, which now sells for 4.5 pesos a pound, was going for 45. Rafters flooded the waters, demonstrators protested on the Malecon. The regime had little choice; in a move some saw as a step away from collectivism, private farmer's markets became legal late in 1994. Prices began to drop, the air began to calm. Hill wasn't doing too badly. He had a small house, a ration book. "I've had it pretty good, better than most

Cubans," he says. "The Cuban government always gives me breakfast, lunch, and dinner. I always worked at whatever I wanted to."

Hill has a twelve-year-old, half-Cuban daughter, Shaunely, and the girl's mother has been riding him hard for support. "Her mother has her heavily oriented toward money," he says. "If I have to buy my child's love, I don't want it."

On the radio, Hill hears the daily news from America. He can't believe his ears. "When I went to high school in East Oakland, it was a nice mixed, Hispanic, black neighborhood," he says. "There was no ghetto. Now the place is run by gangs. People say, 'What's it like in the States?' and I say: 'Can you imagine 11 million Cubans with guns?'"

I cut Hill off. We're standing by the car outside Estadio Nelson Fernandez now, pregame hustle going on all around us. You're in Cuba because of the most violent of acts, I say. How can you of all people condemn violence? "I'm here because I wanted to stop violence," Hill says. "To stop reactionary violence, to stop drugs and shit, you've got to use violence. I say peace comes out of the barrel of a gun. I was violent with purpose. That's what's real scary now: sick fucking violence."

Hill is sure he's right about this, sure about helping kill Robert Rosenbloom, sure that he is the victim of a system gone wrong. "I have to go down with the hardcores," he says. Like all exiles he is stuck fighting yesterday's battles. The only remembrance he has of his son, born after he left the United States, are a few fading pictures. "He was born in June 1972, so my son now is—fuck! twenty-five years old?" Hill says. He goes silent a moment, then says, "No, he's twenty-six this year."

It is just ninety minutes before gametime. Jose Ibar answers the door. He's wearing uniform pants, unbuttoned, a pair of blue canvas sneakers, no shirt. His sleepy eyes barely light up, he makes no effort to suck up his thick, slouching upper body. He is the least impressive great athlete I've ever seen. Yet Ibar went 20-2 with a 1.51 ERA this year to become an instant Cuban legend, and the other night held Metropolitanos to six hits in winning La Habana's first playoff game. We break every pregame rule by merely knocking. In the States, a bodyguard leashed to a pit bull would tell us to get the hell out.

Sure, Ibar says. Come on in.

He is twenty-eight, and suddenly at the peak of his game. Months later, Cuba's home run king, Orestes Kindelan, will tell me, "Ibar has to be the best. His slider is unbelievable and he throws a heavy ball: You hit it, and nothing happens." Ibar has been named to the national team only once in his career, after a 14-2 season in 1995, but after years of waiting he is sure he'll get another shot this season. This is important. For a long time, younger Cuban players soured on the system because some veterans with lesser seasons— but revolutionary résumés—were named to the national roster. Now, officials and players say, only the best players from each year's National Series will be named to represent Cuba. "It's well-understood that the national team will be based on results," Ibar says. "And a lot of the younger players are more motivated. Me, too."

Ibar's father is a retired construction worker, his mother works in an underwear factory, his sister won a silver medal running the marathon in the '91 Pan Am Games. Jose has been living in the industrial hub of San Jose de las Lajas for twenty years, and this latest home is a two-bedroom, tiny concrete box of a house on a cratered street in a neighborhood filled with craters and concrete boxes. He has a wife and two daughters. After his fine season in 1995, some foreign agents contacted Ibar on the national team's trip to Colombia. He says he's not interested. "Country, flag, and family—when those ties are strong, they can offer you all the money in the world and you'll never go," he says.

Ibar lounges in a big comfortable chair, waiting for more questions. It's an hour before gametime, but he seems ready for bed. Behind his head, a red and green Chinese bicycle leans against the unpainted wall. I ask if that's how he'll get to the stadium. Ibar smiles. He has no car. "I'm taking my bike," he says. "Before every game I go to my mother's home, and then I go after the game, too. It's a habit. I've always done it, and now if I don't she gets mad."

A playoff ticket, bought at the stadium window half an hour before the first pitch, costs 1 Cuban peso—about 2 1/2 cents. A white paper cone of peanuts costs another peso. We meander through the crowd and see Yasser Gomez's mother, Lola, waving us over to sit with her. As usual, Yasser's girlfriend looks bored, but it can't be because of the seats: front row, just behind first base.

Estadio Nelson Fernandez has none of Latinoamericano's massive grandeur, but the words on the outfield wall read, "Take my heart for the good of everyone," the roof behind home plate is corrugated tin, and the foul ball netting, briny and well-knotted, looks like it had just been pulled off a trawler. "AMAR-ILLO!" the crowd shouts in unison, yellow being La Habana's color. Nearly full, the place is a chaos of noise—cued by the raucous band rooted in the stands above third base, waiting for any excuse to set off an explosion of bells, horns, and hammering drums. At 9:17 P.M., the ump shouts time and the first pitch is thrown. Lola has put on a pair of glasses. All around us, people are gulping white rum out of an old plastic soda bottle, passing it hand-to-hand.

There are, of course, no air-conditioned luxury suites, and the heat lays over the crowd like a blanket. La Habana builds an early one-run lead but can't hold it, and the game unwinds into a sloppy and dull 5–3 win for the visitors. During the second inning, the band kicks in and the people clap and shout so loudly that the ump calls for a five-minute delay. The band finally stops, the fans quiet. Lola gets out of her seat and walks back down the aisle to a bare-chested man holding the soda bottle. She presents her cup, he pours, she returns to her seat.

The Metro batter steps in. A trumpeter blows a Bronx cheer. The ump steps back, disgusted.

"AMAR-ILLO!"

The Metro batter singles and steals second. Play stops. A girl in spandex canters to second base to present him with an envelope on a plate—movie tickets, a nice meal, some small prize for the first steal of the game. In the bottom of the second, a Habana batter doubles to deep center field and play again stops. A girl in leopard-print nylon runs out and hands him a prize and a kiss for hitting the first double. Sixty people are now sitting on top of the outfield wall, legs dangling into play. No one chases them off.

Yasser leads off the third with a bunt and almost beats out the throw but doesn't. Celebration. I look around at the faces. The eyes all have that unhealthy third-world sheen, watery and bloodshot and buttermilk yellow. But everyone seems so happy.

The highway back to Havana stretches out empty and dark. No streetlights dilute the sky's starry expanse, and within the solemn confines of the old Chevy the knowledge that one stray cow, one shattered axle, can turn a casual drive into disaster sits like an extra passenger. It seems almost sinful to break the quiet, but I mention what the commissioner said earlier about El Duque. Hill chuckles. The driver, a light-skinned man I'd never met before named Javier, peers into the night.

"That's idiotic," Javier says. "Duque was the best. Saying that is like trying to cover the sun with your finger." He shakes his head, his voice begins to rise. "Without information, we're invalids, like a guy in a wheelchair. Everybody knew Duque left, but we had to hear it on the radio from outside the country. There was nothing in the Cuban papers. Whenever they print anything about the United States it's only negative. We're not stupid. This is not what the revolution is about. They always talk about the disinformation put out by the United States, but these guys make the revolution look stupid. Even little children knew Duque was the best. Who's he bullshitting?"

CHAPTER 7

I had heard that Cubans are a deeply religious people. In two days here, I have learned that baseball is their religion.

—SAM LACY, 1947

Javier's Chevy cools off in a shady parking spot outside the Sports City arena. It's Wednesday morning, April Fool's Day, and we're waiting for a ghost. Little Daddy had told me the story days before. In 1982, the sport got rocked by its most serious scandal when the regime found that Havana gambling interests had infiltrated Industriales, the nation's most revered team, as well as Metropolitanos, and paid off at least seventeen players, coaches, and a manager to throw games. Corruption in Cuban baseball was nothing new then; a handful of players had been sanctioned for accepting bribes in the early 1960s, and in 1979 five more, including future Detroit Tigers star Barbaro Garbey, had been banished from playing forever.

But early in 1982, the scale and flagrancy of the corruption had become an embarrassment. It is said the Industriales manager worked closely with bookies, structuring payoffs to the players: $200 for winning, $500 for losing. The players performed so badly—"making errors even a child wouldn't make," as Little Daddy put it—

that rumors trailed both teams all season. When the inevitable roundup began, "they didn't catch them all," one member of that year's Industriales team told me later. "There were about thirty players involved, but they only got half." When the best and last of them, second baseman Rey Anglada, was arrested, cops supposedly marched him out of Estadio Latinoamericano still in uniform and up Calle Saravia for interrogation. There was no trial. The men were banned for life from playing, coaching, or even entering the lowliest of baseball parks. They were left to finish their lives in shame, Cuba's version of eight men out.

One of the lost players, Jose Ramon Cabrera, is an old friend of a man from La Pena named Roberto Cartaya. Cartaya walks with a cane, has few teeth, and takes great pride in the fact that his picture once appeared in the *New York Times*. He says Cabrera has promised to meet us here. Cartaya sits in the backseat staring quietly, and a sweltering hour passes. Javier, still livid from last night, begins talking again.

"I believe in the revolution," he says. "But if there was a free election today, Fidel wouldn't win. After forty years, it's not working. The charisma, the emotion of the revolution is gone. You go to the hospital and there's no medicine. There are retired people here who are close to starving. About a year ago, my son had pneumonia. The doctor gave me a prescription and I went to the pharmacy but they told me I couldn't have it. I had the dollars, but they said I had to be a foreigner to buy it. How can you think of the revolution then? I had to get an Italian to buy me the medicine. In my own country? For my Cuban son? Don't talk to me about revolution. Fuck it.

"People are setting up homemade satellite dishes, but it's against the law now. Why do you think they don't want people to have those channels? They don't want us to know what it's like in the United

States. You look at *Granma*, and it's only about the revolution, about how bad it is in the United States. We know better."

I go looking for a bathroom. The arena is deserted but open, and when I walk into the dank men's room I find myself sprayed by the fine mist of sewage from a broken pipe. When I return, Jose Ramon Cabrera is standing by the car. At forty-four he still carries himself with an athlete's proud reserve, but it's obvious that life has chipped away at him. He is missing the forefinger on his left hand. More than that, Cabrera has traveled the rare path from revered to reviled, and his survival has depended on the reconsideration of himself as victim, a strong man made weak. If he was ever lighthearted, that's gone too. He's a man with a grievance. He wears dark sunglasses, covers his head with a red baseball cap. His striped shirt has "Playboy" scripted over his heart. He says he needs to get to work, but if we give him a ride he'll talk in the car.

"I feel impotent, not disgraced," Cabrera says. "I can do nothing about what has been done to me."

Cabrera played first base in the National Series for thirteen years, and his career was marked by a rare triple: He played his first years with Havana's provincial team, then moved to Industriales for two seasons before playing his final five with Metropolitanos. He hit seventy-eight home runs and posted a career average of .280. He made the national team in 1971 and 1976. In February 1982, Cabrera came home from a baseball tour of Nicaragua and heard that a number of players had been arrested for throwing games. A few days later, on February 23, the police came to take him away. He spent the next year and a half in jail, sentenced, he says, for the catch-all crime of *peligrosidad*—dangerousness. "They never had any proof," he says. "I was always innocent."

Cabrera's life crumbled. All the players were painted, he says, as "delinquents and counterrevolutionaries." He found himself turned away by stone-faced policemen when he tried to watch a game at Latinoamericano in 1986, forced to melt away from the stadium with everyone watching. Even when he once tried to take part in an innocuous softball game at a university, he was told to leave. "That part of my life, they fucked over," he says. But though his name is still tainted, the regime has quietly taken steps to soften the "lifetime" sentence and allow Cabrera to wonder if he's been rehabilitated. His ban has never been officially revoked. He is sure it never will be.

So Cabrera grasps at hints. The day he left prison in 1985, an officer told him that he'd be paid for his time served. He received 2,772 pesos. "When they do that, it means you're innocent," Cabrera says. "But I thought to myself, 'You pay me money, but who'll pay for my life lost in jail? Who pays me this?' I asked him: 'You put on television and newspapers that we threw games; will you now say that I'm being paid?' But the guy just said, 'That's out of my hands.' And that's all that was ever said to me."

In December 1993, without a word of warning, an invitation went out to the banned players from '79 and '82 to come play an exhibition game at Latinoamericano. The state made no public announcement. The players all came early that Sunday, wandering warily into the stadium. It was 10 A.M., but there were some 30,000 people in the stands. Cabrera played first base, and old jailmates like Espudiz Poulo and Eladio Iglesias caught and pitched. The crowd cheered them all. "You could see the people knew we had never done such a thing . . . ," Cabrera says. The men played hard, as if for a championship. Cabrera went one-for–two, stroking a clean double into the grass of right field, feeling the cheers wash over him as he stood at second base.

"It was very emotional," Cabrera says. "A lot of us thought we'd never play in that stadium again. A lot of us were crying. I was crying, too."

Soon after, a car smashed into a motorcycle Cabrera was riding in Havana. He flew off the bike and into a thicket of barbed wire; his finger was torn from his hand. Cabrera has collected odd jobs ever since. He worked at Havana's Psychiatric Hospital for a time, paired with El Duque in an odd kinship. "Many times he came to me very depressed," Cabrera says. "I told him to keep up his strength, that he was being punished for something he didn't do. I'm convinced what they said about him was a lie."

We are out of the car now, standing beside the busy traffic of Fifth Avenue. Since late 1996 Cabrera has been working for INDER, teaching children the fine points of baseball. He says it is time he gets down to the field. He has been busy lately. This season Cabrera has also been monitoring games for Havana's provincial baseball commission, and he goes to Latinoamericano a few times a week to judge talent, see which combinations will work best for the national team. This is, of course, a job he should've had a long time ago. "The only thing I know is baseball," he says.

But if you press him, Cabrera will say he has lost interest in the Cuban game. He lifts his right hand over his head and jerks his thumb to the sky, as if the United States and its fabulously wealthy and accomplished baseball players floated just a few hundred feet above. "The games I want to see are the other games," he says. Cabrera smiles for the first time. He says that he scrambles like a child to hear the baseball coming in from America on the radio. Sometimes he gets lucky. Sometimes a neighbor knows someone who's got a brother with a renegade satellite dish, and he's even able to watch it on TV.

That night, my last in Havana, we head over to Latinoamericano for game three between Industriales and Pinar Del Rio. It is 8 P.M., an hour before gametime. Fans crane over the dugouts, flood the aisles, their excited chatter filling the place with a great nervous hum. Players jog lightly across the field. Pinar has won the first two games; Industriales, coming off a mediocre regular season, must win tonight to stay alive. For no real reason, I'm trying to find out what year the stadium was built, and someone points me to a thick grinning bull named Luis Zayas, now directing traffic in the stands behind home plate. Zayas booms out "1946!," grins even wider and yells, "Ask me a question!" I decide to splurge. If I'm in for more whitewashing, I may as well get it out of the way. I ask Zayas if he feels Cuban baseball has declined.

"Yes, it's down," Zayas says. "We've lost a little love for the sport, and the baseball players are not well looked after. When they go play in the countryside, it's not the way the national sport should be cared for: The food is bad, where they stay is very bad. The Special Period is one thing. Our national pastime is another thing."

I blink. Charles Hill blinks. I'm not sure I'm hearing right. Have I actually stumbled upon a plain-speaking official? Zayas, a career minor leaguer who played one season with the Havana Sugar Kings in 1959, is a member of the Cuban Baseball Commission. I press on, ask if all the defections have hurt. "Yes, it has," he says. "Others won't say this, but mentally all the players here are thinking about this: $5, 6, 7 million." He shrugs. "Maybe not Omar Linares or Kindelan, no. But it's got to be in the minds of these other guys. It just hasn't been proven yet."

I mention the commissioner's harsh comments about El Duque, despite the fact that Duque owns the Cuban record for winning percentage. "True, but Lazaro Valle had a better slider," Zayas says. "Valle pitched against all the best teams. I don't think Duque ever pitched against the Americans, and the logical thing is, Beat the Americans. We can lose to Puerto Ricans, but we can't lose to Americans.

"Now I'm going to tell you a secret: Duque . . . Duque couldn't pitch to left-handers. The team that had three or four lefties hurt him. That's why he could never pitch against Japan or the United States. But I believe he's a great pitcher, very brave, beautiful control, great location. Now in the United States, they're probably training him against that defect. He'll have five or six great years."

I wait for Zayas to rail against capitalistic excesses, but he doesn't. Distanced from the cynical buzz about strikes and salaries, he, like most Cubans, views the major league game with a child's eye, seeing only the players and their games and their great deeds—and responding with a near-religious awe. "I love American baseball," he says. So now I ask him to give me a straight answer. Why it is that Cuba's great ballplayers have begun to throw their lives into the sea? Zayas's grin disappears, and he begins to back away. I follow him and he stops. "There's only one answer," he says. "They just want to play the best baseball in the world, and they were willing to risk their lives to do it. Forget politics or family. They just wanted to play baseball. I'm a coward. I would never do anything like that."

He walks off then, looking uneasy. I scribble down some notes. It is breezy and cooler, the perfect tropical night. A huge billboard for the CDR is mounted on the light stanchion in left field: "We Are All from the Same House." Zayas comes back.

"You have to have courage to say what I said to you," he says. "I'm a revolutionary, I love my country, and I'm going to die here. But that's the truth."

Zayas disappears into the crowd.

"Man," Charles Hill says to no one in particular. "People aren't afraid to talk anymore."

Omar Linares pushes gently through a frantic, blind pack of people scrambling to get to their seats. As usual, there's a Mona Lisa smile on his face; nothing ever seems to disturb him. He is wearing his Pinar uniform with the nifty palm and tobacco patch on the arm, a real ballplayer roaming the aisles. No one notices. I stop him to ask about the pulled muscle in his right leg. He's heavier than I've ever seen him, squirrel-cheeked and looking more and more like Tony Gwynn. "I didn't play a lot this year, but now I'm playing to make sure we win," he says.

He's not talking only about tonight. "Oh no," Linares says, adding a guarantee: "We're going to be National Series champions."

It is 8:20 P.M. Outside the third base line, I see the Industriales pitcher warming up: high kick, sidearm delivery, brim pulled low over his eyes. My double-take is almost vaudevillian. From the stands he looks just like El Duque. Outside the first base line, Pinar's Pedro Luis Lazo is lazily firing the ball to a catcher, face lit up like a jack-o'-lantern. He comes over to the railing to talk. He went a subpar 10–7, 2.30 ERA this season, but attributes that to getting married. Don't worry, he says. He, and the rest of the Cuban team, will be more than ready for the Olympics in 2000.

"We've got to wait till we get there and on the field and then we'll find out," he says, laughing. "But there's no doubt we're going to win. And win and win and win."

Almost time. Bells rattle, men clap tin cans together, one drum keeps pounding this relentless jungle beat. Someone blows a whistle, and suddenly the eerie howl of a hand-cranked police siren flows through the stands, the sound of an air raid, a bomb coming, the end of the world. A man stands on the Industriales dugout with a lion mask pulled over his head. "*Cara de leon!*" people chant. "Lion-face!" Everywhere people are swigging a mean pink concoction from plastic bottles, wincing from the burn of rotgut liquor.

Painted across the outfield fence: "¡Cuba! Land of Love and Bravery ¡Cuba! Land of Purest Youth ¡Cuba! Land of Sports and Culture ¡Cuba! Land of Humanity and Solidarity ¡Cuba! Land of Courage and Tenderness!"

9:01 P.M. All 25,000 fans stand, the players remove their hats. I look around at the cobalt-blue rafters propping up the corrugated tin roof behind home plate. Everyone addresses the flag in center field for the national anthem. Omar Linares steps over to the railing along the first base line and signs an autograph. One by one, the Industriales players trot out to their positions. The game is as important as these things come: Industriales has won seven National Series titles, but a Pinar championship this year will break that record and end the capital's unquestioned place as Cuba's baseball hub. The Industriales players are playing to defend Havana, history, themselves. At 9:09, Adrian Hernandez fires his first pitch. A quarter-moon lies on its side in the inky sky, gleaming like God's toothy grin. I take it as a blessing.

Charles Hill is gone. I am alone. I walk up to the seats along shallow right field, take a vacant seat in the third row. With a man on third and two out in the bottom of the first, a difficult ground ball hops toward Linares at third. I lean forward expecting some magic, but Linares's throw flies so wide of the first baseman it's comical. I've never seen him make such an error. One-nothing, Industriales.

The game is nothing like what I've come to expect. Cuban baseball usually enthralls with its freewheeling display of scoring; discarding the American choice between scrapping for runs or waiting for the three-run homer, the typical Cuban tilt combines both in a manic flurry of steals, hit-and-runs, and cheap homers off aluminum bats, and the result is always some 13–8 monstrosity that bedevils the purist and leaves pitchers gasping. So many times I've seen the Americans or Dominicans stake themselves a tidy, three-run lead while their Cuban opponents calmly built up an irreversible momentum, always confident of launching their inevitable avalanche. "We know how to extend our claws, like a tiger," Valle once told me. "We know when to jump." Watching Cuba play is never like watching the Yankees or Dodgers. It's like watching the 1985 L.A. Lakers come barreling downcourt on a dazzling fastbreak.

But tonight is something else. Industriales, in its classic blue pinstripes, builds a two-run lead and sits there, watching Hernandez keep its season alive. A longtime friend of El Duque, Hernandez is no relation but worshipped him as a boy, modeled his kick and approach after him, even worked with his banned teammate on the sly when Duque was supposedly persona non grata. This season, the twenty-six-year-old Adrian has gone an impressive 10–6 with a 2.95 ERA, but he is no one's idea of greatness. Until now. Mixing pitches perfectly, shutting down Omar, his hot-hitting (.345) brother Juan Carlos Linares, and the dangerous Yobal Duenas in the heart of the order, he has made the National Series' most talented team look pathetic.

Clouds of cheap cigarette smoke drift out of the seats and over the field. The stadium is filled with plenty of American baseball touches: The scoreboard lists Bolas, Strikes, Average, Al Bate, and Outs; a sign stenciled in English next to the dugout insists, "No Pepper Game Here." The game flies by, and not just because it's a pitcher's duel. Here the game is the great dictator: No TV commercials pad time between innings, no at-bats are delayed by some slugger's endless scratches, tugs, yanks, and tics. The umpires keep things moving.

By the seventh inning, when Hernandez strikes out Daniel Lazo and Rigoberto Madera and stands, legs spread, fist clenched at his side, screaming at Madera to sit down, everyone in the place knows he's seeing something rare. Omar Linares fires yet another ball wildly out of reach; no one can ever remember him making two errors in a game. A cloud passes over God's smile, but only for a few moments; it is, after all, Adrian's night. The drum keeps pounding. The siren wails. When he walks Omar to lead off the ninth, the crowd chants louder and louder to Industriales manager Pedro Medina: "Leave him in!" In America, of course, by-the-numbers managing demands the seven-inning start, then a set-up man, then the ace stopper. Nobody goes nine anymore.

But Hernandez has surrendered just four hits. Medina is no fool. He leaves him in. Adrian strikes out Duenas for the third time to get the first out. Then he induces Lazaro Castro to chop an easy grounder to second for a routine double play that ends it. Hernandez tosses his glove into the air and gets mobbed by his teammates. Omar walks slowly off the field. The fans cheer and instantly begin filing out, chanting Adrian's name, ringing bells, singing. The rum bottles are empty.

I feel lucky. It's easily one of the best baseball games I've ever seen. I leave the stadium and allow the peaceable crowd to carry me down to the players' entrance, where for the next ten minutes a pack of people cheer every Industriales player as he emerges. It is a wonderful scene. I wriggle my way closer until I'm standing about two feet from the door, and then I'm hit by an overwhelming stench. I cover my nose. No one else seems to notice, much less care. But each time a player bounds out smiling, he trails behind him the unmistakable odor of a toilet that will never flush.

The next morning, Javier takes me to the airport. "Forty years of this shit," he says. "The Americans: bad, bad, bad, bad. But here it's bad. The only people who do well work with tourists. Taxis, prostitutes,

pimps, fixers, translators. Those who don't, no matter how committed, are fucked."

I sit in an spacious empty waiting room at Jose Marti Airport.
There are rum and cigars for sale, books by Che and Fidel, the photo
book by Corrales, postcards. A television set hangs suspended over
my head, playing music videos, and here it is again: a moment that
in a movie would be jeered as heavy-handed. Between ads for sham-
poo and charter airplane flights, a song comes on, played over a collage of Havana street scenes and antique shots of all the bearded
rebels when they were young. Two men and a woman are singing
softly, over and over, "Por donde vas, Cuba? Por donde vas, Cuba?"

Where are you going?

I board the airplane and head north.

CHAPTER 8

*The picturesque Cuban society . . . was more amusing than any
other that one had yet discovered in the whole broad world, but
made no profession of teaching anything unless it were Cuban
Spanish or the danza; and neither on his own nor on King's
account did the visitor ask any loftier study than that of the
buzzards floating on the trade-wind down the valley to Dos
Bocas, or the colors of sea and shore at sunrise from the height
of the Gran Piedra; but as though they were still twenty years
old and revolution were as young as they, the decaying fabric,
which had never been solid, fell on their heads and drew them
with it into an ocean of mischief.*

—Henry Adams, 1906

The first time, you come home wounded. This is what the exiles
don't understand: Even the most disinterested Anglo, gone to Cuba
for a diverting, mojito-fueled skim along the surface, ends up
drowning in midnight gossip, family tragedy, a flood of tears set to
a salsa soundtrack. Too soon, you find yourself joined in your cab
ride/walk/meal by a teenager who knows more about the workings
of the American Congress than you do. Too soon you hear that your
waiter is a professor of history. Too soon you're engaged in a fevered
discussion about the stupid embargo, about that devil Fidel, about

the bastards in Miami who can fuck themselves if they think they're going to come back and kick my family out of the house they deserted forty years ago . . . and then you're invited to a clean, time-shattered home with that hilarious mami and a flock of neighbors and everyone drinking and now it's 2 A.M. and the songs come snaking out of the little radio, women gyrating their hips and dancing the pain away, and you're wondering how will I ever get back to the hotel?

So you return, again and again. And you come home heavy each time, smelling of diesel fuel and cigar smoke and elated and sad, as if you'd just returned from the best party in the prettiest old prison. You spend weeks thinking about your acquaintances and that stress of living each day in a heightened state of worry or desperation or joy, and maybe you didn't sense this last time that something new has slipped into the Havana air—resignation, a retreat, a fear that the once-ajar window of change has slammed shut. But once you leave, small pieces add up: British Airways will soon start direct flights to Havana, the Dominican Republic reopens relations with Castro, you recall a talk with one dear friend. He's someone you've known awhile, a man of great spirit and massive hands who years ago predicted how the regime would make it through, and if you disagreed you still admired his weight then, the immovable bulk of his believing. Now it looks as if he might be right. But now is too late.

"Yes, I was a revolutionary, but that was before," he said. This last trip he sat in the Hotel Plaza lobby over a soda, CNN playing on the bar TV. For him, the revolution is over. "But I have to be realistic," he said, holding up his hands in a shrug. "I'm fifty. Past a certain age, a man gets used to his life and where he is and it's impossible to change. Otherwise, I'd be living in the United States with you."

You carry all that—sorrow, helplessness, guilt over how easily you drop in and get out—but sooner than they should such pangs begin to fade. Despite yourself, you segue back into the American rhythm. On the flight out of Havana, you'd seen some Yanks. Two men sat a few rows ahead, one in front of the other, and before the plane could take off they were already yelling. "Asshole!" said one; "Asshole!" said the other. "Shut up!" said one; "Shut up!" said the other. Then both slumped, victorious, back in their seats. It was the first argument you'd heard in weeks. The stewardess served drinks. You looked out the window and wondered about home.

In Miami everything moved faster: traffic, lives, time. No one talked about the government much, except in jokes, and the stock market rose and fell and Sosa and McGwire began their season of swat. On April 15, the *Miami Herald* ran a letter written from prison by Martha Beatriz Roque Cabello, leader of the Domestic Dissidents Working Group, a federation representing fourteen of the largest dissident groups in Cuba. Arrested on July 16, 1997, charged with "counterrevolutionary activity" and still awaiting trial, she scribbled her letter on toilet paper. "Those who don't live in Cuba find it difficult to understand that the system maintains its political control principally through self-repression," she wrote. "Each Cuban has a built-in policeman. This complex mechanism whereby one assumes the conscience of a hunted person has been developed and perfected for almost forty years. . . ."

On May 13, I drove downtown to Gerrits Leprechaun Gym to see Joel Casamayor and Ramon Garbey. It had been nearly two years since both boxers defected during a training session in Guadalajara, Mexico, on the eve of the '96 Olympic Games in Atlanta, and they were now deep into their pro careers. Along with eleven other defectors, including six from the ranks of the Cuban national team, the

men had joined the support group/social club/promotional gim-
mick that calls itself Team Freedom—an experiment doomed to
eventual failure if only because of pro boxing's notoriously egoma-
niacal nature. But for the moment, the Cuban boxers train together,
fight schedules permitting, and Team Freedom has made its dent in
the pro game. Along with welterweight Diobelys Hurtado, who lost
a fiercely contested title bout to Pernell Whitaker and remains a top
contender, the lightweight Casamayor and cruiserweight Garbey
make up the cream of the team; both are undefeated at 10-0 and
9-0, respectively, and have begun their rise through the swamp of
pro boxing.

It was mid-afternoon, the gym sticky with the usual ninety-degree
swelter. An American flag hung from the ceiling, the walls were
painted red, white, and blue. Garbey, in black bicycle shorts and a
white T-shirt heavy with sweat, was already in the ring, trudging
through the last moments of a lethargic sparring session with
heavyweight journeyman Phil Jackson. They stopped and went their
separate ways, Garbey to huff and wander the gym, Jackson to
pound on a trainer's handpads. Three other boxers started rat-a-tat-
tatting punching bags. Into the ring stepped junior middleweight
Mario Iribarren and a sparring partner; the two fighters attacking
with all the fire Jackson and Garbey lacked, Iribarren wincing under
a barrage of punches. The air filled with the moist smack of leather
on skin. Casamayor sat on a trainer's table, shouting to Iribarren:
"That's it! Now! Eso es! Huh-huh! There! The right . . . the right!"

The Cuban boxer's transition to America is a blindfolded trek
through the wild. No one trains him how to handle success. "Fifty
percent of the Cuban team could be world champions, but these
guys change," said Jesse Ravelo, a trainer on the '96 U.S. team who
defected after the '67 Pan Am Games. It starts with the weight. The
classic Cuban fighter is broad-shouldered with the waist of a wasp,

inordinately tall—and hungry. The Cuban system constantly chisels its talent, pushing the fighters to drop weight and squeeze their power into lighter weight classes; Hurtado, for example, fought at 132 in Cuba and now fights comfortably carrying fifteen more pounds. But food is the least of the hazards. Heavyweight Jorge Luis Gonzalez defected in 1991 with a great amateur résumé, but his pro career has been little more than a clownish parade of partying, moronic utterances, and goofy haircuts. "There's a lot more temptation, but really, it's just life in general," Ravelo said. "In Cuba, that's all you have: train and train, living the life of sports. Then you come here, and everybody treats you like a baby and hands you things on a silver platter. It changes you."

Casamayor is a small man, of course, with the wariness and wry humor necessary for a small man's survival. He has a face like a ferret. He grew up in Guantanamo, a close friend of Savon, and began boxing at the age of seven. He won a junior world championship at sixteen and, by the time he was twenty-two, an Olympic gold medal and two world championships. Now, at twenty-six, he lives in a hotel on Miami Beach, still bitter over the life he left behind. He has a seven-year-old daughter, Yudeysi, who lives in Cerro, but shrugged when asked if he missed her. "I gave it my heart and got nothing back," he said. "I won a gold medal and I got a Chinese bicycle. There're guys who didn't do as well as me, and they got Ladas.

"Here, when you're a champion, you live like a champion. There, you live like shit."

It is well known that support for the regime is a prerequisite for overseas travel, and Casamayor said that his refusal to join the Union of Young Communists after Barcelona doomed him. But he is no dreamy-eyed freedom fighter. He defected and now fights for the most basic reason. "I came here for the money," Casamayor said. "So I can send it to my family."

Garbey's motives also center on a raw deal. Born in Santiago, the jovial twenty-seven-year-old won a world championship at light-heavyweight in 1991, but never even got the bicycle—much less an old Russian car. He'd already had one firsthand lesson in the unbending nature of the regime; the disgraced baseball player Barbaro Garbey is his uncle. But the real reason Garbey began planning to go early in 1995, he said, was that "there were a lot of stool pigeons in camp who'd say I wasn't working and I was getting tired of it. Third- and fourth-ranked fighters would try to get on the team by squealing on me—then they wouldn't have to beat me in the ring."

Squabbles and politics and ongoing tension between himself and Cuban boxing coach Alcides Sagarra, Garbey said, led him to desert the team "five or six times. But I kept coming back." He planned to defect in Atlanta, but when, at the camp in Guadalajara in late June, Garbey overheard Sagarra talking about cracking down on Garbey when the team returned to Havana, "I thought I'd better not go back."

Garbey called some Cuban friends living in Guadalajara and they took him in. "The only time I got scared was when some other boxers—Maikro Romero and Hector Vinent and one of the trainers—came to the hotel to try to talk me out of it," he said. "I hid from them, and went to the yard of my Cuban friend. There was a room there. I climbed through the window and hid."

Garbey stayed two weeks in Guadalajara. He met up with Casamayor through connections there, immediately attracting the attention of two warring groups of fawning agents, then flew together with him to Tijuana and drove over the border into the immigration station at San Ysidro. Since then, he has gotten engaged, learned to drive, crashed two cars, and made some money.

It was late now. Both boxers left the gym last, and they stepped out blinking into the sunlight. Both said they are happy they left Cuba. Both said they are sure that, as Casamayor says, "there will be more" Cuban boxers defecting. I brought up Vinent, a close friend to both, a fighter many believe is now the best pound-for-pound amateur boxer in the world—but neither wanted to talk about him for the record. Both men promised they will stay in the United States until Fidel dies.

"Things will change," Casamayor said. "Then I will go back with my championship belt."

Eight days later, the Bahamas sent four of the five baseball rafters—Villa Clara catcher Angel Lopez, second baseman Jorge Diaz, pitching coach Orlando Chinea, and outfielder Maikel Jova—back to Cuba with sixty-one other boat people held at a detention center in Nassau. Jorge Luis Toca, the first baseman for Villa Clara and the national team, was granted a Japanese visa because of his Japanese wife and left for Japan. Nicaragua offered to take the remaining players, but the Bahamas said no.

Cuba haunted the summer. The island was all over America in 1998: In New York, Rey Ordoñez won another Gold Glove for the Mets. In Tampa, Rolando Arrojo anchored the new Devil Rays with fourteen wins. In Miami, Livan Hernandez received a restraining order from an ex-girlfriend and led a Marlins staff that lost 108 games. In Baltimore, Rafael Palmiero paced an underachieving Orioles club with forty-three home runs. In Toronto, slugger Jose Canseco, who a decade ago emerged as the first postmodern Cuban curiosity when he became the first player to ever hit forty home runs, steal forty bases, and date Madonna, revived his career by hitting forty-six home runs. At one time, Canseco seemed like the only Cuban playing in America. Now he was barely noticed.

"When you're recognized as the best player in the world and you get the forty-forty and you're Cuban? That's a heavy-ass flag," Canseco said, sitting in the dugout before a June game in Miami. "There were a lot of responsibilities that went along with that, and, really, I couldn't win. But now it's happening everywhere. Now you see Livan and El Duque coming in and Palmiero's having a great year . . . and players are still coming in from Cuba left and right with tremendous talent. They're all carrying pieces of the flag for me now."

I remembered then something defector Rene Arocha once told me about the shoddy conditions all ballplayers endured in Cuba, the lack of showers, the bunks they slept in at the stadium in Pinar Del Rio: "You'd just say, 'This is shit here,'" Arocha said. "There was nothing else to say; that covered it. We all had a saying. Every time we went to eat and the food sucked, we'd say, 'Ah, Canseco, if you were here you'd hit .240 with three homers all season.'"

In 1998, Cuba suffered its worst sugar harvest in forty years. Castro spent much of his time touring the Caribbean, South Africa, returning to Grenada, building new alliances. The U.S. government issued a report stating that Cuba was no longer a military threat to the United States.

On the island, life returned to form. Pinar Del Rio shook off that loss to Adrian Hernandez and, as Omar Linares predicted, won the National Series championship. In June, the Cuban Baseball Commission canceled a tour of Nicaragua by two of its teams because of Nicaragua's offer to the baseball rafters. Savon had been right, too: In July, the International Boxing Federation stripped Ruslan Chagayev of the title because he had boxed professionally; aura and world championship restored, Savon went on that month to win gold at the 1998 Goodwill Games in New York when he whammied American DaVarryl Williamson just fifty-five seconds into the final.

Cuba dominated the boxing, but Hector Vinent wasn't there. Word was that he'd been banned from the national team. No one was saying why.

In July, too, a Reuters reporter spoke to the returned ballplayers in Villa Clara. All complained of harassment by government officials, interrogations, and threats of severe punishment if they tried to leave Cuba again.

"I am desperate to carry on playing baseball," Maikel Jova said then. "Whenever I stop and think, I am inclined, I don't know, to throw myself in front of a car."

On August 2, the Cuban national baseball team—with just nine holdovers from the '97 squad and a pitching staff led by La Habana's Jose Ibar—blitzed through the field in Italy to win its twenty-second World Cup Championship. Refreshed, motivated, and looking like the dynamo of old, the team outscored its opponents 117–14. Cuba has not lost a game in that tournament since 1986. The United States finished ninth.

On August 13, five ballplayers turned up in Nicaragua after again taking to the sea off Pinar Del Rio. Picked up by an unmarked, seventy-two-foot pleasure boat owned and operated by South Florida residents, the men were dropped off in Managua and took up residency at the Inter-Continental Hotel. The ballplayers were Jova, Lopez, Diaz, and a pitcher named Alain Hernandez, plus Villa Clara utilityman Osmany Garcia. Garcia had been one of the banned players reinstated by Cuba in March because, as the baseball commissioner said then, he had the proper "attitude." Evidently, his attitude had changed.

In September, Jorge Luis Toca became the newest millionaire defector. The Mets announced they had signed him to a minor league contract that included a bonus in excess of $1.5 million. His balsero brothers from Villa Clara still hung in limbo: No one expected Jova, Lopez, Diaz, Garcia, and Alain Hernandez to be returned to Cuba, but an effort to get to the United States through Costa Rica, the nation that took in El Duque, fizzled when the five ballplayers neglected to tell immigration officials they'd come through Nicaragua. So they went back to Managua to wait.

I was happy for Toca. Every balsero leaves behind a pile of wreckage, a necessary legacy of bewilderment and loss, but those twelve days when he was missing and feared dead left his family uniquely seared. Toca was a ballplayer, and that magnified everything. Day after day, his fifty-six-year-old mother, Francisca Gomez, would take calls from Japan, the States, the Dominican, Mexico, from reporters ringing in with new rumors, breathing sympathy, and asking how she felt, demanding reaction before she'd had time to react. "We're going crazy because no one lets us have a life," she told me then. "I'm dying not just from the pain, but the press is continually hammering, hammering. . . ."

I hit her, too. Back in March, early on a Sunday morning, I had appeared at her door in the small Cuban town of Remedios with photographer Victor Baldizon. It had been five days since Duque's raucous press conference in Miami. Her son had not yet been found. Francisca hadn't slept. Her dark face was lined and puffy, depleted, a mask of despair. Her one-and-a-half-year-old grandson, also Jorge Luis, waddled about with his father's baseball card twisted in his hand. Later that same day, Francisca would learn that her son had turned up, alive. But now it was 7:30 A.M., and here was another reporter standing on the porch of her cramped yellow house. I fought off the impulse to apologize and skulk away then, because this was the moment of truth, wasn't it? Here was every daughter, wife, mother left behind, the casualty at the moment bullet hits bone. "Eleven days of agony," she said. I could no more walk away than avert my eyes from a plane crash.

Francisca sank into her chair, head falling onto her hand like a great stone. She lit a cigarette. Small columns of ash lay broken at her feet, my feet, all over the floor. "Nobody knows what's really happening," she said. She cried at the mention of her son's name. She pulled out the crinkled page from *Granma*, July 27, 1997, the story announcing her son's ban. He never would've left if he hadn't been banned, she said. She placed her face in her large dark hands. "We've suffered so much and no one seems to understand the pain we're feeling," she said. "I feel at any moment someone's going to knock at the door and say, 'He is here. He wants to talk to you.'"

I carried all that with me back to Miami: the crowing of roosters trickling through the walls; the five boys already tossing a baseball on the baseball field across the street; Francisca saying how Little Jorge Luis looks just like his dad. I carried it because she endured my questions and offered us coffee, because we were hurting her with our presence but she was too polite to make us leave. Francisca even went outside to pose for Victor. On the porch, tears leaking down, baby in her lap—the perfect shot. She trudged across to the ball field, peeked through the fence. "I know he's alive," she said. "I can feel he's alive. God is telling me he's alive. I just want people to leave me alone so I can regain my sanity."

Of everything I had seen and done in Cuba, that morning nagged at me the most. Later, when I saw in September that Toca had received his $1.5 million, I felt happiest for his mother. Some of the money was sure to filter back home, maybe making up for all the uncertainty and strangers. On the way out of Remedios we had passed the usual billboard: "Socialism Has Triumphed Here." I felt like a thief that day. Then I fell asleep.

* * *

Also in September, a week after Toca signed, El Duque beat the Boston Red Sox, 3–0, in Yankee Stadium for the first complete-game shutout of his professional career. Luis Zayas had been right about everything; Duque's weakness for most of his rookie season had been left-handed batters, but the Yankees taught him a new pitch, a four-seam fastball, and he became more and more dominating as the playoffs loomed. The morning after he beat Boston, I showed up at Duque's hotel in midtown Manhattan. I'd called the Yankees and Duque's interpreter, Leo Astacio, had said Duque would be happy to talk. I checked with him twice, Astacio said. Call him at his hotel tomorrow morning. He'll be waiting.

Duque wasn't waiting. No, he said, he knew nothing about any such interview. No, he had no time. "I've got to do my things," he said. "Then I have to go to lunch."

His room was the usual little New York box. A hot iron squatted on an ironing board. Duque leaned over the bed folding shirts, packing for the team's trip to Tampa. I was stunned. The last time we'd spoken, three years earlier, Duque welcomed me into his Havana home, laughed and joked and spoke for hours. I never considered us friends, but I had marveled at his generosity, his open-hearted spirit. Now he wouldn't look me in the eye and spat out short responses. No, he said, shrugging, Leo never told him a thing. I told him I'd seen his wife and kids. "Ex-wife," he said. I relayed what the Cuban baseball commissioner said about him, and Duque loosened up slightly. He even allowed himself to grin.

"You go back to Cuba?" he said in broken English. "You tell him you saw how I pitch in the *Grandes Ligas*."

He invited me to come to the stadium later, but couldn't guarantee he would talk. "Take a chance," he said. I spent the rest of the day mystified.

Getting blown off is a baseball commonplace. The insular nature of the game and its long-hallowed place in American sports have conspired to make baseball players the rudest, crudest, and most insufferable lot of athletes; for every gentleman like Tony Gwynn there're four others like Barry Bonds, Albert Belle, Kevin Brown, Kirk Gibson—self-centered stars who treat strangers like trash and nurse themselves with the assurance that they are "misunderstood." The most common retort, when a writer raves to colleagues about his chat with some nice, eager rookie, is, "Yeah? Give him time." But behind such a cynical logic is the fear that it will indeed come true, that too much money and too much worship will conspire to ruin another refreshing soul. I wasn't perplexed because Duque lied or blew me off. He owed me nothing. I was just marveling at how quickly he'd been infected.

My first impulse, then, was sadness. I had, after all, been exposed to the openness of the Cuban player in Cuba, and it's impossible to be there without becoming infatuated with the grubby charm, the simple accessibility of sports. For years now, I'd hit the island to do more than report stories; the place had become my personal antidote to the diseased state of the American game, a haven from the relentless blast of big money. Every instinct I had as a fan in 1998 told me that here was how sports should be, because here was how sports was once-upon-a-time. No luxury boxes, no exclusive parking, no agents, no teams moving, no tickets selling for the price of a car. Old stadiums, old dynamic. I was sure I hated the values of spoiled American athletes and pined for the good old days. I was sure now that El Duque had lost himself in our awful new world.

He told me to meet him at Yankee Stadium at 3 P.M. He showed at 4:13, wearing a fine gray suit and a cell phone on his belt. He didn't apologize. He was polite but guarded. He announced that the one off-limit topic was the escape to Anguilla Cay; movie negotiations were ongoing and he didn't want to just give that away. As Duque undressed to work out, in a locker room far finer than his Havana home, I took in the cluster of gold chains dangling around his neck.

It wasn't a warm interview, lasted twenty minutes or so, but I found myself recalling it often over the next two months. Duque got better and better as the 1998 season wound down, winning his last three starts to finish 12–4 with a 3.13 ERA, and like his brother the year before, Duque went on to become a playoff hero. In the Yankees' most crucial game of the season, with New York down two games to one to the Cleveland Indians in the American League Championship Series, Duque started against Dwight Gooden—the man he worshipped when young—fired a crucial three-hitter over seven innings in game four, and gave no sign of the big-game jitters that Cuba's baseball commissioner had seen in him. "The commissioner? He didn't even play," Duque said that September day. "It's all political. That shows no respect to say I wouldn't win a big game here. Do you know why he's wrong? Because the person who doesn't know must be wrong. The person who doesn't know has to show respect when he speaks. He has no ethics. No class."

Then, in game two of the World Series, with his agent's hype machine cranking into overdrive, Duque again pitched seven superb innings to win. By then, his dominance was almost expected. The surprise came when, just after the Series, Castro went against type and abruptly allowed Duque's mother, ex-wife, and two daughters to travel to New York on a six-month visa. It was the final piece of the story; when I'd asked what he missed most about Cuba that day, Duque said, "My family, my two daughters and my mother. I don't know if I'll be able to ever call this home." No one expected Duque to allow his daughters ever to go back now. Home had come to him.

It was, indeed, perfect grist for a movie, despite the fact that some details of Duque's trip were later found to be embellished. The facts remain: Duque was the best pitcher in Cuba, he was banned because his brother defected, he found himself twice interrogated for twelve hours by State Security at its headquarters at Villa Marista. He refused all his food there, even water, "just in case." He did not want to leave. "No," Duque said. "I always said I would never leave my daughters behind. I had to do it. They were trying to humiliate me too much, the police and everyone else. The police would come and stop me in my own yard, asking me for identification. They'd tell me, 'You used to be the Duke. Now you're no one.'" Had he been caught trying to escape, Duque would be in jail today.

The first signal, though, that told him he had fallen into disfavor came in the months after Livan defected in 1995. "There were four times when they gave out cars," Duque said. "I was the top pitcher on the national team. I never got anything." In one sense, nothing rankles Duque more about his treatment than that. When asked who was the better pitcher, he or Lazaro Valle, he ended the interview by walking away and shouting over his shoulder, "Valle. I consider him better. I consider him better because he has a house and a car."

At first, so cynical a statement left me cold. It seemed to confirm my worst fear about the souring of El Duque. But the more I turned the facts over in my mind, the more disturbed I became by my reaction, not his; the more I couldn't get past the fact that my disappointment grew from the same place as the nostalgic blubbering over sports now dominating the American scene, and that such a halcyonic view was patronizing at best and hypocritical at worst. Fans keep asking, "Where have you gone, Joe DiMaggio?" But it struck me as ironic that the more conservative one is—the more wedded to the ideals of free-market capitalism and small government—the more likely one is to despise the rootless, overcompensated athlete of the nineties and yearn for some fifties golden age when all the power in sports resided solely in the hands of owners and autocratic commissioners, when players had no say in where they worked or how much they made. It became obvious that the only place where such a thing could happen now is a place like Fidel Castro's communist Cuba, where the regime makes all decisions and muffles all dissent. Joe D. is alive and still playing. I have seen him in Havana.

I'd never been naive enough to ignore the flood of athletic defectors voting year after year with their feet. But I'd come to enjoy the life and games of Cuban athletes more than their American counterparts because, like most American fans, I was both a closet tyrant and a closet bomb-thrower. Not only did I want players controlled, to stay with one team and actually represent their community, but I reveled in the idea of sport's classlessness, its place as one of our society's few stretches of common ground. For much of the century, you could attend a game and cheer with CEOs and truckers and everyone in between. You could take random snapshots of the crowd and examine them later and not be wrong in thinking, "Here's America. Here's what the country looks like." But in the 1990s, the gap between have and have-not fans became oceanic. Ticket prices and parking costs shot so high that only the rich could afford a day at the ballpark. The losers got ghettoized. We could watch on TV. We might even get a chance to cheer at the parade.

I'd resigned myself to resenting all that, taking solace in the friendly jostle of thousands milling through stadium portals across Cuba. But then I kept thinking about El Duque, and something he said about the teammates he left behind. "I'm worried about those players getting old and having no future," he said. "Their true future is here in major league baseball, because there's always a reason to play." He was speaking of money again, of course, but the more I considered it the less it bothered me; because what El Duque's actions and words described were a man's right to make his own decision, free agency in its purest form, and who can argue with that? I tried in vain to distinguish between a Cuban pitcher taking the defector's leap from Havana to New York and an American taking the free-agent jump from, say, Chicago to Atlanta, and it became clear that America's dollar-dominated, modern sports scene is not some aberrant development, a wrong road taken. It's the inevitable fruit of a society based on the principles of individualism and a free market, for good and bad. We may not like free agency and franchise movement and the buying of championships, but these are only the sporting expressions of what Americans deem most crucial: individual freedom and money. If, in the process, the United States has somehow become far more of a workers' paradise than a place like Cuba, so be it. Even leftists can like American sports: In no other industry does the common laborer—albeit one, like El Duque, making $1.65 million a year—hold so much power.

For those who find this kind of sport too rich to stomach, Cuba is the only alternative. "Professionalism has been eradicated," Castro declared in 1975.

But that was long ago and some plagues never die. Joe DiMaggio is tired now. Joe DiMaggio has had it with being a throwback, a weapon, a symbol, a hero. He wants to get paid.

PART TWO

CHAPTER 9

I would find a proper legal cover and I would go in. There are several justifications that could be used, like protecting American citizens living in Cuba and defending our base at Guantanamo. I believe that the most important thing at this point is that we do whatever is necessary to get Castro and communism out of Cuba.

—RICHARD NIXON to John F. Kennedy, April 1961

Change has come again, gaining speed. It has been nine months, but even before I touch Cuban soil I can smell the difference. Instead of the usual Soviet castoff, the Cubana jet out of Nassau this time is a newly minted Airbus A320, staffed by three Irish stewardesses. One of them, so emerald fresh and antiseptic she seems shrink-wrapped, tells me that there are two Cuban steward trainees and two more pilot trainees on the flight deck, commanded by a Canadian pilot—the whole mishmash a result of some new $30 million joint venture between the Cuban government and the Irish airline TransAer. I buckle up, begin reading my *USA Today*, December 8, 1998: "DiMaggio Clinging to Life, Doctor Says." Inside, there's a small piece about Connecticut Senator Christopher Dodd, fresh off a six-hour chat with Fidel, declaring the U.S. policy on Cuba a failure and calling for new talks.

Three men come down the aisle and seat themselves in a pungent cloud of two-day-old sweat, and within thirty seconds a Cuban with a head and face eerily resembling the Jose Marti bust found in every Cuban hamlet sidles past spraying deodorizer from a can. The pilot begins rasping into the intercom, and it takes a moment to realize he's speaking in perfect corn-fed English. "Welcome aboard our flight to Havana," he says.

We land at the city's new, modern international terminal, breeze through baggage claim and customs. As I walk outside, a woman touches my arm. "Do you want to rent my apartment?" she says. I'm traveling this time with Victor Baldizon, a Costa Rican photographer who has visited the island two dozen times, and as we jostle along in the Habanatur shuttlebus to our hotel we both remark on the empty streetcorners. No *jineteras*, anywhere. "Thirty days ago, overnight, special forces came and picked up everyone," the bus driver says. "They closed all the discos, even in the hotels. They took all the girls to a clinic, gave them blood tests and a vagina test to see if there're any diseases. If a girl is picked up and she's a hooker, she gets five years hard labor. The pimp gets eight. They closed the clubs and then they hit the streets and that's where we are now: It's a ghost town.

"They started hitting private places after that—anywhere there are *extranjeros* with girls. They come in with dogs and if a dog likes you you're gone. Say you're wearing a shirt from the day before: If there's even a whiff of a drug? You're gone."

We whisk past restaurants, drop passengers at hotels, and I'm seeing more neon, more renovation, more new signs than ever before—all that European seed money finally beginning to blossom. We check into the Copacabana, out in Miramar, and the bellman tells the same tale.

"You've got to understand: Everything had gotten too far out of hand," he says. "The Cuban woman wasn't even looking at a Cuban man; he was nothing. The government had to step in. If some old woman wants to be a whore, fine. But at fourteen or fifteen? Forget it."

I'm not convinced. I need definitive proof. Since the mid-nineties the jinetera has become such a staple of Havana life, and for many the hub of a vital, decidedly unsocialistic black market economy, that eradicating her would change everything—scare off male tourists, push the girls toward less lucrative work or desperation, defuse the nation's sexed-up aura. We take a cab into Vedado, then trip down to the Malecon. The night is thick with humidity, but quiet. We stride toward El Morro, sea tumbling against the wall below. Only once, when a glassy-eyed girl backs out of a pack of men, wiggles her ass, and grabs my crotch, does the city seem itself again, but in light of what I've heard that gesture seems hollow, like someone leading a cheer when the game is long over. Still, I know where to go. I pick up the pace and turn right, plunging into the arbored darkness of Paseo del Prado, the most direct route back to the red-hot core.

Seven guys huddle beneath the unforgiving shower of light at Castillo de Farnes. They sit on stools, hurtling toward fifty and drunk, puffing cigars, eyeing the door. The atmosphere has shifted, as if some variation on the neutron bomb had recently dropped, killing women but leaving men alive, bewildered, mute. The parade of girls has disappeared. Jinetera Central is dead. Victor pulls out his camera and holds it beneath the bar, snapping, snapping. "I'm going to call it *La Isla de los Hombres Solos*," he says. "The Island of Lonely Men."

With one exception. I can't believe it at first, but nine months after I last saw him, my ponytailed acquaintance from Victoria, Canada, remains propped at the same table with the same black teenage girl. But even here something has changed: His face bears a fresh sunburn, but there's no hiding the exhaustion, the fleshy sag around the eyes and jaw. She stares off at the ceiling and kneads his lap with her left hand. He smokes a cigarette. It's as if there's been some kind of erotic short-circuit, all of last spring's manic lust replaced by the calm of ruin. Next to the door, a twelve-year-old boy scrawls off-the-cuff caricatures of whatever face takes his fancy.

Out the window, ten feet away, four cops wearing black berets square off around a police car. Each is upbraiding a fluorescent woman. I walk over to Victoria and reintroduce myself, and he focuses and apologizes and says he can't remember. A string of puka shells circles his right wrist; he's wearing a new green T-shirt embroidered with a leaping marlin. I ask him how long he's been back. He tells me two and a half months, then explains how he's in the process of building an apartment atop the back end of some house here in Havana to cut down on expenses. "It's only costing me $700," he giggles through teeth the color of chicken fat. "That's like, seven months' rent. It's illegal, but if it all goes bottoms-up I'm still ahead of the game."

He seems content, and I try to remember the last time I'd met a man who'd actually realized his life's ambition. I move back to the corner of the bar. Victor is talking to the bartender. I feel something jabbing me in the side; a man on crutches is poking a pen through the latticed window. "My friend . . . for you . . . for you," he says. "I hungry. Give me a dollar." He shows me the infected gash on his right leg.

The bar begins to fill: sixteen men now, two women. The bartender smiles. "Cuban men . . . we're back in demand!" he says.

Outside, a cop leads a girl in a floral dress to the car. The boy appears at my side and silently drops a piece of paper on the bar, my picture: big nose, big chin, big head, big grin. The face of a fool. I hand him a dollar.

Wednesday morning rises smeary and gray, the air utterly still—hangover weather. After breakfast, on a wall of the Copacabana bar, I notice a bronze plaque with a bizarre bas-relief likeness of a man's face. The inscription reads, "To the memory of young Italian Fabio Di Celmo, whose life was cut short in this place by a bomb planted by a Salvadorean mercenary Sept. 4, 1997 at 12:22 P.M. This imperialist barbarian cannot stop the people of Cuba or the family of national sport from remembering Fabio."

The bartenders, waiters, and hotel clerks grimly explain. Fabio, a thirty-two-year-old soccer fan, businessman, and resident of Montreal, Canada, who'd been in Havana two months trying to arrange a new venture, had been sitting alone at a table sipping coffee when a bomb planted in an ashcan at the foot of the bar ignited. That same day, bombs exploded across the city at the Bodeguita Del Medio—Hemingway's old mojito haunt—as well as the Chateau Miramar hotel and the Triton hotel, in the latest salvo in a six-month campaign of bombings directed at Cuba's tourism industry. Starting in April and ranging into the fall, eleven bombs exploded or were defused at various Havana hot spots in 1997, a terror tactic designed to scare off travelers whose dollars kept the regime afloat. The regime blamed anti-Castro exiles, others speculated about counterrevolutionaries based somewhere in the city.

Either way, those responsible couldn't have designed a better victim. Di Celmo's father had come to Havana from Italy to visit. Italy and Canada rank first and second in the world in the number of tourists sent to Cuba each year. Di Celmo's links to both countries guaranteed frightening news coverage in both countries.

None of the other bombs that day, or the ones that blew up previously at the Nacional and the Capri, or out in Varadero, or at the Melia Cohiba, caused serious injury.

But at the Copacabana, all the lobby windows shattered. A huge splinter from the hardwood bar snapped into the air. A cabinet fell on top of a female cigar roller. A shard of metal from the ashcan rocketed thirty feet across the floor and sliced open Fabio's neck. The father arrived just in time to watch his boy die.

I stop by Ana Quirot's place. The elevator still works. She sits in a giant rocking chair in her living room, serves coffee. She finished fourth in her last race, the Central American and Caribbean Games in Venezuela in August. An injury to her right foot hampered her, but Ana Fidelia admits that losing doesn't bother her as much as it should. She is more determined than ever to retire. "The biggest crown, the biggest trophy I could have now is a baby," she says. "I've been successful as a woman athlete. I want to be successful as a woman."

I stop by Parque Central to find Little Daddy. He's there, naturally, dapper and cool in the same boxy sunglasses, and we shake hands, sit down in the shade. He tries to catch me up: Jose Ibar, who won last night to lift his record to 8–1, is again tearing up the league. Industriales' Adrian Hernandez dominated Pinar Del Rio again last night, and is now 4–1. Our guy Yasser Gomez has left Metropolitanos and is playing center field for Industriales. This last one throws me. But before I can get him to explain, Little Daddy asks if I've heard about Lazaro Valle. "I think he's back from Japan, but no one's seen him," he says. "His brother-in-law killed himself. Lit himself on fire."

* * *

Now I don't know what to expect. The drive out to Playa Guanabo, a beach town twenty minutes east of Havana, is something I normally relish, for spending any time with Lazaro Valle, the one-time pitching star of the national team, is like boarding the front seat in a roller-coaster: You walk away wide-eyed and grinning and happy to be alive. There is no funnier man in Cuba. With his bullfrog voice, rat-a-tat-tat delivery, and harmlessly filthy mind, he quickly turns the most innocent conversation into a riotous free-for-all. Five years ago, in my first lengthy interview, he politely endured twenty minutes of ultra-serious questioning before finally exploding, "What is this guy, a monk? Hey, don't worry, be happy! Do you eat pussy? You suck? You fuck?" With the slightest prompting, he'll jump to his feet and do a perfect screaming imitation of Livan Hernandez winning the World Series MVP award: "I love you Miami!"

But Valle is more than a circus act. As he once put it: "Every time I got the ball, I laughed, and every time I fucked and drank I laughed. But I knew what I was doing the whole time." Smart, emotional, and perceptive, he's the first Cuban athlete I'd ever spoken to who didn't fall back on the usual black-or-white posturing. While on the island players mouth the party line to American reporters, then rip the system once they defect. Experience has taught me to be suspicious of both answers, to recognize each as a necessary response to the dictates of the powers in Havana and Miami, and to understand that ideology more often than not serves as intellectual or romantic window-dressing for the more mundane universals of family loyalty, religion, money. I see the appeal of dramatically taking sides; who wants to come off as a mere bystander when there's a war on? But I've also learned not to believe a word.

Valle chose to be different, and I always saw this as an act of courage. He wasn't afraid to drain himself of grandeur. "I'm not with God and I'm not with the devil," he says. "I'm a man." He has acknowledged that he'd often considered defecting—the mere thinking of it is a crime punishable by sanctions or worse—and has refused to disown the teammates who'd left. Dismissed by exiles as an obvious *militante* because of his constant spurning of offers from agents and major league teams—not to mention rumors that he conned at least one agent into thinking he was ready to jump and pocketed whatever cash he could get from him—Valle always bragged that he was the only superstar in Cuba who never joined the party. "I am not a communist," he says. "But I don't want to play in the States if I have to run. There's not enough money in the business to make me turn my back on my family."

That he has lost millions of dollars is unquestionable. Armed with a ninety-five-mile-per-hour fastball and a mean slider clocked at eighty-seven, Valle was the number one pitcher in Cuba for eleven years before an elbow injury forced him to bow out of Cuban baseball in 1997. When I first saw him pitch, against the USA in Millington, Tennessee, in 1993, he dominated the Americans and chuckled while doing it. Major league scouts pegged him as a twenty-game winner. "He had the stuff to be a number one or number two pitcher in the majors," Preston Gomez, a special assistant with the Anaheim Angels, told me. "One of the best." Valle's lifetime record of 131–58, with a 3.09 ERA, is second only to Duque's in the modern era, and Duque—as well as every other Cuban player who made the majors—testifies that Valle would succeed there, too. He spent the last two seasons pitching in Japan, and insists that his arm troubles are behind him. "I'm as good as ever," Valle says. In September 1998, on his way back from his second season in Japan, Valle stopped for a layover in Vancouver. There, he says, an official with the Seattle Mariners showed up with a check for $2.5 million bearing his name. Someone else from the Toronto Blue Jays offered him $25,000 just to consider defecting.

Why not go? "You know the answer," he says once we all sit down at the stone table behind his garage, and crack a bottle of rum. "Because my daughter is here, my wife—and my mother is very sick. Because I'm one of the few players who feels that their family needs them."

His eyes are veined and weary, and as the night draws on they don't clear. Valle is thirty-five now, with another birthday coming in a week, and within minutes I realize I'm watching a man's career slip away. He's smoking more. His gut has ballooned. Still possessing a dark and delicate Hollywood handsomeness, he makes the same jokes but bears a new heaviness that threatens to cloud every conversation. His mother, Lucia, has had two strokes, his sister Mercedes lies in a hospital struggling with lung cancer. He made $7,500 playing this year for the Shidax semipro team, lived in Tokyo, and compared to Duque he lives like a king here, too. He has three bedrooms, two bathrooms, a swimming pool, a Lada, a yard encircled by a six-foot wall and patrolled by three yappy dogs. But his grudging satisfaction with the regime soured last spring when the authorities decided to scrap the policy of renting retired players overseas. For the moment Valle is refusing to make appearances. He is not playing in the National Series. He is furious.

"A lot of the players are angry: That was the only way to get money, the one window of opportunity, and if they take Japan away there's nothing," Valle says. "That's the reason we felt betrayed. It's like giving candy to a kid to stop him from crying . . . and then taking it away.

"The problem is that there've been so many great stars in Cuban baseball, and now we're getting older. All the big stars have a nice house, but what happens when we can't play anymore? How do you know if you can afford to keep it up? How do you know if they'll let you keep the house at all? You go to the U.S. and play and make $10 million, you know you're set for the rest of your life. You know you'll be able to provide for your kids. We have coaches going overseas and making a killing, but there aren't that many slots. What are we going to do? Linares, Orestes Kindelan, Antonio Pacheco, me—what are they going to do to us? Take all our medals away? Take away all we've done?

"Look at it this way: Rene Arocha—St. Louis Cardinals. Osvaldo Fernandez—San Francisco Giants. Rey Ordoñez. Toca. Livan Hernandez. Arrojo. They're all big stars in the U.S., but they weren't considered really good players here. Today those guys are shitting money. And the guys here are saying, 'What's happening?' That's why we're all mad. The government sees this and they're not doing anything about it."

Valle has always loved the American game, measured himself against it. He has read two books about Tom Seaver, another about Dave Dravecky; he quotes Ted Williams as if reciting holy writ. He can do an uncanny imitation of Greg Maddux's windup, then describe the Atlanta ace's approach like Hemingway discussing Fitzgerald: equals. "Remember in 1993, when I pitched against the All-Stars in Puerto Rico? Carlos Baerga. Javy Lopez. Juan Gonzalez. Ruben Sierra: twelve strikeouts in seven innings," he says. "In 1994 in Venezuela they called me 'The Jet'—the press, the people, the players. Those were exhibition games against AAA players. I've been to the States eighteen times, I've seen twenty-six states, and I've kicked ass wherever I went.

"People say to me, 'You've been the best pitcher in Cuba for eleven years. . . .' And I say no, I've been the best pitcher in the world for eleven years. Why? Because I pitched against Frank Thomas and Robin Ventura. I remember seeing a sign in Millington once: 'Today's USA team, tomorrow's major leaguers.' I pitched against the best in the world and I pitched great against them. I'm the only pitcher to throw two perfect games. The same night Nolan Ryan got his 5,000th strikeout off Rickey Henderson on a 3–2 pitch in the fifth inning? I pitched a perfect game against South Korea in Ponce, Puerto Rico. 1989. It's in the record books."

He tips the bottle, topping off our glasses. We drink at a leisurely pace, but steady. Valle wears a red T-shirt with "Winston" emblazoned in white, sweatpants, socks, flip-flops. Though it isn't inordinately hot, he is sweating. Those types of performances, he says, are what insulated him from pressure to join the party, to keep quiet. But they didn't protect him forever. Arocha was his best friend. After he defected on the eve of the '91 Pan Am Games, Valle became instantly suspect. He believes that some careless words, spoken soon after by a covetous American scout, reached the regime, and for the next two years, he says, "Life became hell for me.

"They really squeezed me. When Arocha left, they took me into a room at the airport and said, 'We know you're going to go. Think about it. You're going to hurt yourself.'" For two years, Valle was barred from traveling overseas with the national team. He didn't know if he'd ever pitch internationally again. He traveled the streets on a bike. He became depressed.

Valle stops, calls in his wife, Margarita, from the kitchen. Ask her, he says. Then he does so himself. How bad was it for me in those years?

"He suffered and cried over the situation, the whole time," Margarita says. Then she goes back inside.

Finally, in 1993, Valle rejoined the national team on a trip to

Japan, Italy, and the United States. He concocted this bold, strange plan. First stop: "I don't go out and I don't buy anything," he says. "All the guys are buying TVs and refrigerators, but I just pocket the money. Then we get to Italy, and guys are buying clothes and still I don't buy anything. Now security is very concerned: *He's leaving, he's keeping the cash, he's not going home.* The plane lands in Miami, and an umpire—Ivan Davis—defects. Two other players are rumored to be jumping. Everybody's nervous. We got to the hotel and I grabbed my bags and took off; I went to a big party of some friends in Hialeah. Security didn't sleep; they looked for me everywhere, all night. The next morning I went to the gate at the airport. When the team arrived, here I am holding a drink and the old commissioner says to me, '*Cojones!* I thought you were gone! What are you doing here?'

"I came home and they interrogated me and kept asking, 'Why did you do that? Why?' And I said, 'I wanted to show you that I have bigger balls than you'll ever have. I left and I came back. I stepped outside because I felt I had the right to taste the water. Now you all know I could have gone if I wanted. Now get off my fucking back. If that's not enough to show I'm not leaving, fuck you.'"

He stops to light another cigarette. The night presses in from all sides, smelling of salt. Victor leaves to go to the bathroom. Valle turns to me and begins to cry. "My sister," he says. "It's very bad. Very bad."

When I try to say something soothing, Valle grins, brushes it off, "No, don't worry man!" The mood shifts again. Valle begins talking about how, ever since '93, he has made it a policy to speak his mind. He smiles at this memory: Four months later, at the Central American Games in Ponce, forty athletes defected. Valle did an interview from there with Miami's exile mouthpiece, Radio Marti. "That station is the greatest public enemy of our revolution, and Castro later asked me, 'How can you talk to these guys when nobody else from here has talked to them in thirty-five years?'" Valle says. "I told him, '*Jefe*, I couldn't pass up an opportunity to show them what you taught me.' I have a degree in social sciences. What good is an education if I don't use it?

"People here say the Americans are bad. But who in the world hasn't smoked a Marlboro? No one knows what's going to happen tomorrow, but you have to be ready. How can you not talk about radical changes here? What's going to happen when the whole thing drops? The people who didn't speak their minds . . . how are they going to feel in the future when they didn't speak out in the past? Politics has always been dirty. The friends I have outside Cuba are closer than the best friend I have here. It's deeper than just knowing them. I feel them. El Duque, Arocha, Euclides Rojas—all the guys who left—we shared everything: The girls, the drink, the wind, life. We tasted juice when everything was dry. Now they're gone. Havana is empty. But how can I feel lonely when all of them are in my heart?"

I begin worrying about reprisals. I ask if he's sure he wants to say this. Valle stares, shrugs, but he does not stop.

"It feels great not being afraid to talk, to say what I want," he says. "I could get put in jail, but it doesn't matter. They can cut my hands off. I'm not going to stop talking. They can cut my feet off. I'm not going to stop talking. They can cut my dick off. They're going to have to cut out my tongue. I still have my degree. I'm not just a ballplayer. I *think*."

It has gotten late, 11 P.M., and no one has eaten. Margarita and Valle's twelve-year-old daughter, Yuleysys, sit quietly inside. We pack into a tiny tourist cab, five of us, cruise around the quiet lanes of Guanabo a bit. We finally settle on the Caporal chicken restaurant out on the road to Havana.

The place is the size of a ballroom. Only three tables are occupied. A Michael Bolton video screeches at top volume from the TV. A Christmas tree squats in the corner, complete with lights, ornaments, candy canes; this year, after entreaties from the Pope, the party reinstated the holiday for the first time since 1969. Valle, wearing his Chicago White Sox hat on backwards, orders three different main courses for everybody. The food is passable, the bill comes to $79.

Victor places a $100 bill on the tray. Without a word, Valle grabs it, stands, strides over to the cash register. He returns with the change, leaves a $2 tip on the table. The rest of the money he puts into his pocket.

We drop the family home. On the way out of Guanabo, the cab driver stops at a bar to talk to someone. Victor steps out, leaves his wallet on the seat, and asks me to watch it. I place it on the seat next to me. In five minutes, we begin the drive back to Havana, exhausted and silent.

We stop in the Copacabana lobby for a drink. Ten minutes later, the cab driver walks up to the table and asks Victor to follow him. They go outside and talk a while. I almost nod off.

When he returns, Victor is shaking both his head and his wallet at me. I'd left it in the backseat. He sits, thumbs through his visa, his credit cards, his cash . . . and stops. "I'm missing $600," he says.

I feel like an idiot. Losing cash in Cuba is like losing a tank of oxygen underwater. American credit cards are worthless here. I apologize, grovel, promise to pay him back when we get home. Victor shaves his head and wears a beard like Colonel Sanders except it is very black. He can be quite charming until he gets angry; then he looks like death. He stands up to go to the bathroom. I apologize again, try to make a weak joke. "You want me to watch your wallet?" I say.

Victor doesn't laugh. "You've got a better chance of holding my dick than holding my wallet again," he says.

CHAPTER 10

I wish Castro all luck. The Cuban people now have a decent chance for the first time ever.

—ERNEST HEMINGWAY, 1959

"Tell me about the baseball," the boy asked him.
    "In the American League it is the Yankees as I said," the old man said happily.
    "They lost today," the boy told him.
    "That means nothing. The great DiMaggio is himself again."

—ERNEST HEMINGWAY, *The Old Man and the Sea*

The phone rings at 9:30 A.M., waking me up. "Mr. Price! This is Manuel Zayas. I must talk to you. I will wait in the lobby." Zayas is the Cubadeportes official in charge of foreign journalists, and Olga's boss. He is not happy. I didn't call to tell him I was coming to Cuba, and I didn't call to tell him when I arrived. I roll out and shower. Half an hour later, he is saying that his bosses have chastised him, wondering how I can get into the country without him knowing. He winces like a henpecked husband. He has been told that we've been traipsing around Pinar Del Rio, talking to baseball players. I tell him this isn't true. He waves it off. I don't bother to ask how he found me.

We sit downstairs in the bar, sipping tiny cups of Cuban coffee. Zayas says he wants to make some points about sports in Cuba. He is a small man of indeterminate age, a cold smile, a cadaverous mien. He has always treated me with exceptional grace, and he is less afraid than most officials to utter subversive thoughts. I don't trust him at all.

"The Cuban thinks he knows everything, especially about sport," Zayas begins. "It's ingrained. We feel we are managers, directors, scientists—and we criticize everyone. There are situations where a winning manager has been dismissed just because of this. The manager of Santiago managed the national team in Indianapolis at the '87 Pan Am Games. Cuba won every game. In the final against the U.S., Jim Abbott pitched and Cuba played terribly. In the eighth inning, people were saying the manager was terrible. Then they took out Abbott and brought in Cris Carpenter and Cuba won in an agonizing ninth inning by one run. By the time they came home, he could never again manage the national team. He was finished.

"The woman's volleyball team has won two world championships in a row. The men had won a World Cup before, but they didn't play well this year. They struggled to finish third. Criticism got so bad that the team manager knew changes had to come. It's not a peaceful time for him. We Cubans believe we are experts in games like volleyball—even if we never played the game ourselves."

Zayas stops to light a cigarette. Then he brings up El Duque. I'm not surprised: Duque is still the specter hanging over any conversation about Cuban sports, and not just because he was the biggest fish to slip the net. Duque is the ultimate personification of the regime's helpless struggle to fend off American values, and his forced defection revealed better than any other incident how badly the ideological battle has been lost. "Anybody who works with the government is not going to talk about Duque," Zayas says. "But the general public is wiser. The people feel happy for him, feel good about him, they say this guy is one of us, he played here and trained here and overnight he became the greatest in the U.S. The public knows more than any government official."

I mention what the baseball commissioner, Carlos Rodriguez, said about Duque in March. Zayas lifts an eyebrow. "It's like a dog and his master," he says with a shrug. "The athlete understands everything he says, but he can't talk back. The dog is mistreated but he can't say a thing."

Zayas understands the commissioner's blindness. But he says that the regime has since softened its stance on defectors. "The politics have changed," he says. "The government now figures, 'If you don't want to stay here, then go. Find your way out. You want to come back because you're nostalgic and you miss it? Come back.' It's a new philosophy. Anybody who left in the past was a traitor. We don't say that anymore. There's some sadness, but we're not going to crucify them."

That evening, we drive over to Cerro. It was Victor who first told me about Rey Ordoñez and the family he left behind, and I want him to see the other half of the story. We glide by cops talking to girls, cops clustering on one street corner after another, cops watching crowds with blank eyes; I've never seen such an obvious show of force here. Jackbooted police snake past on sleek black motorcycles, shiny and new Moto Guzzis from Italy. We pull up in front of the darkened apartment building. The door is locked. So much for discretion: I shout up to the third floor like Brando yelling for Stella. Hilda pokes her head over the balcony, nods, and a few moments later opens the door. We troop up a pitch-black stairwell amid the stink of fresh urine.

Inside the apartment, Little Rey sits on blue plastic chair six inches from the TV, sucking his raw left thumb. He's watching a show featuring little boys dressed up as bumblebees and singing in front of a giant sun. He's wearing a T-shirt dominated by the word "Spitball." Hilda's mother sits on a couch beneath a painting of a bare-breasted woman. Hilda smiles warmly and says that, no, she hasn't heard a word from Rey Ordoñez since last we spoke. He has sent no money. Worse, she says, Rey's brother and father don't talk to him anymore, either. Every time they call his home in the States, the operator says that the Ordoñez phone does not accept calls from Cuba. "Now they're as screwed up as I am," Hilda says. "He hasn't done a thing for them. If you go there, they'll be protective, but just look at how they live. There's nothing there."

She sits in a straight-backed chair upholstered in red vinyl. Little Rey stands and wiggles into his grandmother's lap. I ask Hilda if she has found a man yet. She has gained weight.

"I think I'm in love," she says. "But sometimes I see Rey playing on TV and I feel pretty good about it—especially when I see he's doing well. I don't know if I've forgiven him, but half my life is incomplete because I have a kid who loves his father and his father doesn't even look back at him."

Hilda says her mother, Maria Elena Naranjo, is traveling to the United States on a six-month visa in January. "The only reason I'm going is to have a conversation with Rey," Maria says. "I'm going to say, 'Get my daughter and grandson out of there. You know how they're suffering. Please, just get them out of there.' Everyone who comes here and spends a few weeks leaves saying how beautiful it is. But no one really knows how tough it is, how much suffering there is in this country."

Hilda mentions El Duque, how he maneuvered to get his ex-wife and daughters out and into the States. That's the least Rey can do, she says. But she's expecting more.

"I feel something is going to happen," Hilda says. "I'm sure I'm going to see him again. My mother is going, so my chances are much greater. And if I can have just five minutes with him, I know he can't be in love with that woman. I know that. Once he sees his son and me, I'm sure he will snap out of it. I was his first love and he was my first man; we were in love, totally in love. I'm sure that will come back to him. I'm sure things will be just like they were before."

I don't bother to argue. It is 7:15 P.M. Hilda thanks us for coming, and points the way to the apartment of Rey's father, uncle, and brothers down the block. The walk from stairwell to unlit street is like emerging from a cave at midnight; only a shift in the air lets you know you've made it outside.

We climb three flights of narrow stairs, bang on the slats of a yellow wooden door. Nothing. We bang again. A minute passes. Then a twist of the knob and the door opens halfway: An old man, painfully thin and wearing a ragged T-shirt, peers out defiantly, forefinger clenched in the pages of a thick book. His eyes narrow. Behind him is a spare room, distinguished only by the half-empty liquor bottle on top of the refrigerator. Neither the brothers nor the father is home. The uncle begins an angry stream of babble.

"He'll be here Monday morning at 6:30 for five minutes . . . They're not coming. . . . They're all going to be gone for a month. Where's Rey? He'll be back with the others. But you have to go now . . . you have to leave. Go. No, no, no."

We try to ask a question, but the uncle won't listen. "He'll be back at 6:30," he says, closing the door. "But go on, fuck off. Get out of here."

*   *   *

Friday morning, December 11, is checkout day. Everyone keeps talk-ing about cheap houses for rent in Guanabo, so we're moving there for a few days. I turn on the TV to CNN. The announcer says that DiMaggio has gone into a coma. His family is flying in to gather at his bedside.

I stare at the screen. I never liked DiMaggio. My father wor-shipped him, singing the "Joltin' Joe" song and extolling the man's endlessly celebrated virtues of class, grace, and reserve, but I grew up in the age of Ali and Namath and found such qualities dull. To me, DiMaggio was a stuffy and overrated coffee pitchman, hyper-pro-tective of an image no longer relevant. I always found myself drawn more to bombastic, profane, tortured, self-destructive Ted Williams; I was sure heroes should be men, not statues, and Teddy Ballgame was always too busy battling himself to worry over what the kiddies might think.

Still, accidents happen. I was working for the *Miami Herald* in December 1992 when I'd heard that Joe D. had lent his name to a children's hospital. I needed a column and he was a name and two phone calls later I found myself in the Hollywood, Florida, office of his lawyer, sitting across a table from the man himself. I'd been given just one ground rule: Don't mention "the M-word." But I had no need to speak of Marilyn Monroe. I just wanted to know why DiMaggio had become a cultural icon, and he answered the absurd question with a dig at himself. "Lefty Grove told me once, 'You've got the kind of kisser people will remember for life.'" DiMaggio laughed. "And he's right. I have got an ugly kisser."

There were photos of him all over the walls: DiMaggio swinging from the heels, DiMaggio with George Bush, DiMaggio hitting safe for another day or with his brother Dom, DiMaggio and that ugly kisser serene amid a black-and-white storm of hits and throws and fans screaming for another glimpse of such easy elegance. He saw these pictures, saw himself, every day, but fifty-one years after his famed hitting streak ended he still had no answer. "Why they picked me as being a . . . a . . ." he said, grasping for a word he could never find. "No, I still don't know why."

It was a sweet hour. DiMaggio relaxed, rambled on and laughed plenty, told stories about Lefty O'Doul and General Douglas MacArthur and Hemingway, about bombing through the Pacific Coast League in the 1930s, hanging jockstraps out the bus window so they'd dry in time for the next game. I asked him if he could remember the last time he could walk down the street like anyone else, just some guy named Joe. "I guess just before I played professional ball," he said, and suddenly he was there again, a teenager watching the San Francisco Seals. "I was fourteen, fifteen, sixteen, and I saw the pitchers there. I was behind home plate, and I saw them throw the curve, the fastball, and I said, 'Hell, I could hit that crap.'"

He talked more, about how some people didn't like his demeanor—"'Aloof' is the word they used," he said. "But I was just bashful"—and how he got Ronald Reagan and Mikhail Gorbachev to sign a ball for him. But what I remember most vividly as I sit in a Havana hotel, a stack of folded shirts in my lap and sadder about the news than I ever expected, was DiMaggio's mystification over his own autograph—how much people were willing to pay, how men would come to his table and drop pens in his salad, how women and kids demanded he stop and sign whenever he was rushing through an airport.

"You can be running like hell to make that plane, and by God if you don't sign—right there on the counter . . . 'Hey, Mr. DiMaggio, can I get your autograph?' and I'll say, 'I'm sorry, I have to catch a plane.'" He shook his head in exasperation. "But the thing that bothers me is that they walk away, and they must be saying, 'That no-good' . . . You can't satisfy them . . . "

And I wonder what the Great DiMaggio must've been thinking then, last winter, when he got one of the strangest requests of all. Word came through some Americans back from Cuba that Fidel Castro would love a signed baseball. DiMaggio mulled it over, and as one friend told a New York newspaper, "He figured if it helps relations between Cuba and the U.S., then OK."

But I prefer to think that DiMaggio wasn't thinking politics then. I like to think that he was bewildered by the idea: a sworn enemy of America coveting the ultimate piece of Americana? It makes no sense, but then, how could DiMaggio know that the most intense, awestruck love for American baseball rises off the streets of Havana? How could he know that it long ago infected even communism's greatest survivor—and then survived El Jefe's every effort to convince himself and his nation of the evil lurking in the American game? I like to think that DiMaggio wondered a bit and never understood this, but eventually shrugged and signed simply because he didn't want Fidel Castro to walk away and call him "That no-good . . . "

The ball arrived in Havana in the middle of March, just before the start of the Cuban playoffs.

We go to lunch with Olga to request some interviews we'll never conduct and some information we'll never get. It is all very pleasant. She sits in the backseat as we head back to her house, and we're bouncing down Fifth Avenue in a postmeal stupor when she suddenly starts screaming, "Here he is! Here he is! There goes Fidel!" Three black Mercedes, going in the opposite direction, pass us on the other side of the median. All other traffic has stopped. Olga grins widely, alight; it's a rare moment when she lets her guard drop like this.

"I thought we might be seeing him," she says. "We Cubans can feel it when he's near. Something happens. You'll be seeing all these special police, talking into their walkie-talkies, and you just know El Comandante is around somewhere."

Friday night is still fight night, but not at Kid Chocolate. I'm disappointed until we pull up at this week's venue—the Rafael Trejo Boxing Gym in Belen—and I realize I've found an arena even more satisfying than the Kid. Ranking Cuba's finest boxing halls is not easy. All possess personalities as singularly quirky as America's old ballparks, but whoever loves Fenway Park loves Wrigley Field and Yankee Stadium for the same basic reason. Still, Rafael Trejo, a tiny bandbox tucked away on Cuba Street, has the two incomparable virtues of obscurity and nearness to heaven. It sits across from the eighteenth-century church and convent of Our Lady of Merced, and its boxers work outside under the stars.

We get there early. I'd love to see Ariel Hernandez or Savon fight, but the man in charge tells us the card is weak, full of second-raters. But Hernandez does fight tomorrow, he says. Where? The man has no idea.

Victor, Little Daddy, and I step outside into the narrow lane. Julio Mena, a round, pumpkin-faced trainer with the national team for twenty-two years, stands by the door. Mena tells us that Ariel and some other top talent will box tomorrow on a street in Punta Brava. He says everyone on the team is fighting well lately. I ask about Vinent. "Oh, Vinent's the best," Mena says. "But he's working in Santiago. He's not with the national team right now."

I look to my left. There, thirty feet away, with its two left tires rolled onto the sidewalk, leans a yellow bus with "Boxeo" printed in the destination sign above the driver. "Equipo de Campeones" is scripted proudly on the side, and out the door, one after another, pours a stream of large, young black men. They don't make a sound. I stop talking. Little Daddy, Victor, Mena—all stop to look at the quiet tide of muscle flowing our way, and for a short instant there's something odd about the moment, holy even. It doesn't matter that there are no champions among them. This is the Cuban national team, the best boxers in the world, and here they come walking to the ring, bags over shoulders. They glide to my left, my right, slipping past to go inside. It's like suddenly finding yourself standing amid a pride of passing lions, just fed. They glance at me out of the corner of their eyes, and move on.

"The whole team was working out once when they came to get him, and they took him for twelve hours," Valle says. "Everybody on Industriales got pissed off when they took Duque away. This is not a criminal. After Arocha defected, I went to see his kids. Same with Luis Alvarez, same with Alberto Hernandez, and those kids all asked about their fathers. 'Valle: Why did my papi go?'—and many times I was forced to lie. I want to say something big about Duque. Once when Duque was playing here, Luis Alvarez's kid sent a letter to his dad through El Duque and he asked, 'Papi, why did you do this to us? Why did you leave us alone?' After Duque read the letter, he talked about it and he was so emotional; he said, 'How could any of us leave our kids? How can any of us go?' It hurt him. Duque is one of the most disciplined athletes I've ever met. He's one of the best teammates I ever had."

We are out back again, the stone table behind the garage. Valle wears a red-white-and-blue tank top he picked up in Japan; in one of those bizarre, lost-in-the-translation goofs over American cultural slang, the shirt, instead of saying "The Boss" in woven white letters, says "The Boos." He is laughing more tonight, joking about the uncanny knack Cuban ballplayers share with insecure women: Both can turn back time. "Listen," Valle says. "I am thirty-five. Duque is thirty-five. Oh, I know: Not now he's not. Now in the States he's . . . what? Twenty-seven? Come on, man!"

Valle watched the '98 World Series across the street at a neighbor's house. He saw what Duque did to the Padres in game two, disarming a lineup with seven left-handed batters, striking out seven, retiring ten in a row at one point, forcing the dangerous Greg Vaughn to pop out with the bases loaded and two out in the seventh. He saw Duque give the lie to everything Cuba's baseball commissioner once said about him, win on the biggest stage against the toughest hitters in the world, give the major leagues its most distinctive windup since Cuban legend Luis Tiant mesmerized hitters in Fenway Park. "I was alive with every pitch he threw," Valle says.

"I felt so much joy. This was a moment of glory, a moment when he represented us. He wasn't just pitching for himself. He was pitching for us all. Sure, I had a few moments of fantasy: What if it were me? I'd be lying to say I didn't. I'm a dreamer. What if it were me? Could I have done better? But that was pure. It was such a pure feeling."

He had a lifelong rivalry with Duque, both sharing the colors of the nation's premiere team, Industriales, but wanting to be recognized as Cuba's best. Now that game is over. "He is the greatest pitcher, and he's showing the world how great we all are," Valle says. "I shouldn't be saying any of this because he's been banned; I'm not supposed to be honoring Duque, but I'm saying it because I've got big balls." He grabs his crotch and squeezes, slaps his chest. "I've got heart."

He won't say the same about Rolando Arrojo. Arrojo, the Tampa Bay pitcher who left the Cuban team in Albany, Georgia, just before the '96 Atlanta Olympics, was the team's number one starter at the time—and teammates who knew his intentions implored him to stay and pitch a few Olympic games to ensure that Cuba would again win the gold. Arrojo refused. He hopped in a car with the waiting Joe Cubas in front of the team hotel—and never looked back. Politics has little to do with the bitterness Arrojo left behind. "It was the way he did it," Valle says. "He betrayed everyone. The way he defected involved a lot of other players; he sacrificed people and a lot of them got hurt. His own manager, Pedro Jova, got hurt. Even if he makes $100 million, he'll never be a hero in Cuba because he was like a Judas. He sold everybody out."

I get up to go to the bathroom, passing through the room Valle and his wife have set aside for their shrine to Chango, the Yoruba deity of fire and war. Both are devotees of the Afro-Caribbean religion of Santeria, a mix of Catholicism and Yoruba, that quietly dominates the island. Pope John Paul's visit earlier this year focused attention on the struggling Catholic Church in Cuba, but as one English professor put it to me, "The Catholic Church is the face of religion here, but behind that face is Yoruba."

Valle has dedicated his entire career to Chango. The night before a start, he places his glove on the altar. Before leaving for the park the next day, he always shakes his rattles over an altar bearing an amalgam of beads, shells, coconuts, dollar bills, coins, a large sword, a small drum, candies in a dish, and two barbells, and chants, "Chango, I need your strength. . . . " Initiated at the age of eleven, two years ago Valle broke through to a new level when he became a *babalao*, or priest. People come to him for advice and guidance. As I walk back through the room, the measure of Valle's devotion sits out for all to see; there, on the floor in the middle of the altar, are two baseballs. One comes from the last regular-season game he pitched and won, against Pinar Del Rio in 1997. The other comes from the last strikeout he ever threw in the National Series.

I sit back down at the table, and figure there's no more avoiding the subject. I ask Valle about his brother-in-law. He doesn't even flinch. It happened a week before he made it home from Japan, on September 7, he says. The man, Juan Ricardo Reyes, was married to Valle's sister, Maria. He was thirty-five years old, and one of Valle's dearest friends. "He was the godfather of my daughter," Valle says. "That's how close we were."

It was no suicide. It was a cliché: Juan was drunk and smoking and fell asleep in his bed. "The fire started on his head. My daughter saw him walking out of his room in flames," Valle says, and then he shouts into the house. "Yule!"

His daughter comes out, twelve years old and tall and sweetly unaware that she will soon be beautiful. Valle theatrically sticks a cigarette in his mouth and lights it, eyebrows dancing. "Yule, how did your uncle die?" he asks.

"Smoking," she says. Valle chuckles, teeth shining, and kisses her on the cheek goodnight.

At moments like that, it's easy to see why Valle may never leave. All his feelings of competitive pride are balanced by the absolute warmth of his home; Valle is the virtual mayor of this neighborhood called Little Miami. Neighbors constantly shuttle in to pay homage, to trade bullshit and barter, to chat with Margarita. "I've got a great country, a great wife, a great daughter," he says at one point. "Even if they don't ever let me leave the country again, I'm happy."

But that isn't completely true, no matter how many times Valle repeats it. He is caught in a depressing limbo now—in need of cash but unable to go overseas, officially retired but still capable of pitching, in love with his life and unsure he can keep it together. He is anchored to nothing. Foreign friends come to visit, and he hits them up for $5 here, $10 there. "That's not me," he says. "I don't know how long I can let this continue."

For the moment, Valle refuses to go near Estadio Latinoamericano. He doesn't want to see the commissioner, or anyone connected to the baseball authorities. He doesn't want to talk to the people about his greatness. He stays in Guanabo, far from the ballpark, waiting at home for something to change.

"I feel like an alien," Valle says. "I've been here for a while. Nobody calls me. Nobody talks to me. My opinion doesn't count. I'm an alien in my own country."

CHAPTER 11

*Why we ever engaged in this asinine Cuban adventure, I
cannot imagine.*

—DEAN ACHESON to Harry S. Truman, 1961

Little Daddy sits in the backseat, trying to explain how Metropolitanos is eternally damned. Yes, he says, the team made the playoffs
last year and constantly produces great talent like Yasser Gomez
and, no, they have absolutely no chance of ever winning a National
Series championship. Their fans are the pathetic chumps of baseball, suffering an endless heartbreak that makes the troubles of
Cubs and Red Sox devotees seem minor. "They suffer all the time
because they're always losing all their great players," he says. "We're
always telling them how shitty they are."

Just before this season began, five players—Yasser Gomez,
first baseman Antonio Azcul, catcher Ivan Correa, pitchers
Amauri Sanit and Jorge Luis Machado—and manager Guillermo
Carmona—were unceremoniously transferred to Industriales by
the Havana Baseball Commission. How can this be? I bleat.
That's like the American commissioner stripping the Mets of
their five best players and sending them to the Yankees. Wasn't
there a great outrage? "No, everybody knows that's just the way

it is," Little Daddy says. "Every two years or so, Metro gets fucked."

We are on our way to Punta Brava for the boxing. It is late Saturday morning, December 12, sun and black clouds. Today's *Granma* announces a triumphant close to the twentieth Latin-American Film Festival, which drew luminaries like the directors Francis Ford Coppola, Costa-Gavras, Ethan and Joel Coen, singer Harry Belafonte, and actress Frances McDormand. It also announces today's doubleheader at Latinoamericano between Metro and Industriales—nothing, Little Daddy says, to get excited about. This is no great rivalry. Everybody in Havana wants to see Industriales, with seven National Series championships to Metro's none, win again.

"Let me get this straight," I say. "Even though Metro competes in the premiere league against other teams like Pinar Del Rio and Villa Clara, even though Metro and Industriales both have minor league teams in the Liga Desarollo, its only reason for existence is to keep Industriales strong?"

"*Claro.* Remember when we went to see Metro last March? That's why there was nobody in the stands. If Industriales had been playing, the place would've been packed. Industriales has a radio broadcast, Metro doesn't. Why?" He shrugs. No one ever asks why.

Sure, it's idiotic, he says, and no other team in Cuba suffers the same weird existence. But I have to understand that Havana is the only city in the league with two clubs. What matters in Havana is keeping Industriales on top, period. Although officially organized as two distinct regional teams—Metro for players hailing from the center of the city and Industriales for the industrial communities ringing Havana—no one takes that distinction seriously. Little Daddy saw Yasser at Parque Central just before the season began, when both teams came to pay their annual honors to the statue of Jose Marti and mix with the boys at La Pena. Yasser was not happy.

He wanted to keep playing for Metro. But it's not important what Yasser wants.

"Look: A few years ago Villa Clara and Industriales played in the final. After being down three games to one, Villa Clara won three in a row and took the championship in Havana," Little Daddy says. "The fans came out of the stands with rocks in their hands, and the police had to stop them from flinging them at players. One fan attacked Lazaro Vargas, and Vargas ended up hitting him with a bat. The fans are very intense here in Havana. They don't care about the players. All they care about are the letters: I-N-D-U-S-T-R-I-A-L-E-S."

I turn back in my seat. We are heading southwest, through the gritty squalor of La Lisa, and I sit for a minute contemplating the absurdity of a system that would countenance such blatant disregard for . . . what? Fairness? Competitive spirit? Uniformity? Then I start thinking about the Florida Marlins and how they bought a championship, and the dominance now of the big-money teams from New York and Los Angeles. I try to remember the last time the Montreal Expos, who spent the last decade developing the best young talent in baseball and then losing almost all of it to free agency, won a championship. The answer is never, of course, and I suppose the Expos never will.

"Hey, remember that guy you talked to, Jose Ramon Cabrera?" Little Daddy says.

"Si . . ."

"He died about a month ago. A stroke."

I'm stunned, naturally, but I have no reason to be. I didn't know Cabrera—the Metro first baseman banned for throwing games—apart from our one interview, but I hoped that he'd find a measure of public redemption one day. I ask if there had been an announcement, any clearing of his reputation whatsoever, but Little Daddy shakes his head. So Cabrera dies, without his finger and his good name, officially just another casualty of the ongoing war between capitalism and the revolution, one man who couldn't resist the money. I tell Victor the story, and we rehash the scandal of '82. I mention how Little Daddy helped find Cabrera for me, and the conversation begins to range, as it always must, toward the state of Cuba today. I tell about Little Daddy's assertion that most *jineteras* come from the countryside.

"The farms have really got it rough," Little Daddy says. "In Havana, we're getting seven eggs a month. They only get rationed two eggs a month, and a little bit of fish—but the fish are so skinny they've got bones in the eyes. Those people are starving. You kill somebody here in the city, you get four to five years with good behavior. But you kill a cow out there? You get fifteen years. They're hungry out there.

"Everybody knows there's millions to be made from tourism. It's not being used for the people. The houses are falling down, the streets are fucked, the whole situation is fucked up. Forty years after the revolution, and nothing has changed. This is a dictatorship in the true sense of the word. This is not a free country at all. You want an example? I have a home, but I can't have guests. I have to get permission. I can't have a car even if I have the money. The only ones who can get a car are the ones he wants to get a car. The volleyball team got $1 million for winning the world championship; he takes the millions and gives them an old Lada or $5,000 or $50—but he keeps the rest."

We pull off the main drag, take a right, ask someone where the boxing will be today. We're not far; we drift slowly past groups of men on the corner, kids chasing each other—a barrio mired in the exhausted lull of Saturday before noon. No one working. No one hurrying. "Everybody here is high," Little Daddy says. "There's nothing left for them to do but take whatever money they can scrape together and get drunk."

Havana City Champion, age thirteen. Roberto Balado Boxing Gym; February 1999.

TOP: *Morning practice, Developmental League. Santa Clara; January 1999.*
BOTTOM: *Omar Linares, the greatest player in modern Cuban history.*
Monterrey, Mexico; July 1997.

TOP: *Boxing Day. Punta Brava; December 1998.*
BOTTOM: *Los Olmos Gym, the cradle of Cuban boxing.*
Santiago de Cuba; December 1998.

Rainier Virulichy, age thirteen, Cuba's number one track prospect at the warmup track at Pan American Stadium. Havana; February 1999.

TOP: *Ana Fidelia Quirot on the Malecon. Havana; December 1998.*
BOTTOM: *Ana Fidelia Quirot, four-hundred-meter finals, Pan American Games.*
Havana; July 1991.

TOP: *Basketball class at Domingo Portela Rural School. Santiago de Cuba;*
December 1998.
BOTTOM: *Waiting to play. Trinidad; February 1999.*

Hector Vinent at El Morro. December 1998.

We pull up at a small park bordered by four streets, various three-story apartment buildings, a water tower. A gazebo squats in the middle, shaded by thin leafy trees. It is still more than two hours before fight time, but there's no sign of a ring or any preparation for an afternoon of world-class boxing. A pack of a dozen boys clustered at one end assure us that, yes, this is the place. We park, and Little Daddy wanders out to sniff around. Thirty seconds later, he's hurrying back to the car with Ariel Hernandez. The boxer looks relieved to have someone to talk to.

Once, Ariel Hernandez thought he could stop death. It was July 2, 1994. His dear friend Roberto Balado gasped on a bed in a Havana emergency ward, blood gleaming from the many cuts on his skin, and Ariel took a useless white cotton pad and waited and watched for the next gash to bubble and shift and spread like a living stain. It made sense somehow. Ariel's hands were so fast then. He was twenty-two and an Olympic and world champion, and his career, his life, stood at the precise intersection of innocence and experience. Who better to stop the blood? Ariel kept daubing the cuts. Nothing helped. A passenger train had blasted through Balado's car and nosed into the man, shattering six ribs, stabbing a hole in his lung. Roberto Balado lay dying.

Not since the Martyrs of Barbados had Cuba's sports community suffered such a loss. Balado, the superheavyweight champion at the '92 Olympics, a world champion whose name had been placed on the ultimate place of honor in Cuban boxing, the Wall of Champions, with Teofilo and Savon, a winner of fifty-six straight matches, had been a quiet hero. "It was a national tragedy," Juantorena told me once. "He was very much loved. Charismatic, very simple. Everybody took it hard."

But no one more than Ariel, who knew Balado for more than a decade, moved to La Lisa from his home in Pinar Del Rio just to be close to him; who spent every day with him, loving the man's modesty. "He helped me with everything; he taught me boxing and life and women," Ariel said. Two days before Balado died, he told Ariel to take care of his wife should anything ever happen. When he heard the news, Ariel was taking a bath at La Finca. He ran to where the crumpled Lada sat near the tracks. Balado had already been taken away. He rode a bike to Balado's house and told his wife there'd been an accident. He went to the hospital, dabbing and panicking as doctors tried to keep Balado alive. Ariel whispered, *Get strong. You're going to be all right.*

Balado was the only fighter Ariel ever looked up to. He always told Ariel he was the best in the world. When it ended, Ariel left the hospital and traveled back across town to La Finca. He undressed for a shower and found the cotton in his hand, blood drying to black. He put the pad down, and stood a while under the cool water.

"For all my fights, I remember him," Ariel says.

For a time, Balado was right. A defensive expert with knockout clout, a lefty who befuddled opponents into making disastrous mistakes, in the mid-nineties Ariel used Balado's death to push him to even greater achievement. American trainers and agents called him another Sugar Ray Leonard, compared him to Roy Jones Jr., anointed him the best pound-for-pound amateur on the planet. He won another middleweight world championship in Berlin in 1995—beating American Eric Wright, 16–2, along the way—lost just one fight in four years and in Atlanta again easily won Olympic gold. He prized his '92 gold a bit more; it was his first and, besides, he'd beaten Chris Byrd of the United States in the final. "To beat an American is the most important thing," Ariel said. "Knocking out an American is better than knocking out a better boxer. It's transcendent."

When I spoke to him in early 1996, Ariel was living in a two-room shack in La Lisa; the only towel in the tiny bathroom hung on a rusted nail. A T-shirt hung on top of it, bearing the message in English: "Float Like a Butterfly, Sting Like a Bomb." He pulled up in a white Lada, given him the year before as reward for his world championship. Music blared out of the windows, loud enough for the neighbors and the gargantuan pig next door to hear. Later, when he told me how he'd rejected offers of "millions" from agents after Barcelona and Atlanta, I knew that the reason lay in that tiny car. Ariel had been given a choice of colors when offered the Lada, but he wanted it to be white like the car that carried Balado to his death, wanted people to see him and think of the bigger man. He went to the cemetery after it arrived, as he often did when he wanted to speak to his friend's bones. He told Balado what he had done.

I'd seen Ariel again last March, at Kid Chocolate. He was wearing black patent-leather shoes and a fresh, pale blue buttoned-down shirt with the collar unbuttoned, and I asked about defectors, and he declared, monotonously, that he fought for the people, not money, because "they adore me, they talk to me on the street, they love me." When pressed, though, he spoke passionately about his six-year-old daughter Yatisledy, how he dedicates every fight to her, salutes her before and after. "That's my heart out there, my love," he said. It is she and the memory of Balado and his grave, too, that keep Ariel's feet planted in Cuba. "They can keep their money," he said. "I'm going to die here. I don't want to earn millions. Many things happened in my life that I feel I can't do without. I just can't afford to lose them."

By then, though, much had changed. At twenty-five, Ariel was no longer considered the best in the world. He had lost much of 1997 to appendicitis; in late January of that year he doubled over with a searing pain in his stomach, was rushed to the hospital and rolled into a five-hour surgery. The appendix had been just minutes from bursting, and there were complications. It took six months for him to recover. In July, after just fifteen days of training, he lost to a Cuban middleweight, Jorge Gutierrez, who'd never beaten him before. He began to round into shape, but not soon enough: At the '97 World Championships, Ariel lost again in the final to a Hungarian. "It feels horrible," he said. "I'm not used to this."

Now, nine months later, I'm baffled by what I see. I barely recognize Ariel when he first walks toward the car; his classically handsome face has expanded into a puffy, bearded mask. He looks bone-weary, ten years older and fifteen pounds heavier. But, later, sitting in an empty restaurant two hours before the boxing, he assures me that he is slowly climbing back. In July, he won the gold medal at the Goodwill Games in New York, beating an unranked Frenchman by just one point in the final, and he has beaten Gutierrez the last two times they've fought. He vows to win the gold in Sydney. At lunch, he refuses to eat or drink anything: too close to fight time.

I ask Ariel what he was doing, wandering around the park alone. He shrugs; he doesn't understand that it might be strange for one of the world's great boxers to drop out of the sky on an unsuspecting street. His car had broken down with carburetor trouble, so he'd taken the half-hour bus ride out from La Lisa. Until we showed up, he'd planned to just walk around some more and wait for something to happen.

I ask him how he thinks the Cuban team will do in Sydney. Six Cubans top the most recent world rankings and eleven more are scattered among the twelve weight classes. Ariel, the third-ranked middleweight, figures that he, light flyweight Maikro Romero, and Savon are locks to win, but that the youth and inexperience of the rest of the Cuban team make these Olympics more unpredictable than usual. I point out that he didn't mention Vinent. "Vinent is banned," Ariel says. "He missed weight so he was banned. It's temporary."

He is wearing a pair of black nubuck Spalding sneakers, red Cuba warm-up pants, a Tommy Hilfiger tennis shirt. I ask about his old shack in La Lisa, but Ariel tells me he's moved to a high-rise and wants to move again. His eyes are bloodshot, but he is friendly, unhurried, open to any question. It is 12:30 P.M., and I worry that Ariel needs to get back to the park. I'm not sure that walking into a swarm of boxing officials just minutes before the bell would be a good thing for either of us. I ask again if he wants something to drink—water, anything. He smiles and says no. A silence falls over the table. I ask if he wants to leave.

"No," Ariel says. "Let's stay here awhile."

The ring squats in the middle of Calle 249, looking like the hurtled residue of some Kansas twister. Workers leisurely pin a purple apron around the edge of the canvas. A pack of boys hides in the trees, tossing sticks at the unsuspecting. Their legs dangle off the branches. It is 1 P.M. The yellow bus stands some twenty feet away, engine quiet. Ariel climbs aboard. There will be seven fights today. Through the windows, six fighters can be seen pulling on shirts, lacing up shoes. On the back of the bus is a sign: "On the Road to Victory."

Castro has always viewed sport as a prime tool—popular and more easily understood than ideology—in the fight against what he considered a corrupt ruling class. "In the capitalist era, professionalism prevailed in Cuban baseball and boxing," he once said. "They were hang-outs for traffickers, bookies. Ball fields and clubhouses were not open to the masses. About 15,000 played organized sports, but that wasn't promoted. Instead, horse races, dog races, jai-alai got great play in the press. The lottery, craps, roulette, slot machines and the whorehouses—that was the kind of activity promoted by the capitalistas in Cuba. . . . "

The revolution erased racial and economic barriers to the country's exclusive sporting clubs. Sports was made "a right of the people." Physical activity became a required part of the blossoming educational system. Admission prices for sporting events were eliminated. "The goal is to develop sporting culture, artistic activities and culture in general for the people as well," Castro said in 1960. "To create centers of entertainment for the people—something that in the past was only for the rich."

Today, I am seeing the idea in action, the revolution in one of its rare, pure forms. Economic conditions have forced baseball games to require a 2 peso admission charge, but today's event is for anyone willing to make the walk. Some five hundred people have begun to gather at Punta Brava park for an afternoon's entertainment: Three world champions—including Ariel and Olympic silver medalist Juan Hernandez Sierra—will fight with eleven others in a scrappy neighborhood for free. It is no publicity ploy. There are no television cameras, and few outside Punta Brava even knew the card had been scheduled. Today's boxing is indeed for the people.

The hour crawls by. One fighter sits on a stone bench, punching, rubbing, massaging his headgear. Boys follow the bored fighters all around the park; finally Ariel puts a friendly hand on the shoulder of a tubby kid in a red shirt. "Hey, you want to be a boxer?" The boy doesn't even bother looking up. He shakes his head no and swings an imaginary bat. Ariel throws up his hands in disgust. "Ahhh, pelota," he says. We sit away from the rest of the fighters, and despite some dark looks from the Cuban trainers, Ariel insists on staying put. He introduces us to his good friend, a smiling heavyweight with ropy veins on his arms, named Yulkis Sterling. I think of Balado. Boxers in the same weight class never become friends. A pack of teenagers walk past. "Look at that girl's ass," Ariel says.

Two o'clock comes and goes. Black clouds drift overhead. Six men descend the bus steps in red satin shorts and navy blue tank tops bearing three white stripes. At 2:20, the sky cracks open with an apocalyptic deluge, drenching the park, bus, ring, cars, and pavement. Ariel, the other boxers scramble back up the bus steps. Little Daddy and I sprint to the car. Victor has gone up to a ringside apartment he has borrowed to shoot the fights. For the first time in days, the moldy, dieseled air washes clean; torrents of brown water rush in gullies down the street. For fifteen minutes rain pounds the hood of the car. I'm sure the boxing will be canceled, and Little Daddy shakes his head over yet another sad example of how the people get jobbed.

"Cuba *enferma*," Little Daddy says.

The rain stops, the ground is streaming. No one has left. The boxers step out. The canvas is soaked but nothing changes. After a few minutes, the first two fighters dip under the ropes and begin to dance in wide circles, warming up. A man strikes the bell with a small hammer; gloves begin whistling through the air. Fighters slip on the canvas, fall, get up. No one makes any move to protect the nation's precious boxers from hurting themselves. "Hit him!" says one male voice after another from the growing crowd.

I go to watch with Victor, snapping his Hasselblad from a third-floor balcony. Juan Hernandez wins easily. Sterling, our new friend, beats the veteran Freddy Rojas for the first time in his career. Ariel climbs into the ring with his opponent, Edelfonso Castillo of Santiago. The sky is lit up like a Turner seascape, scarlet-tinged and exploding sprays of blue and gray. Ariel wears a lime-green mouthpiece. His face spurts out of the headgear like an orange squeezing out of its skin.

The first two rounds, he looks sluggish, unsure, his punches non-committal. Ariel is the classic Cuban counterpuncher—cautious, planting a foot close to his opponent and bobbing his head in and out, searching for an opening. His one concession to style is a nod to Ali; he keeps his hands down at his waist, leans back away from punches like a cobra dancing. Before the fight we joked that once he knocks out Castillo, he must look straight up at us, into the camera—and we've all but forgotten that until, suddenly, standing in his corner just before the third, Ariel throws a glance our way.

He tries. He takes the fight to Castillo now, moving twice as fast, sticking his face with quick jabs, peppering him with combinations. But Ariel can't finish him off, and the fight ends as a desultory 3–1 decision. The applause is light and brief. People instantly begin drifting home. Ariel doesn't take any time to celebrate; standing on the edge of the ring just outside the ropes, he inclines his head in the universal gesture of "Get over here." Victor explains: We're giving him a ride. Ariel needs to go find a part for his car.

It is 4:41 P.M. By the time we get downstairs, Ariel is already dried off and in the street, waving his arms, arguing heatedly with the national boxing commissioner about his need for a new house, one-story, somewhere in La Lisa. The sun begins to dip behind the buildings. A cool breeze eases through the thinning crowd. Workers break down the ring; within two minutes the canvas is gone, and all that's left is a spindly platform on wheels. A few boxers join the effort, gathering in a pack to shove the panels of the ring into place so it can be carted away. Not Ariel, though: He points to me, then our car, and he starts walking.

The three big men squeeze into the back of the rented Toyota: Little Daddy, the giant Sterling, Ariel. "Stop at the next street," Ariel says. "Some guy's going to give me a bottle of rum." We ride half a block. A drunk shoves his face into the rear window, and there's some kind of dickering until Ariel finally yells, "Just give me the damn bottle!" Sterling grabs the clear bottle of label-less yellowy liquid, takes a swig, hands it to Ariel. He throws back his head, hands it to Little Daddy, who swigs and hands it to Victor, who swigs and hands it to me.

We drive, stop at a Servi gas station in La Lisa, searching for a $4.50 part for his carburetor. Ariel and Sterling walk past the pumps in their satin shorts and boxing shoes, two champions out on a Saturday night. No one approaches them. No one has what Ariel needs. We leave. I ask why he was arguing with the commissioner. "I needed him to know how much I need a new place," Ariel says. "I don't want to live up in the air like some bird. I'm a world-class athlete. I don't deserve to be living there."

We meander through the dusk, pulling into one gas station after another, passing the jammed pink buses dubbed "camels" because of their distinctive humps. The bottle empties. The shelves are spare. No one has what Ariel needs. Defeated, he gives directions to his home, where his wife and daughter wait. We pull up outside a ragged block of apartments that has all the charm of a government project, its chipped white facade fading fast in the gathering night. Victor asks for his phone number.

"There's no phone," Ariel says, then he disappears up the stairs.

Near midnight. Valle walks a rutted dirt road on the southern edge of Guanabo, White Sox hat jammed on his head, flip-flops kicking up stones. He is accompanying Victor and me to our house for no other reason than a chance to catch some air. We pass an empty field off to his left, and the sky expands into a sparkling dome.

Overhead, electrical wires hum and snap. Soft voices travel along the sea air.

We step on the porch, and without warning every dim light on the street goes dark. "Oh my God!" Valle shouts, and then he coughs and bends over and unleashes a huge laugh. Our landlady mutters, "Third time today," and goes to fetch a candle. Valle looks off toward his home and the dark walk back. "Ay, *cojones*," he growls in resignation. "Cuba, Cuba, Cuba."

CHAPTER 12

At 11 A.M. the next morning, Lazaro Valle takes the mound again. He's standing under the low ceiling on his front porch, face tight with concentration. Slowly, he lifts his left leg high, draws back his right arm, bites his bottom lip. The arm comes whipping over his head, cuts the air with an audible hiss. He grunts. The cigarette butt flies into a bush at the base of his concrete security wall. "Fastball," he says.

He is just back from visiting his mother in Havana Vieja. Today, December 13, is her sixty-third birthday, and Valle left at 5 A.M. to see her, carrying a small box of cigars and an even smaller box of candy. There was no celebration. Tomorrow, his sister Mercedes will undergo surgery for lung cancer, and no one has told their mother for fear of inducing another stroke. "We don't know what we're facing here," he says, and then he points inside, toward the shrine to Chango. "I'm going to be praying a lot tonight."

We have come to say goodbye, and perform a favor. It's time to get out of Havana. We plan to drive fourteen hours to Santiago de Cuba, the heart of the revolution and Cuban boxing, and then on to Guantanamo. Valle's wife has a friend who needs a ride to Ciego de Avila, and by bus the five-hour trip takes two days. We've agreed to drop her. Victor carves out a place in the backseat, sees her two bulky bags and a framed poster, then tries to carve a bit more. The woman is fat, wearing the fat Cuban woman's inexplicable uniform of Lycra stretch pants and a clinging tank top. She wedges herself into the back of the Toyota like Houdini ducking into a steamer trunk, without complaint, as if somehow pleased by the confinement.

We drive back toward Havana, pick up the Via Monumental, and eventually head East on the Autopista Nacional, the eight-lane highway that bisects the island like a concrete spine. The woman is twenty-seven, though her tubbiness makes her look younger, and lives in the hamlet of Violeta outside Ciego with her four-year-old son. She works in a factory that processes sugarcane; she came west to pick up supplies. "In Havana you can find baloney, cooking oil, beef, fish, rice," she says. The noon sun beats down on the roof. Victor hits 110 kilometers per hour and holds it there; a constant stream of air whips strings of hair into her eyes. "But outside Havana it's like a different island. We get nothing. Salt, sugar, and rice. Three pounds of beef a month, three eggs for every kid under three years: That's it."

A hurricane destroyed her house in 1995. She immediately took out a loan to rebuild, and began paying it off. She's still waiting for the construction materials to arrive. "Every day they tell us, 'Mañana,'" she says.

The woman is very calm. Her voice never shifts out of its plaintive monotone. She says her father fought in the revolution. I ask how people under thirty, the ones with no memory of life under Batista, feel about Fidel's revolution. "Very bad," she says. "The only ones who feel comfortable with the system are the children of *militantes*. They don't have to worry about anything; they've got a car, house, food on the table, money—everything they need. But the people who are eating shit? We see plenty on TV about problems around the world, but you never see the truth about life in Cuba. Nobody left in Cuba feels good about the revolution, but especially young people. There is nothing here. The system is exhausted. They used to promise things, but now they promise nothing. They just take. We don't want to go to school. We don't want to work. All we want is to find a tourist to help us leave the country.

"When I was fourteen or fifteen, I thought I was in the greatest country in the world. I would die for it. But then, if I wanted to drink juice or get food? I'd get it. Now my son is four years old and he doesn't know what good juice is. Everything is bad, bad, bad. Everyone knows the system doesn't work. They give everything away to the tourists and there's nothing left.

"I took my grandmother to the hospital. She was dying and I didn't have the $10 to pay the doctors. She had a feeding tube and shit was coming out of it and she was choking on it. They wouldn't get out of bed to come see her. They want you to believe that there is no capitalista here, but this is as capitalista as anyplace else. You go to a hospital now and you're sick, they're going to let you die. Because what good are you?"

This reminds me of a joke Valle told the other night. What's the difference between an American doctor and a Cuban doctor? The American comes in and says, "How's my patient today?" The Cuban doctor comes in and says, "Holy shit! My patient's alive!"

We pass a man standing under a bridge, yelling as we pass. Soon we will be in Villa Clara, where forty years ago Che Guevara led the army that seized an armored train and shattered the morale of Batista's troops in the revolution's final military triumph. "That guy's selling gas," she says. "Stealing it and selling it. That's the only way to be happy here—to live like that. To live decently, you always have to decide: If you eat, you don't dress. If you dress, you don't eat. Or you steal from a *turista*. That's why crime is way up. It's the new fashion."

A billboard flies past: "Villa Clara—Here You'll Find Enthusiasm, Hope, the Revolutionary Spirit." Victor pulls into the Che monument just a few minutes off the highway. They buried Guevara's bones here last year, in the shadow of a massive statue and the steel and concrete reproduction of his farewell letter to Fidel. We are the only visitors; the place sits eerily silent under a pale denim sky, light breeze passing. Victor grabs his camera and hurries away. We've been driving three hours. I make peanut butter and jelly sandwiches. I ask if she wants to get out and stretch her legs, go to the bathroom. She says no. The poster cuts into her legs; it's one of those dime-a-dozen Miller Genuine Draft lithographs you see taped up in dorm rooms and sports bars all over America. She has no intention of being left behind.

We pull into Ciego at 10 P.M. She tells us to drop her off at a shelter, where she plans to sit until a bus comes to take her to Violeta at 6 A.M. We insist on driving her the thirty extra kilometers home. On the way, she points to the bus stop where she would've waited; already four people are stretched out on benches there. Victor wonders aloud why she just wouldn't walk home, but she doesn't answer. We arrive at her house, and as she finally scoops herself out of the backseat I'm curious to see if she'll be able to walk. She smiles, thanks us, hoists her bags. She grips the framed poster and ambles through her gate. Victor begins to drive, but about a mile on he suddenly brakes. "Here's why she wouldn't walk," he says, clicking off the headlights.

The world dissolves to solid black.

We don't know where we are. Victor pulls into a dimly lit roadside food shack outside a town called Gaspar. It is 11:30 P.M. Sunday night, and everything about the stop feels wrong. What I mean is that Cuba is a notoriously safe place, one in which it's easy to forget that you're an obvious American in an obvious rental car, and a real triumph of the country is that you can walk the streets alone for weeks or show up at some obscure, crowded corner and never be menaced by the mean fact that your presence changes the wind like a fresh piece of meat. Face-to-face assaults on tourists are rare. So rare, in fact, that my instincts are blunted; it's only after I climb out of the car that I take in the drunken dozen men singing loudly, or the six other people lolling about—everyone out far later than customary—and note that we are, indeed, the only outsiders here.

We walk through an open door into a cavernous room, with only one stretch of countertop lit up and ready for business. Three women sit behind it. One finally pulls herself up and lugs her body forward. We've been driving twelve hours, but we're still hoping to make Santiago by dawn. We lean elbows on the plastic, order tiny ham sandwiches and coffee. Someone steps through the doorway behind, breezes into place at my right, and begins to speak. I turn, and for a moment I can't tell if it's a bony woman with light facial hair or a flamboyant black man in a skin-tight, purple Lycra top, mincing as if this were San Francisco on Gay Pride Day. It soon becomes clear he is the latter. He leans in, extends a long and delicate finger. He asks in a high feminine voice if we are from Texas.

I don't know whether to laugh, cheer, or mumble. I want to ask him what he is doing way out here, so far from Havana's toler-ance, tonight and every day with all these drunken machos. I want to know how he keeps himself intact. But as I begin munch-ing the too-salty sandwich, I notice that the guitar playing has stopped and some men have stumbled in behind us. The room begins to fill and I'm hit with that vaguely sinister feeling again. Victor shoves the sandwich whole in his mouth and I ask for the bill.

The woman looks us up and down and says, casually, $5.50—an absurd price for the product and she knows it. I pull out my wallet and see I've got four $1 bills and a $100, and my instincts kick in sharp and I just know that presenting a $100 bill here and now would be tantamount to whirling about, waving a wad of cash in the air, and laughing, "Don't you wish you had this kind of money?" So I tell Victor I've got four bucks and hold it up and the woman raises an eyebrow, and that's when our friendly queen grabs the bills and throws them on the counter and glares at the woman and snaps, "That's enough, that's enough, that's okay," and pushes us through the men to the doorway.

We calmly but quickly move to the car, get in; one drunk has fol-lowed and won't let Victor close the door. Finally Victor puts the car in reverse, saying, "No thanks, papi, no thanks, no," and then we speed away amid the clichéd cloud of rocks and dust. And as dark-ness envelops us again, I wonder aloud about what might happen to the samaritan we left in our wake, why he bothered to help us and how he's bearing up under a sure barrage of hostility. It strikes me that I've never seen a stronger man in Cuba, one so willing despite all the forces arrayed against him to be exactly what he wants to be, and it strikes me as odd that such a man is laughed at to his face and behind his back, is called El Maricon—the Faggot—in that casual Latin way of labeling someone *Gorda, Negro, Rubio,*—the Fat One, the Black Guy, the Blond.

A half-hour later, Victor, blinded by yet another oncoming driver who delights in flashing high beams at the last possible moment of passing, takes a sharp curve that comes too fast, and we suddenly fly off the road like a rock released from a slingshot and the car spins and screeches and grinds to a stop. The headlights sweep the pavement from an odd angle. The engine hums, the stars gleam, oblivious. Victor and I start breathing again. We decide to drive another half-hour, and spend the night in Camaguey.

There's been a shift in attitude somewhere. I can feel it, subtle but distinct, scraping the sensibility like one of those California tremors too small to worry anyone at the time. But then some seismologist wanders into deserted hills and finds a crevice the size of the *Queen Mary*, then the big one hits and buildings start to fall, then they all look back to see where it began. I say something began sometime in the middle of 1998.

When I'd come to Cuba in the desperate days in the mid-nineties, and even as recently as last March, the typical Cuban still carried himself or herself within a wall of pride. I'm not speaking now about the taxi hawk or pimp. I'm speaking of the Cuban man walking the street in his clean guayabera and thick black mustache, the housewife who'd never so much as glance your way unless you came to her first. They didn't watch you, looking for a way in. They didn't size you up for money, not blatantly, and they did not beg. An *extranjero* could walk unmolested, yes; but there was more to it than the natives merely minding their own business. The man in the guayabera was sure he was as good as—or better than—you would ever be. People in Latin America constantly remark on Cuban arrogance, but if Cuban self-regard was so high that it took forty years of fear and a decade of privation to erode away, then there's something in it worthy of respect.

The arrogant Cuban is dead. Modern capitalism has evolved to a stage in America where getting and spending can be a discreet exercise, hidden behind a facade of fashion or coyly ironic advertising ploys. In Cuba, there is none of that. The dollar is oxygen, an object of naked need. Everyone needs money and will do most anything to get it. You offer a customs officer, a government official, a good friend $5—and he will take it. He can't afford dignity. He can't turn it down anymore. Victor tells me something I didn't know: The other day, Valle pulled him aside and said, "If I was the Lazaro Valle I used to be, the one everybody saw, I wouldn't have to ask. But I don't have 50 cents. I'm so ashamed of what I'm going through. I need $20 to be there when they operate on my sister."

We are riding on the road to Las Tunas, three hundred miles west of Santiago. We woke up groggy in the hotel, watched Shannon Sharpe on ESPN talking about the Denver Broncos' first loss of the season until a blackout shut down the set. Then we had a cold, paltry breakfast, checked out just as the morning *jineteras* were checking in, and pulled through the Camaguey town square past the most chilling revolutionary scrawl I've seen yet: "Consistency Is Based on Surveillance." The first time Victor came to Cuba, he accompanied an uncle who'd come to interview Fidel.

He counts it as one of his great moments. In Latin America, Fidel was never the devil he is in Miami; for no other reason than the fact that he dared take on the United States, had the *cojones* to challenge the world's greatest power, he will remain a hero to many forever.

"But there's no hope now," Victor says. "I can feel it, papi. It's painful for me, like never before. It's painful because I was not expecting it. The Cubans were always so positive their problems would change. My first year here was 1970. You couldn't rent a car then. Nobody could drive you. Everybody had hope that the revolution was working. I got really involved in it. I need to talk to them—that's how I get my pictures—and I always learned the truth. They thought the revolution would win out, and then? *We're all going to win that great respect.*

"In 1991, when the athletes helped with construction and they got the facilities built in time? I liked what was happening. I was brought up so that you don't work for money; you get compensated for a good performance. Here I saw people with the same principles: Everybody pulling together. In the seventies and eighties I'd seen it getting purified, getting cleaner. But nothing was as strong as what I saw in '91: They were making it work. I was thinking about becoming a party member. I became fascinated by Olga; she was so very disciplined. Guys would say, 'She's brainwashed,' but it was never like that. There was too much pride, and pride is not something you can brainwash into people. Pride is strength. I saw them suffering and winning medals like never before. I saw them and I said, 'These people are for real. They're this far from pulling it out.'

"But then they shot down the Brothers to the Rescue planes and Clinton turned tough and that was it. They gave up. I watch people's eyes, and I can see they are totally hopeless now, empty. In the past you'd always see some sad people, but now it's a general thing. Even Lazaro Valle, his watery eyes . . . I look at him and he gives nothing back. That's why I'm not taking so many pictures. There's no mirror in the eyes, and to me it's a big defeat. I thought this was the hope for humankind and this was the last place a common worker could work and live. Now it's over. Totally over."

The sun bakes the highway's pale surface. Shirtless men fly by the car on bicycles, riding wobbly and slow. One man walks, dragging a cartful of firewood. Potholes infect the road like a spreading virus. Once, for his thirteenth birthday, Victor's stepfather gave him a black-and-white, fourteen-by-twenty-one-inch photo of Che, Fidel, and Cienfuegos chopping sugarcane. He carried it with him every-where. "Look at this: They were always building roads for the future, but El Comandante is getting weaker," Victor says. "They're just maintaining the roads now."

Driving Cuba is nothing like driving the USA. Highway signs, streetlights, warnings of upcoming hazards—all are luxuries here, and almost nonexistent. Taking the American road is an exercise in freedom, a grand monotony punctuated by explosions of magnifi-cence. In Cuba it's the opposite—a frantic vigilance, punctuated by moments of peace. You travel amid anarchy. Everyone warns against driving at night, because it's like finding yourself trapped in a hor-rible video game: You must watch always for bikes veering into your path, lampless horse-drawn carriages trotting along in your lane, slow cows wandering onto the road, eyes ablaze like egg-sized jewels, unmarked fuel trucks, oncoming speeders flashing their beams. But the daytime is little better. If a sudden onset of moonscape doesn't get you, the abrupt finality of concrete ending—the highway went from eight lanes to four; didn't you see that turnoff?—will. The Cuban highway is a white-knuckle prison. You're lucky to get out alive.

We are driving a Toyota Tercel, unglamorous and egg-white. When we pass through the town of Guaimaro, men stare as if we ride in a golden chariot. A billboard features a picture of Che: "Forty Years and Counting." We enter the province of Las Tunas, childhood home of Teofilo. Victor begins speaking of the day Arrojo defected in Albany, Georgia. He happened to be there, visiting with Omar Linares at the Quality Inn, when the agent Joe Cubas pulled up in a big black sedan. Seven Cuban ballplayers stood watching. It was dusk. "Arrojo walked up and threw his bag in the back," Victor says. "He got in, and they kept the car doors open, waiting to see if anybody else wanted to go. I could hear Arrojo in the back, saying, 'Vamonos! Vamonos!' The driver stood outside looking at the other players, saying, 'Come on, it's the chance of a lifetime. Let's go.' Finally Arrojo pulled his door shut and they were gone."

We pass a baseball field to our right, in miniature. The outfield fence is only three feet high, but on it is written, "Sport Is a Right of the People" and "We Believe in Youth." We are listening to a cassette tape of Manolin, "The Salsa Doctor," and his daring and infectious hit about Cuba's new reality. *Mami, hay que vivir para ver los tiempos cambian tu vez . . . Yo tengo amigos en Miami.*" Mama, you have to live to see that times do change . . . I now have friends in Miami." Little Daddy has said that Manolin is pure *partido*, that his daring music is only a ploy to make the world think Castro has loosened up. I don't know what to make of it, really, but I can't stop singing.

"Look at all these faces, man," Victor says. "Expressionless. No curiosity, nothing. Who's going to be their next hero? Who's going to liberate them? Americans? Fuck no. Their Cuban brothers in Miami? Fuck no. God? No God here."

We pass in and out of the charming, shady town of Las Tunas, the prettiest I've seen in Cuba. My *Lonely Planet* guidebook calls it "a provincial capital with an exuberant population that will be pleased to see you," but we exit unscathed and stop at a Servi for gas. A man is passed out on the pump platform, left hand dangling, throwing a crisp inky shadow on the pebbly ground. No one seems to care, so we assume he isn't dead. Inside, it's possible to buy Close-Up toothpaste and gold-scripted license plates that say Merry Christmas.

Past Bayamo, the air begins to cool and the country fades to green. The ride becomes smoother, passing field after field of sugarcane, seven feet tall and shooting fluffy white blossoms into the sky. A cropduster swings high, wheels, and flies right above us, dumping chemicals of cancerous intent. We cross a bridge five hundred feet above an unmarked river; horses and naked men swim, a couple embraces in the muddy brown water. The sun hits the surface, exploding glints of light like a prism. We don't stop. To our left, the purpled bulk of the Sierra Maestra looms like a low-hanging storm.

We cross the border into the province of Santiago de Cuba, and I see the day's first and only sign of ambition. A boy, eleven or twelve, squats flat atop a bareback horse on the side of the highway, and they are flying together in full gallop. The boy's legs, chest, neck press so close to the horse's skin that they seem glued; his face is oddly serene. He whips the horse's flank hard with a fraying rope. The horse is ribby but strong, the color of fresh coffee with a touch of cream, and the boy urges him to outrun the cars—our car now—whistling past. It is so futile I laugh out loud, but then my heart begins to pound and I stop; suddenly I want nothing more than for him to win. I turn and watch him ride until we round into a curve and pull away.

At 4:54 P.M. Monday evening, we pass the sign "Santiago, City of

Heroes" and then a blowup of Fidel with his arm upraised and the slogan: "Rebels Yesterday, Hospitality Today." By 6 P.M. we've hit the center of downtown. It is already past nightfall. A blackout has hit, buses spew thick smog, our headlights struggle to pierce the darkness. The air has the grainy look of newsreel. People scamper across the street, cut through traffic, faces obscured and their clothing waving loose. They glow for an instant, and then the city swallows them whole.

I have become obsessed. I must see Hector Vinent. The obvious facts are reason enough: One of the world's great boxers has been banned from Cuba's national team, and I know he is here, somewhere, in Santiago. I even tell this to Victor and Jorge and Evelio—two local English professors and friends of Little Daddy—the next morning. But truth be told, first and foremost I just want to see Vinent, read his features and remember. Ever since last March, when that man identified himself as Hector Vinent near Parque Central, I've needed to find the truth. Was that him? Was it a fraud? Information is the journalist's currency, and I'm embarrassed to think I took counterfeit bills. I hate not knowing. I hate being conned. Finding out is payback. Finding out, I win.

We take a short ride to the boxing gym in Los Olmos. Vinent may well be there, but that doesn't matter yet. The Los Olmos gym, called "The Cradle" by aficionados, is considered the national launching pad for Cuba's boxing success. Nearly every great fighter in Cuban history, from pros like Kids Chocolate and Gavilan, Doug Vaillant, and Casamayor, to amateurs like Reguiferos, Teofilo, Savon, and Vinent, all spent time here as boys, beating each other bloody and daydreaming about gold.

Victor and I walk in. Two older men sit as if waiting for us. Carlos

Semanat, thin and dark with a tiny mustache, huddles in a folding chair clad in slacks and a pullover shirt. Alberto Feria, lighter and looser, sprawls on the steps leading up to the gym's naked ring. Sunlight cooks Feria's face, and his shirt is off. He has a proud little potbelly. The men are doing nothing. They spend five minutes ticking off the names of great champions, arguing over when they fought and what they achieved. "You're not going to have enough paper," Feria says with a laugh.

"This gym has such a great history," Semanat says. "But as you can see, we lack equipment. We rigged up all this stuff to keep going, and we ask everyone to give us supplies because we've got to keep on. Because this is a gym that has given glory to the world."

It sits in the open air, no bigger than a strip mall shoestore. A corrugated tin roof shades the small pavilion dedicated to the boxer's lonely time, but instead of speed bags and heavy bags, four tattered rice sacks stuffed with more tattered rice sacks hang suspended from two steel Ts. An old tire dangles from the ceiling. Five barefoot boys—ranging in age from eight to twelve—dance, jab, glide around the bags, their soles slapping time on warped slabs of plywood.

This is the boxing EIDE of Santiago. Some three hundred kids from five to eighteen come daily to learn from Semanat, who has been working here nineteen years, and Feria, who has been here thirty-two. The two men get little payoff. The nation's acknowledged boxing genius is national team coach Alcides Sagarra. "We start with these kids and when someone looks like they'll develop, they get taken away to Havana," Feria says. The look on his face is simultaneously resigned and amused; what am I going to do?

I ask for the bathroom. Inside the small outbuilding that houses a jerrybuilt museum of news clippings and frayed black-

and-white photos—there's the first picture I've seen of Vinent, sitting at some kind of desk and far darker, more intense, than the man at Parque Central—is a Black Hole of Calcutta locker room, crusty and dripping. Outside, stenciled on the wall, a blue boxing glove punches the word "Bloqueo": Boxing beats the blockade. I walk out and ask Feria whom he would call the best fighter on the national team. A rooster, five hours past dawn but unconvinced, crows and crows.

"No question," he says. "Vinent."

The five kids finish working out and climb up, hanging on the ropes to catch every word. Others begin filtering in off the street. A lone barbell, with two uncollared weights, sits on the ground. The ring is sturdy but old, with sweat-stained canvas sheets laid over wood. In one corner, hanging off the side, a broken black bell waits for someone to ring it.

"This local gym is known all over the world," Feria says again. We tell him we should go. His face again folds into that expression. "If we had gloves, I'd put on an exhibition for you," he says. "But we have no gloves."

On the way to the car, I see one of the boys who'd been drilling inside. He looks about twelve, and he passes before us, running barefoot on the rutted pavement with the authority and ease of someone wearing a spongy pair of Nikes. He doesn't look around. He doesn't wince. We cross the wide, grassy divider between lanes, and I glance to my left. Two dozen boys and girls in Young Pioneer uniforms have split into two groups and lie facedown under the trees. Someone gives a signal, and they start doing pushups.

Feria said that Vinent may be working out at the INDER complex near the baseball stadium, and I'm beginning to think my answer is finally at hand. We drive past Guillermon Moncada Stadium and the Sports Hotel where the baseball players stay and through a fence and up a hill, past one building that says, "Down with the Helms-Burton Law," and a gym that says, "'All the World's Gold Can Fit in a Kernel of Corn'—Marti."

We park. I can see the heavy bags of the boxing gym off to my right. An official comes out and asks what we want. "Vinent isn't here," he says. "He left yesterday. He went to Havana."

Everyone in the car is silent. I have no time to be deflated. Victor steers past the ballpark, and Jorge, voluble and large to Evelio's contained and scrawny, shouts from the backseat, "There's Omar Luis!"

So it is. Cuban kismet never takes away without giving back, and now here's Omar Luis, one of Cuba's finest pitchers, killer of the USA in the '96 Olympics, coveted by major league scouts since he announced himself with a nineteen-strikeout no-hitter against Korea in 1995, wandering alone after a morning workout. It's noon on Tuesday, December 15, Camaguey's game against Santiago doesn't begin for another seven hours—and Luis isn't pitching. Our timing is perfect. Luis wears the red uniform pants of the national team, a sweat-drenched long-sleeved shirt. His glove dangles from his left hand. He is about to cross over to the hotel for lunch. Could we chat?

"Sure," Omar says.

He turns around and walks over to the shade of a jaguay tree, the branches above dropping thigh-thick roots into the earth. Jorge, who prides himself on being the most knowledgeable baseball fan in Santiago, whispers to me, "His brother just died in a car accident. He played for Camaguey, too."

Omar says he is twenty-five, though the official record says he'll be twenty-seven in July. He dropped off the baseball map for six months in '97, after a springtime freak accident demolished his left elbow; he was driving a car near home with his arm hanging out the window when another car crashed into him. Luck: Omar is a right-handed pitcher. He lost nothing. He came back to strike out 147 batters in 137 innings and finish 13–5 with a 1.77 ERA in 1997–98. He has been less dominant since; after striking out eleven in eight sterling innings in Cuba's run to the '98 World Cup championship last July, he has gone 3–4 so far this season. No one believes the slump will last long. "He has great command of his pitches, can throw them all for strikes," said New York Mets assistant general manager Omar Minaya when I asked him later about Luis. "And he's a great competitor. He reminds me of a younger El Duque."

Luis is quiet but open, a serious man with dark skin and somber, bloodshot eyes. He has five pitches—a ninety-five-mile-per-hour fastball, a change-up, a screwball, a slider, and, most dependably, a terrifying curveball. "The batters all call it unhittable," Omar says.

His older brother, Andres, pitched for Camaguey, played three years on the national team, and in 1989 put together a magical year of 11–1 with a 0.67 ERA. He taught Omar everything he knows about baseball. He also convinced the manager of Camaguey to put Omar on the team. "And not because he was my brother," Omar says. "Andres would help anyone who he thought might need it."

On September 18, while riding his bike home after a party, Andres crashed and hit his head. He'd been drinking. His head dropped into a hole; the hole was filled with water and he drowned. He was thirty-five years old. The next day, Omar was running sprints in the outfield with his Camaguey teammates, getting ready for the '98 season. The local baseball commissioner strolled out to talk.

"I still can't get over it," Omar says. "He was the oldest. He taught us everything. He was the family's right arm. He supported everybody.

"Now I'm the right arm. Now I feel my brother is pitching in me. I have to help my family. I'm the only one."

Omar always loved watching El Duque pitch in Cuba, because he admires anyone who, like himself, has mastered the curveball. He made sure he saw El Duque pitch live in the '98 World Series on a friend's TV, and he also owns a World Series videotape that he prizes. "There's a lot of pride," Omar says. "He's Cuban. He's one of us."

Enough of commissioners and fans, enough politics, I finally have an expert who lives pitching and has studied both men closely. Who's better? I ask. El Duque or Valle? This has become an oddly important question for me, and as I pose it to Luis I finally realize why. Duque's growing fame in the States—his stature as the island's best, his role as anti-Castro symbol—threatens to bury the exploits of those left behind in a flurry of fevered rhetoric and pinstriped hype. Had Valle gone to America with Duque, their rivalry might well have played out on the greatest stage. Instead, like every other baseball great who chose to stay in Cuba, Valle will eventually fade away now, a mere footnote in someone else's story. Few will know how great a pitcher he was.

"For me, it's Valle," Omar says. "When Duque pitched, he'd have good days and bad days. But any time Lazaro took the mound, the opposing team knew it was going to lose: It's over. That slider and that fastball? Over. He's the greatest pitcher we have."

Have? But Valle hasn't pitched in the National Series for two years. He's been in Japan, no? Omar pulls apart a golden leaf into well-considered little strips. "Lazaro hasn't lost a thing," he says.

"He could take the mound right now and dominate. Any time. You just can't hit the guy."

Scouts have tried to lure Omar away. During the '96 Olympics, he and Pedro Luis Lazo fielded constant entreaties from agents. During last spring's playoffs, a scout called him to his hotel and asked if he was willing to jump. He said no. He says now that there's not enough money for him to betray the revolution. Yes, there are problems in Cuba. "But there are problems everywhere," he says.

"There's a saying: Money makes the world go around. But not for me. My father died, my brother died, but my mother is alive. What good is money if you can't enjoy your family? What if she gets sick? What about my daughter? What good is money if I can't come back?"

CHAPTER 13

President Kennedy tried to get Castro, but Castro got Kennedy first.

—LYNDON JOHNSON to Joseph Califano

Baseball could have saved the world a lot of trouble. That's the story, anyway, and one that nobody has much interest in disputing anymore, for baseball people love myth as much as children, and a game rich in apocryphal lore like "Say it ain't so, Joe!", Babe Ruth's called homer, and Ted Williams's ability to read the label on a spinning phonograph record has grown fond of the idea that young Fidel Castro was a pitcher of major league caliber. American press accounts on Cuban baseball invariably recount how Castro was scouted by/offered a contract by/had a tryout with the Washington Senators/New York Giants/New York Yankees, and while no one ever goes beyond that point to explain how such a promising career fizzled, the idea that a dictator who brought the planet to the nuclear brink once dedicated himself to the intricacies of the curveball is too juicy to resist.

Magazine writers, baseball hacks, the *New York Times*, TV commentators, at least one short story writer and one novelist, any serious American biographer of Castro—all have revisited this well-trod ground with surreal result: Long the country's final answer and everyday fact, the Maximum Leader has also realized Cuba's ultimate male fantasy. He is now the most famous Cuban baseball player in history. In the late 1990s, an American company began peddling vintage baseball hats from Cuba's prerevolutionary past. Each cap came with a small pamphlet explaining Latin baseball. Martin Dihigo, "The Immortal" who is considered the greatest Cuban player of all time, is pictured once in a business suit. Castro, who actually never proved himself beyond the high school level, is shown twice: once in his Barbudos flannels and once, oddly, topless and playing Ping-Pong. "Latin baseball history is rich and evolving with wars, elections, dictators and presidents all playing major roles," the pamphlet explains.

I'm no less guilty. When I wrote a lengthy piece for *Sports Illustrated* on the Cuban sports machine in 1995, the opening photo showed Castro in mid-windup, face encased in thick spectacles, two fingers on his right hand lightly riding the seams. I brought the picture back with me from Havana. And, yes, when I saw it the first time in a store, I could not put the baseball cap down. I own it still.

Lately, Castro's baseball reputation has taken quite a beating. Robert Quirk's 1993 biography derides the quality of Havana high school baseball, attributes any scouting of Castro to the shortage of talent during World War II, and states that Fidel "was never as talented as he thought he was." A 1987 article in the *Miami Herald* dug up some of Fidel's ex-high school teammates at Belen; all, enemies now, called him a wild pitcher of questionable merit. Tad Szulc's 1986 portrait reports Castro "forcefully" denying a rumor that he'd once wanted to play ball in the States. In 1981, *Atlantic Monthly* quoted Minnesota Twins owner Calvin Griffith as saying that the Washington Senators—presumably through Joe Cambria, then the top judge of Cuban talent—had scouted Castro in the 1940s, but that his fastball wasn't the stuff of major league dreams. "You always hear rumors that he was going to sign, but that was not true," Preston Gomez, an executive now with the Anaheim Angels, told me. "I was scouted by Joe Cambria with a lot of other players, and if he had been we would have known. I knew the baseball coach at Belen, Reinaldo Cordeiro, and he never mentioned Castro. We never heard his name. We never saw him."

Yet the idea of Castro as talented ballplayer endures. "Baseball will not bring Castro's regime to an end," read a *New York Times* editorial by Tina Rosenberg on January 11, 1999. "But had Cambria been more patient with a developing prospect, baseball might have prevented it." This is partly because Castro himself has regaled American visitors with boasts of his pitching prowess, but two other props keep the story up in the air. The first is a statement made by then-Giants owner Horace Stoneham to revered New Yorker baseball essayist Roger Angell in 1975. Stoneham said that one of his scouts had seen Castro play and sent a report—now lost—to the States. "A good ballplayer," Stoneham recalled of the report. "I think if he'd stayed in the game, he'd have made it to the majors."

The second is a comical account by former Pittsburgh Pirate third baseman Don Hoak, a ten-year major league veteran and vital member of the 1960 World Series champions, that ran in the June 1964 issue of *Sport* magazine. Recalling his days playing for Cienfuegos during the 1950–51 season, Hoak describes one Havana evening when he was just about to step into the batter's box against Marianao. Firecrackers exploded, banners rose, horns blared, and then some three hundred anti-Batista demonstrators swarmed the field. A tall skinny, twenty-four-year-old dressed in street clothes imperiously demanded the ball and glove from the pitcher, whirled his pitching arm over his head a half-dozen times, and looked, Hoak said, "kookier than any southpaw I have known." The civilian tossed a few warm-up pitches. Then he yelled "Batter up!" It was Fidel.

"Castro gave me the hipper-dipper windup and cut loose with a curve," Hoak told sportswriter Myron Cope. "Actually it was a pretty fair curve. It had a sharp inside break to it—and it came within an inch of breaking my head."

The umpire called it a ball. The demonstrators began to grumble. The ump told Hoak to start swinging or he'd have to call strikes. Hoak fouled off two fastballs—the first "a good fastball, a regular bullet," and the second "scorched its way to my eyeballs." Then he decided he'd had enough, and demanded Castro's removal in a cry that has echoed in various forms through Miami for the last forty years. "Now just get that idiot out of the game," Hoak said.

Hoak's tale stood as fact for decades, filling out baseball anthologies and lending melodramatic color to a life that ended as baseball tragedy. In 1969, Don Hoak collapsed at the age of forty-one. "He died the day he thought he'd be named manager of the Pittsburgh Pirates," Jill Corey, Hoak's wife at the time, told me. "But it didn't happen. Someone else got the job. They called it a heart attack, but I say he died of a broken heart."

In 1994, Hoak's famed at-bat came under attack for the first time, when Cuban native Everardo Santamarina wrote a piece in *The National Pastime*, the journal for the Society of American Baseball Research, called "The Hoak Hoax." Declaring that "Castro and Hoak? Never happened," Santamarina dismantled Hoak's recollection as a host of factual errors, citing that no such protest happened and that Hoak didn't even play in Cuba during the winter of 1950–51. During the one verifiable season Hoak did play Cuban ball, 1953–54, Castro had been locked up for his failed attack on the Moncada barracks.

If Hoak was perpetrating a historical scam, he never told those closest to him. His first wife, Phyllis Hoak, told me that, no, Don did not play in Havana in the winter of 1950–51 as he had told Cope; the two had been married at home plate in Fort Worth, Texas in August 1950 and spent their first winter in Puerto Rico. But, she says, Don played the following year's winter ball season, 1951–52, in Cuba—and she went with him. While Santamarina says that no serious student demonstrations occurred in Cuba until 1955, Fidel had been arrested in November 1950 for taking part in a student demonstration in Cienfuegos and, a year later, he was indeed stirring up attention and trouble in a bid to position himself for the June 1952 national congressional elections. In January 1952, Castro even went so far as to file a lawsuit against the nation's president, Carlos Prio, charging abuse of power. Quirk's biography details a Havana then bristling with the aftermath of the recent public suicide of popular senator Eduardo Chibas and "signs of political and economic unrest." Szulc's account shows Fidel organizing protests against both the president and Batista in the spring of '52, and who can say if a baseball stadium didn't catch his fancy?

In the ensuing years Hoak not only stuck by his story, he expanded on it. According to his daughter, Kimberly, Hoak would talk about how Castro "was a decent pitcher" with "great potential," and how he'd become friendly with and even played poker with the Cuban leader. In her home, she says, she has an old sock containing twenty silver dollars Don won from Fidel at cards. Phyllis, Hoak's son Jeff, and his second wife all say that Hoak insisted that the at-bat happened, and he never deviated until the moment he died. "He did talk about it," Jill Corey said. "He loved Cuba and had the great honor of hitting against Fidel. He believed he hit against Fidel Castro."

Considering the play it has received in the United States, the most curious aspect of Castro's supposed brush with the big leagues is that no one in Cuba mentions it. Not once, since 1991, has anyone ever informed me that Fidel might have had an above-average arm. The Hoak story is met only with blank looks; one press official said that it sounded invented to him. In a place that adores baseball, prides itself on its defectors' success in the majors, and has built a cult of personality around Castro celebrating his every move, this has always struck me as significant. Castro himself has been preaching against professional baseball from his earliest days in power. "It doesn't surprise me to see those miserable men coming over to offer money to our ballplayers and our ballplayers tell them to go to hell," Castro said in 1966. "That's a man of high integrity, dignity, a man who doesn't surrender, doesn't sell himself. They can never convince him." But he has never used himself as an example.

Instead, Castro's athletic image in Cuba is both broader and more shallow. A good all-around athlete in high school and college, he excelled not only in baseball, but basketball and track and field, running the four hundred meters and competing in the high jump. When the regime was just finding its legs, he made sure to be photographed with successful athletes in any and all sports, wearing boxing gloves, playing hoops; they are tacked up at the offices in Havana's Sports City complex, at La Finca, in gyms nationwide. After the volleyball team won the gold medal at the 1971 Pan Am Games in Cali, Castro went on court to play with journalists and spiked a ball for photographers. In 1980, he published a book of 640 musings, quotes, excerpts on every aspect of Cuban athletics, called *Fidel on Sports*. In America, he'll always be a wannabe pitcher. But inside Cuba, Castro prefers to paint himself as the country's number one cheerleader, umpire, general manager, and coach, and his interest is considered so intense that it can even spill over into policy.

On January 17, 1996, then–New Mexico Congressman Bill

Richardson, who went on to become UN ambassador and secretary of energy in the Clinton administration, flew to Havana to negotiate the release of ten political prisoners with Castro and discuss the two countries' relationship. Before his second meeting, Richardson attended a National Series championship game between Pinar Del Rio and Industriales at Latinoamericano—where he met Omar Linares and teased him, saying, "You know, I can get you a good contract, Linares." When he met with Castro, Richardson, a former pitcher once drafted by the Kansas City Athletics, began an hour-long discussion about baseball and boxing. "I had a design in mind," Richardson told me. "I knew he was a very avid sports fan—and I was too—and that and the fact that I was speaking Spanish to him, warming him up, was part of any negotiator's objective. I wanted to use sports as a way to have him think: This is not just another gringo negotiator. This is somebody who relates to us because he's got part of our 'Latin Culture'—and he knows his sports."

But Richardson also wanted Castro to know he wasn't trying to curry favor, and to accomplish this he chided Castro—pitcher to pitcher—on the inferior quality of Cuban pitching. The ploy almost backfired. "It set him off," Richardson said. "I won't say he was offended, but it was close. I got him a little agitated. . . . But I think that helped me warm Castro up. He was a little offended, but he could think, 'At least this guy is not sucking up to me.'"

Richardson left Havana with a concession from Castro on reducing fees charged to Cubans who legally emigrate to the United States. He returned to Havana a month later and the next day left with three political prisoners released by Castro. Asked if he thought his sports discussion helped the two men come to an understanding, Richardson said, "Absolutely. Look at the results of the trip—we got prisoners released, we got the emigration agreement, so yeah. It was great."

But Castro's high-level meld of politics and sports was nothing new. He set the tone as soon as he took power. In 1959, the AAA Havana Sugar Kings, a member of baseball's prestigious International League and Cuba's last link with the majors, won a place in the minor league World Series and a chance to play the Minneapolis Millers. Castro had supported the Sugar Kings all season, working out with the club and pitching to fellow revolutionary/baseball fanatic Camilo Cienfuegos for the crowd before games. No one thought it strange that a politician would spend so much time at the ballpark. "The year they took over, everything smelled like roses," Preston Gomez, the Sugar Kings manager that year, told me. "There was free admission to the games. To me, it was not a terrible time because everybody thought he was God. Everything seemed good." On July 24, Castro pitched in the now-famous Barbudos uniform in a Havana exhibition to benefit agrarian reform; he struck out two and allowed no runs in his one inning of work. "You can't beat Fidel," Cienfuegos said. "Not even in baseball."

Because of cold weather in Minnesota, five of the seven games in the '59 Little World Series were played in Cuba, and Castro attended them all—even when that meant canceling a cabinet meeting and bringing his ministers to the park with him for game five. Every night, fifteen minutes before game time, he would come striding through the center field gate. "As a baseball fan," Hoak later said, "he belonged in the nut category." Castro told the Sugar Kings' president, Roberto Maduro, of their need for "another right-handed pinch-hitter." For game six, he insisted on sitting on the bench. Press accounts at the time reported that Castro then demanded that Gomez allow him to take over for a few innings, and ranted at the players when the team fell behind. But Gomez insists that Castro never overstepped his bounds. "He came and sat for a few innings. But he never took charge of the team," Gomez told me.

"Anybody who knows Preston Gomez knows that if he told me that, I'd take off my uniform and go sit in the stands." The Sugar Kings lost the game, but won the series. A year later, the team moved to Jersey City.

Despite his efforts to appear impartial, nothing ever supplanted baseball as Fidel's favorite sport. Quirk's biography is studded with references to Castro asking questions about Warren Spahn and the '59 World Series during the revolution's final military push, and later trying to keep up on baseball scores while traveling to Chile or the Soviet Union. Arocha says that Fidel was reputed to go to Latinoamericano for batting practice "at two or three in the morning. The story is that Fidel would be at the plate yelling, 'Throw it fast!' while an escort would stand next to the mound whispering, 'Throw it slow.'" When I asked El Duque in New York if Castro had a deep knowledge of pitching and the overall game, Duque nodded and said, "He knows."

Richardson agreed. He asked Castro about some older Cuban ballplayers who'd left the country long ago to play in Mexico, and Castro reeled off what happened to each. "He knows everything," Richardson said, adding that he found Castro's attention locking in any time the conversation turned to sports. "This was when he was smiling," he said. "He was clearly in his element." Richardson also learned something else.

"Castro is a fanatical newspaper reader," he said. "He told me he never had an appointment before 3 P.M., mainly because he stayed up all night. And what he'd do for several hours before he saw anybody was read the newspapers. So he knew all the standings, the batting averages—in the U.S. He was a prolific follower of baseball—U.S. baseball. He said that."

But the national team is his baby. In 1993, at the athletes' reception after the Central American and Caribbean Games in Puerto Rico, the victorious baseball team met, as always, with Castro first. Lazaro Valle didn't show up. When Castro noticed the nation's top pitcher was missing, he asked players and officials, including Duque, why Valle didn't come to see him. "He doesn't have a car," Duque said. A day later, Castro called Valle to ask him himself. "After that," Valle says. "They gave out seven cars to guys." Richardson also hit a raw nerve when he brought up Linares, telling El Commandante that he had to let the national team third baseman prove himself in the United States before he got too old. "No, Richardson, *no se puede*," Castro replied. "We can't do that. I'm not going to permit that."

Knowing all this, I still wasn't prepared for what I saw a few hours after bumping into Omar Luis. In the back of a small room under the stands at Moncada Stadium, beyond the glass cases full of dangling medals and news clippings and curling photographs in the newly opened Museum of Santiago Sports, stands an astonishing piece of craftsmanship. It is a life-sized panorama of athletic exertion, extending across the entire back wall for more than twenty-five feet, rising from the floor to above eye level—all of it carved out of a native wood. At first glance, the frieze seems just a generic celebration of athletic exertion: Unknown sports heroes jumping and throwing and sprinting, movement and faces frozen in an oaken gasp. But as I follow the lines, sort out the arms and legs, I begin to recognize faces and feel the thing's surreal idea overtaking me. There, in the midst of this nod to sporting excellence, I see the revolution taking shape. Camilo Cienfuegos has on a catcher's mitt. Che Guevara is playing chess. Fidel swings a baseball bat. Everyone playing for keeps.

Havana may be the cosmopolitan center of Cuba, its hub of politics and culture and business, but I've come to Santiago de Cuba because no one can even begin to understand the island without knowing the east. Cuba's narrow physical dimension evokes a Rorschach-blot reaction—conservatives describe its shape as shark-like, liberals see it, more benignly, as a cigar—but I liken it to a slender leg stretched provocatively across the Gulf of Mexico, just daring the world to ignore it. In that context, it's only appropriate that the province of Oriente ends up looking like the country's solid big foot—with Santiago, its de facto capital and Cuba's second largest city, lodged in the arch like an annoying pebble. The people of Oriente pride themselves on toughness, simplicity, and bravery to the point of self-destruction, and I've heard Habaneros casually dismiss Oriente, in the manner of a New Yorker referring to Appalachia, as a land of savages.

Part of this is, I suppose, a racist reaction to the region's predominance of blacks, but it's also a matter of respect. The people here like to battle. Much of the War of Independence against Spain was fought in and around Santiago. Castro's revolt took root with a 1953 assault on the Moncada Barracks, grew in the piney crags of the Sierra Maestra and takes nourishment here still. There's no place where the revolution burns brighter. It was in Santiago that Fidel, a son of nearby Biran but schooled in the city, first claimed power in 1959, and it is here, less than a month after I leave, that he'll return for the fortieth anniversary and declare himself a man "who dresses the same, who thinks the same, who dreams the same." Santiago is the only place I hear people regularly call one another "companero," a term as obsolete nationwide as giant beards. "Havana is full of people against the revolution," Jorge says in one of the few moments he gives his smile a rest. "But in Havana they are scared of us, because they know we'll come down on them hard."

Aside from the parade of superb boxers, Oriente has produced a disproportionate and dazzling array of athletes. Juantorena was born in Santiago, and pitcher Jose Ibar spent his first eight years here. Some thirty-five years ago, the outlying town of Palma Soriano, population 150,000, produced, near simultaneously, Cuba's greatest woman track star in Ana Quirot, its greatest home run hitter in Orestes Kindelan, and its greatest second baseman in Antonio Pacheco. All came from poor families. "It's the work," says Juan Trenal, the head of the Santiago INDER. "This is a city of labor. The people have always been used to working hard."

It is 1 P.M. Trenal takes us over to the cafeteria, located in the stadium under the left field bleachers. Kindelan sits before a heaping plate of rice and beans. We walk in to say hello, he glances at us and says to Trenal, "What are you doing, letting these guys in here?"

Fifteen minutes later, Kindelan reclines in a seat overlooking the field. He has a bandage on his left ear from some recent acupuncture treatment for a sore leg. Kindelan is thirty-four, and for someone who has hit a record 431 home runs in his eighteen seasons in the National Series, he's slimmer than I expected, less the thick-waisted slugger—it must be in the hands and thighs. In Atlanta, Kindelan hammered opponents for nine home runs in nine games, and in the recent World Cup he hit .560. We talk for about fifteen minutes, but it is like fishing without a pole: Kindelan is quiet, suspicious of American journalists, and known to be strictly *partido*. He gives me party line on the game's recent reforms and the revamped national team's continued greatness.

"The new team is just as strong," he says. "We're not as consistent, but in two years we will be."

Kindelan does reveal one bit of news, though: After a bit of tinkering, Cuba will resume renting out players overseas. The difference now, he says, is that the national team comes first: No capable players will be able to retire just for the purpose of making money. Instead, the players who go to Japan will be only those who don't make the national team—but they will be required to continue play-ing in the National Series. It's a clever hedge against defections, because more would share in the meager rewards. National team players get the prestige and advantage of traveling overseas. Impa-tient backups who might otherwise jump now get the chance to pick up cash.

I thank Kindelan. Trenal gives a smiling handshake and apolo-gizes. "I'm sorry you didn't get a chance to talk to Vinent," he says. "He's one of our best."

At 4:45 P.M., we walk back into the stadium like a pack of dogs, slowly, sniffing the air. Now there are five of us: me, Victor, Evelio, and Jorge, and a tiny and gracious twenty-six-year-old singer named Arelis Morales. We had all converged on a downtown paladar for a late lunch, where I learned that Evelio had fought in Angola in the early eighties and Arelis, who'd been sitting alone at a nearby table, confessed that she is both one of the city's premiere guaracheras—a singer of the high-energy musical form of guaracha—and not the woman she used to be. A recent attack of peritonitis, caused by a burst appendix, sent her into a hospital and close to death. She lost seventy pounds in a month. She's only been back in circulation a short time, singing little, trying to gain strength. Her mother and three uncles fought in the revolution and killed people. She decided she'd love to go to a baseball game.

Through an open door, the ball field expands in murky shadow. Only the outfield wall catches the last stream of sunlight, burning from left to right in a mellow orange: "Santiago de Cuba: Following the Path of Champions," "Healthy Hit," "We Are More Interested in Honor than in Medals," "For a Long and Better Life, Sport is the Best Option: Exer-cise It," "Mass Participation Guarantees the Quality of Sport."

We stand along the rail off shallow right field. Near home plate, two men work alone. One drops into a squat and begins walking, ducklike, toward first base. Then he turns around and goes back. "There he is," Jorge says. "The captain of captains."

Antonio Pacheco is the soul of the Big Red Machine. The Santiago second baseman has been Cuba's national team captain since 1986, when the great Antonio Munoz stepped aside because he knew that this quiet, intense twenty-one-year-old should be handed the reins. Pacheco had already been on the national team for three years—one of two players (the other being Omar Linares) to be named directly out of school—and he is acknowledged as the steady, disciplined presence that guided Cuba to a dizzying string of 152 straight victories, two Olympic gold medals, and its current supremacy. Pacheco never protests calls, and at thirty-four shows little sign of slowing. He hit a typical team-high .348 with ten home runs during the 1997–98 season; in the '98 World Cup he hit .450, drove in seventeen runs, and was named the ten-game tournament's Most Valuable Player. Valle says Pacheco is the toughest hitter he has ever faced.

The coach begins slapping ball after ground ball to Pacheco, who with each one takes another step forward until he is close enough to touch the man. Pacheco stops and picks up a bat, and begins hitting batting practice in the most efficient way I've seen: Instead of standing at home plate and spraying balls all over the field, he faces the backstop while the coach kneels and flips up the ball. Pacheco cracks rocket after rocket—Chung!—into the backstop. The balls tumble into the dirt at the base of the wall, easy to retrieve. His manager, Oberto Nunez, comes out and stands in the infield grass in his street clothes, picking up the occasional stray, pleased. Pacheco has been out of the lineup for twenty-five days—the longest layoff of his career—with a mystifying bronchial ailment that forced him all the way to Havana for treatment. It's not surprising that, during that time, Santiago sank to last place in its division. Pacheco is the glue.

"I'm working out twice a day," he says. "I want to show the guys I'm ready to come back."

We sit in the Santiago dugout. Pacheco has showered, put on a royal blue "Cuba Beisbol" pullover, and thanked me for talking to him. He is known as one of Cuban sport's prime *militantes*, a man so loyal to the regime that even a stalwart like Linares is hesitant to speak freely in his presence. One interesting aspect of the defection of baseball players is that it began, like all trends and any expected opposition to Fidel, with players primarily from Havana—Arocha, Ordoñez, Euclides Rojas. Lately, it has spread like a contagion, east into Santa Clara—Arrojo, Toca, Maikel Jova—and I'm curious to see whether it could ever take hold in the loyal bastion of Santiago. I ask Pacheco about El Duque.

"I didn't see any of his games, but I'd be lying to say I wasn't proud of him," Pacheco says. I hide my surprise. Pacheco's hands are folded in his lap; the outfield lights shine on his light brown, pockmarked face. "He's showing the world Cuban baseball. I love playing here. This is my place. But if a guy decides to go, I respect it. We're all products of the same system. We all feel the same way."

Except about Arrojo. Like Valle, Pacheco resents Arrojo's pre-Olympic jump. He sees it as something beyond politics, the breaking of a code. "He could've waited three or four games so we'd have a solid lead. I feel very empty about it," he says. "But it's not just about the winning. It's about friendship, about being a great team. What he did wasn't just a blow to Cuban baseball. It was a blow to his friends. Ask anybody on the team. We were all hurt."

He is wearing a denim baseball hat, Levi-Strauss label on the crown. He says he was proud of how the team responded in Atlanta, how Luis stepped into Arrojo's place, started the most crucial games against the USA and Japan and went 3-0. "Tremendous," Pacheco says. "That's what the Cuban people are all about: We fight back. We don't ever give up."

It hasn't been easy. When Japan snapped the national team's giant winning streak in the final of 1997's Intercontinental Cup by the overwhelming score of 11-2, Pacheco sat in the dugout in Barcelona for many long minutes, trying to come up with something to say. "My biggest concern was, 'How do we face the Cuban people?'" he says. "This is the national pastime. It was painful to lose like that, and then we had to come home and see the people. I felt awful." The new national team is young, but, he says, "We're ready" for Sydney.

"Everything we do is directed toward winning gold. It's going to take more effort than in the past, because some of our other teams have been stronger. But I have no doubt. As long as the pitchers keep throwing the ball where we can see it—and not underground— we're going to hit it." Pacheco pauses and allows himself his first tight grin. "And even if they throw it underground, we're going to hit it."

Moncada is an elegant affair, the model for what a Caribbean stadium should be. The first ballpark built by the revolution, in 1961, Santiago's home field has a unified, intimate feel, a contained spiffiness that Latinoamericano lacks; and if people in Santiago wonder where their money is being spent, they'd do well to look here. The rich field unrolls, impeccable, unmarred and green, the foul poles gleam neon red, the cement stands rise in alternating pastels of pink and blue. One dugout reads, "Home Team" in English, the other says, "Visitador." The Santiago players sprint, chat, warm up in their big baggy uniforms, white with red trim, black pinstripes. I succumb to a wave of contentment. I drink my first beer, a frigid Cristal.

Something begins to happen. We are sitting in front-row seats, just past first base. It turns out that Arelis, far from being a baseball neophyte, knows every player who trots by. Each one comes and smiles and kisses her on the cheek. They ask about her family, her singing, her health. Victor and I tease her about her popularity. She glows like a happy teenager. But then one player approaches, glaring and refusing to stop. "I hate you," he says to Arelis and then he walks away.

She blinks, isn't sure what to say. At that moment, eight of the fourteen light stanchions silently fizzle out, leaving half the field in darkness. Fans cry out, but the players act as if they don't notice. The hyper-romantic strains of Dominican merengue continue their milky flow from the loudspeakers. As always, I notice the scoreboard; where in America it would read R-H-E—runs-hits-errors—here it reads C-H-E—*carreras*, hits, and *errores*. A constant reminder: Che lives.

Kindelan comes over, says hello to Arelis, and I find it curious that he doesn't even nod in my direction. On the field, right in front of us, three groups of players begin playing pepper, three players each fielding sharp ground balls from one batter. I don't notice at first, but soon baseballs start flying over the railing and into the seats, just to our left and right. I look out at the pepper game taking place directly ahead. Facing us, smacking ball after ball at his trio of teammates, is the sour-faced player. He's not looking in our direction. I ask Jorge his name. "Eddy Cajigal," he says. "Second base."

The nine players before us chase the ball with ridiculous ease, snagging and firing it with that casual, buzzing, big-time velocity. I'm again struck by the thought that at least twenty Cuban players I've seen could play in the major leagues. I'm so filled with admiration, in fact, that I don't realize my moment has arrived. A ball skips like a stone off the blue railing, and before I can think I react, stretching my left hand out and behind me in its furthest extension in years. The ball jets smack into the web of my fingers as the crowd behind me leans away in fear. I hear them yell, "Ohhhh!" I feel the scuffed leather, and without thinking or changing my expression, I fling the ball back out to the field. Arelis grins at me and yells, "Five points!" It may well be the coolest single act I've ever performed. Cajigal stares for a second, and then starts hitting again.

The lights fire back to life. At 7:45, the four umpires walk in perfect cadence toward home plate. Wilson Lopez takes the mound for Santiago, and as I'm watching this it slowly dawns on me that the stray balls, the pepper game, Kindelan's snub, Cajigal's glaring—all were of a piece. Victor and I are two extranjeros who abruptly arrive in the company of one of Santiago's best young singers, a friend to the players, a prize. Is she with us for the same old reason? Sniffing dollars like everyone else? In Havana, the native hostility to foreign power is a subtle grumble. But Santiago is not Havana. Cajigal is not happy. I, naturally, decide to despise him.

It is a superb game. Though in last place, Santiago had won six in a row coming in, and 20,000 fans show up because they sense a turn in fortune. In the second, Santiago's Rey Isaac scores on a triple and hands Lopez a 1-0 lead, and that is more than enough. He blows through the Camaguey lineup inning after inning, growing stronger, limiting it to just three hits over eight. His opponent, Neudis Fernandez, is just as effective: A pitching duel. My luck continues to hold. Someone in the crowd cranks up an air-raid siren.

Baseball's appeal lies partly in its complexity; you can watch thousands of games and still come away surprised. Tonight, I see two things I've never before seen live. One, twins. Camaguey has two titanic twin brothers, Loidel and Laidel Chappelli, hitting back-to-back. Loidel is the new national team first baseman and hero; he drove in two game-breaking runs in Cuba's win over Korea in the '98 World Cup final. Two, the hidden ball trick. In the fourth inning, Kindelan walks and takes second on a balk. Fernandez peers home, and when Kindelan steps off the bag, the second baseman tags him out. Kindelan walks off the field, hands up as if to say, "What can I say: I'm a idiot!" Then there's the customary umpire break, a practice so civilized it always leaves me agog. At the end of five innings, two girls walk onto the field bearing trays laden with cups of coffee and water. The umps walk over, take a few dainty sips, and return to their positions. It's nice.

Coming off the field for the bottom of the sixth, Cajigal deviates from his usual second-to-dugout route, walks straight over to Arelis, says, "You got something for me?" and jogs away. I now wish him ill-fortune. I want to see Eddy Cajigal look bad.

One inning later, I get my wish. With one out and two men on and a chance to break the game open, Cajigal slaps a weak grounder to second for the inning-ending double play. The game ends beautifully. Camaguey threatens in the ninth with men on the corners and one out, but Santiago brings in two relievers to dispose of the Chappelli twins and they do so, the last forcing Laidel to chop a weak grounder to short for the force-out at second. Cajigal deftly pulls in the ball, steps on second to end it, and then slaps the base with his glove for emphasis. The fans cheer, and begin filing out. A dozen kids jump the rail and start running bases. No one minds.

By the time we get outside, the players are already working through a tide of fans under the broad gray trees in uniform, heading for the hotel. Jorge goes home. We return to our lunchtime paladar for a late dinner, but the day's frenetic randomness, the close game, and the late hour all suddenly collapse on Arelis. She goes silent at her seat, frail and dizzy, nearly passing out. We wonder if we should take her to the hospital. Two women wait on us—the first fiftyish and crabby, the second our lunch waitress, dark and early-thirties and dressed more formally for evening. She brings bread, then food, and Arelis nibbles quietly, gaining color and assuring us she'll be fine.

Midnight hits, closing time. A Lada pulls up, filled with six heads. The crabby waitress walks outside carrying two bags, ignoring us, opens a car door, and begins squeezing herself in. Then she turns and says, in English, "See you tomorrow!"

"She wasn't talking to me," Evelio says. "I'm Cuban."

We drive Arelis home. She asks Victor in, but he declines. Evelio asks if we want to see the Morro now, so Victor negotiates some inky hills and curves, rolls past a lighthouse, and stops. We get out and separate in the 1 A.M. quiet. Built in the seventeenth century, the fortress looms 180 feet over the entrance to Santiago bay, catching the freshest air in the city. Wind courses around my ears, blowing over the headlands in an endless rush. Far below, fishing boats reveal themselves in a quickly doused wink of flashlight. A faint cranking of truck gears, a car horn, drift in from somewhere. The lighthouse sends its massive beam slow across the grass, over the ancient stones, out to the empty Caribbean. I stretch out my arms. This should be some kind of moment, melodramatic and cleansing, but the whole world looks spent from here. It feels like the end.

CHAPTER 14

*PRESIDENT KENNEDY: "But I'm just wondering about whether
. . . Obviously Castro's response would be against
Guantanamo. If he overruns Guantanamo, we're going to
have to invade."*
*GENERAL TAYLOR: "He won't overrun Guantanamo or he'll
have a good fight around the place. By the time we get the
Marines in, with the carrier-based aviation, we'll hold
Guantanamo."*

—WHITE HOUSE TRANSCRIPT, October 18, 1962

The boxing coaches sit in a salmon-colored gym under the stands at Nguyen Van-Troi baseball stadium. One after another, long-muscled boys troop into the room, change their shirts, ransack the rattling tin cabinet for gloves and headgear. Early afternoon Wednesday, December 16. Outside, the city of Guantanamo sprawls under the relentless sun like the victim of a beating, quiet and covered with dust. No one comes to this city much. It is an arid, whitewashed grid of 200,000, charmless and hardly protected by scrubby vegetation and scrawny spikes of cactus. The U.S. naval base, nearly one hundred years old, sits just twenty minutes away, but the expected armed-camp, Yanqui-go-home spirit seems subdued for a place that could conceivably be overrun any day. Van-Troi Stadium—in a classic

enemy-of-my-enemy-is-my-amigo gesture—was named for a
North Vietnamese soldier killed in action against the United
States. Just one jingo billboard guards the city's edge: "They'll
never conquer Cuba."

Aside from "Guantanamera" and the base, Felix Savon is Guantanamo's most famous product. His six world titles and two
Olympic gold medals spark arguments like the one unfolding
before me now: Savon's early mentors, Salvador Lamoth and Juan
Alvarez, disagree on Cuba's best-ever heavyweight. Salvador says
Savon, because of the quality of opponents and Savon's need to
destroy them all. Juan says Teofilo, because of his technical bril-
liance, elegant style, and knockout power in the days of lighter
gloves. Salvador agrees that Savon is not the prettiest fighter, that
both Hector Vinent and Ariel Hernandez carry themselves with
more grace. "They all look better, but in the end it's about winning," he says. "When it comes to results, no one touches him.
Savon is it."

Savon has always relished beating the Americans. He trained in
Caimanera, the last Cuban hamlet before the borders of the naval
base on Guantanamo Bay, in a gym that has since been converted
to a girl's school. While resting between sparring sessions, fifteen-
year-old Savon would stare at the stately, clean American ships
chugging through the water. "I could see them having military
maneuvers," he said to me once. "We would watch the cannons go
off. A lot of times you could see one white cannon pointing toward
Cuba. I'd see the planes flying low, breaking the sound barrier." At
night, Savon would entertain himself by watching a lone American
spotlight flash through the dark. "I don't like having the base
there," he said.

As the two men speak of Savon as a teen, I notice that they don't
lapse into wistful nostalgia or color his every early move as a har-

binger of greatness—and it strikes me that this is common. Sports heroes are different in Cuba. Unlike in the States—where stars live on in romanticized decline until they depart and fans then identify them with their happiest years—the passing of some great athlete into retirement doesn't evoke questions about "Who'll pick up the baton?" or "How will the sport survive without him?" These are questions that can never be asked, in fact, because they would be akin to asking "Can the regime survive?" Since Castro endows them with symbolic power, making them virtual stand-ins for the state, each Cuban athlete holds a position never quite equaled by his counterparts in the United States. In a sense, the athletes are bigger than the mere game they play. "The place of honor our boxers hold in the world—we cannot let that be taken away," Castro said in 1977. "Let them know that their boxers will have their most horrible battles against our fighters."

Yet there's little sense of loss when an athlete departs, and, though constantly celebrated while he competes, no awe-struck self-congratulation by other adults about being in the presence of someone rare. Part of this is because the Cuban athlete is never an industry unto himself, can never place himself above the system or "the people." Part of it has something to do with the value placed on maintaining the common touch. "The system is that way because that's the way we are," two-time world champion long jumper Ivan Pedroso once said. "We are more considerate of each other here."

But it's when Salvador mentions his belief in the innate competitiveness of the people from Oriente that I think I understand fully. "We fight. It's all around us: in the land, all the colors," Salvador says. "It's in the people—the way we grow, the way we talk. It's in our blood. It's already there: All we coaches have to do is train it. We could pick up anybody in the street and make him a fighter. He's already got it."

So Savon is quite special in Cuba—but then again he's not. An athlete can be bigger than sport, become a symbol, but he always ends up smaller. For he's only the latest in a long line, part of a continuum that began before him and will continue once he's gone. As such, Savon's every win is but a nod to the system—official line on defecting athletes: "We made them, so they owe it to us to stay"—that produced Felix Savon, just a new example of what communism can do. He is something the machine spit out. The machine is the hero.

Van-Troi Stadium is actually the center of a concentrated cluster of playing fields, pools, volleyball and basketball courts, dorms, gyms, classrooms, offices, and a hotel for the visiting ballplayers—the physical core of Guantanamo's sports factory. Here, some eight hundred children from ages eight to eighteen become engaged in the two-stage process that develops Cuba's athletes. The first stage, the Guantanamo EIDE, is one of sixteen schools of sports initiation, handling an estimated 10,000 kids, that are sprinkled throughout the country. Some EIDEs have as many as 2,000 kids or as few as, in this case, 450. With philosophy lifted directly from its former allies in the Soviet Union, Cuba built its first EIDE in Havana in 1963. By 1976, every province had one and the teaching had evolved. "Cubans are more dynamic than Europeans—we have more speed, more rhythm—and a bit more aggressive," one Havana sports instructor told me. "We took ideas from the socialist countries. But we adapted them to the Cuban character."

At the age of eight, after a child has been spotted excelling in school games or special tryouts or on the street, he will be sent here, where he lives during the week, takes a full complement of academic courses from 8 A.M. to noon, and plays sports ranging from basketball to shot-put to Ping-Pong to tennis from 2 to 5:30 P.M. Many kids apply and are turned down. Many kids, like Juantorena or Ana Quirot, who both started in basketball, find themselves switched to different sports once they come under the organized scrutiny of an EIDE. You don't argue when you are, as Yasser Gomez put it, captured and placed in a particular sport. Instruction is intense; the children sit silently. In Guantanamo, there's one coach for every eight kids.

At the age of fifteen, the best athletes get funneled into one of fifteen ESPAs—schools for athletic improvement and perfection—and then the nation's top 1,000 end up at Havana's CEAR, the center for high-yield training. Some, like El Duque, slip through the cracks and emerge on their own—but fewer and fewer. It's estimated that more than 90 percent of Cuba's Olympians now emerge from an EIDE. I remember something Yoelbi Quesada, the 1997 world champion triple jumper, told me last March: "We're going to keep getting better," he said. "For 2000 and 2004, we've got some new kids people don't even know about yet. We're going to surprise the world."

The machine never shuts down. This, I realize, is why the coaches seem almost bored talking about Savon. For them, he stopped mattering long ago.

"We don't worry about 2000," Juan says. "We've already won that. We're thinking about 2008."

Besides, both men say, if you really want to know about Savon, you shouldn't be talking to us. We got ahold of him late. Savon nearly didn't make it here at all. You need to go up in the hills, deeper into the country. A man is waiting for you.

Cuba is America reversed. Its defining urban center squats in the West, dirty and crowded, its far East is the land of wide open spaces, cattle, endless tracts of wavy blond grass, a sky so blue and overarching that it borders on the oppressive. Now the ground begins to rise; we turn onto a rutted dirt road, twist past the gray hulking ugliness of the Paraguay sugar processing plant, slow as we hit the rickety center of what is clearly a company town. Hugo Fernandez, dark and greyhound-thin, his jaunty straw hat the only mark of style in a place scrapping for basics, is standing outside his office. He says hello, but doesn't dwell on pleasantries. He invites us in and sits. He extends his arms, reveals weathered palms, and says, "Many champions have come through these hands."

Before we talk, though, Hugo insists on a demonstration. The Paraguay sports school is even more ramshackle than Los Olmos, with four bald tires and a limp bag dangling from the peaked rafters, a bent basketball hoop nailed up on one wall. But Hugo has invested the place with discipline. He blows the whistle hanging around his neck on a ratty sneaker lace, and four barefoot boys leap side-by-side into a line, left foot forward. "Uno!" Hugo barks. The boys all extend a left, perfectly synchronized. "Dos!" The boys step forward, execute a left-right combination. "Tres!" The boys fill the air with a whirring series of hooks, jabs, uppercuts, and Hugo keeps counting all the way to twenty-two, orchestrating a seamlessly choreographed display of any and all fistic options. The boys look to be twelve years old.

Hugo exits, returns to his office, and sits down again behind a small desk. He removes his hat, placing it on the desk near his left hand. It's a nice hat, a cream-colored fedora with a snappy gray and white band. Hugo is forty-eight. He has trained nine world or Olympic champions, including Casamayor, but gets little credit for that because he handled them when they were eight or nine or ten years old, and how many Little League coaches ever become legends? But the fact is, Hugo has the most important job in the Cuban sports system. He gathers the raw material. He cuts the cane. He is one of Cuba's vast network of bird dogs, one of the many scouts who sift through schools, streets, and vacant lots looking for the next Ana Quirot, the next Duque, the next Teofilo. And in 1980, he actually found him.

When I ask how, Hugo reaches into a drawer and pulls out a sheet of paper with detailed names, dates, fights. He has been waiting two decades for that question. He begins: At the time, Savon's sister Eneida was the more accomplished athlete, a volleyball player and very tall. "When I saw her size, I got curious and I pulled her aside and said, 'Do you have a brother?'" Hugo says. He is wearing a gray checked shirt. He reads down the notes, scanning with his finger. "She told me yes, but that he doesn't like boxing and neither do his parents. I asked for his age and size. I asked where he went to school. Then I got on my motorcycle and went to the school in Jamaica, and I asked the teacher there, 'Do you have any athletes?' But my secret thing was to find Savon."

Jamaica is a tiny town in the Guantanamo hills. The kids all stared at Hugo as if he were an apparition. He told them who he was, then asked the class to stand. "There he was," Hugo says. "I knew it as soon as I saw him." Hugo kept talking. He didn't want to come on too strong, so he circled. He walked over and talked to Savon's buddy about sports. He ignored Savon, then casually turned and asked if Savon liked boxing. Not really, Savon replied. But I do like that big guy who jumps over the ropes into the ring. Teofilo.

"You have to understand: Savon had been recruited already to become a rower," Hugo says. "He was just getting his paperwork together. He was all set. So I tried to talk him into it, but he said he'd only come to boxing if we'd take another of his friends. I said yes.

That kid was strong, but no good. He lasted one round and after two days he was gone."

Savon was twelve then. He began training on the sly, hoping his parents wouldn't find out. His father, also Felix, had been a superb baseball player for Guantanamo, and when he heard his son had gone into boxing he grew livid. "Very angry," Hugo says. "So I tried to discover his father's weaknesses. I found out he loves food, so I began taking him to a food-supply center and I said, 'Here, eat all you want.'" Hugo smiles at this, golden eyes sparkling behind thick glasses. A bushy mustache, a pair of mutton-chop sideburns frame his teeth. He is balding, but his face glows with the knowledge that even here, in the hills, he can figure people out.

"After about three months, the father comes to me," Hugo says. "He's never home. He's drunk. He never really cared about the boy before. But he says he's doesn't like it. I tell him: Let the boy decide. When Felix comes in, the father tells him he is forbidding him to box. And Felix tells him, 'These people treat me better than anyone, even my own father in my own house. I'm staying.'"

It didn't end there. The rowing recruiters still had their hooks in Savon's mother and she, too, tried to pull her thirteen-year-old son out of boxing. Hugo was about to surrender, to leave the boy to his parents, but Felix stopped him. "Don't go," he said. "You have to hear what I have to say." Then Felix turned to his parents and said, "Don't take me away from here. These people have become my family. I'm sick of you. I love them and I want to stay."

Hugo began working with Felix even more intensely. At the age of fourteen and a half, Savon began making a name outside Oriente, announcing himself at an exhibition in Camaguey by knocking out one opponent with a right to the chest. "The guy never fought again," Hugo says. "He got convulsions and everything." At sixteen Felix won the youth national championships, and at his next tournament, nationally televised, he won every fight by knockout. "The whole country was talking then, and the ESPA picked him up right away," Hugo says. "From then on, it's out of my hands."

Not quite. Even now, after every major fight, Savon comes home and seeks out Fernandez. The two sit and watch videotapes. Hugo critiques. "He doesn't want to hurt opponents enough," he says. "I don't know if it's in his heart. That's something I insist on: Just go in the ring and beat the shit out of the guy and that's it. You can't be nice." He doesn't feel Savon is Cuba's best. He refuses to say who is.

I ask Hugo why so many greats emerge from Oriente. He lights a cigarette, holds it over his hat, streaming smoke. His red eyeglass frames are too big for his gaunt face, his chest sinks when he sits.

"That's complicated," he says. "This is farm country. People work here from the time they are three years old. They carry water miles to their houses. There are salt mines here, and that's good for the skin, toughens it. The terrain is broken; you have to go up and down, work your legs a lot, and it's high and it's hot and the people are hot-tempered. Explosive. Very brave.

"Plus, the technical development in sports has been tremendous over the years. The country has put a lot of effort into it. So the athlete is used to working, and we teach that sport is all about tactics, psychology, and discipline. Everything is based on perfecting each of those aspects, and the results are obvious. Anyone who gets stopped along the way? There are fifteen to twenty more waiting to take their place."

Dozens of faces hover outside the office, watching Hugo talk. He has been in boxing twenty-eight years, and just as I'm starting to wonder what he is doing here, in the first place I've ever been that qualifies for the term "middle of nowhere," Hugo says that last year he got the opportunity to go to Colombia and make some money and coach there. But he did too fine a job. Three of his fighters won gold in a major junior competition, beating Cuban fighters each time. After two and a half months, the regime yanked him back home. He had no time to make any cash. He had no say in any of it. His mouth twists, he changes the subject. Would we like to see the gym again?

Hugo places his hat on his head. We follow him next door. He points to one boy, shirtless, shoeless, and wearing shorts with a broken zipper. "I predict he will win gold in 2008." He pulls two ragged yellow pieces of foam onto his hands and holds them up; another boy begins dancing, jabbing. "To the right!" Hugo says. "Go to the right!"

Suddenly the floor clears. Hugo wants a fight. He calls two brothers, fourteen-year-old Rainiel Rodriguez and thirteen-year-old Yunielky, and they tug on the gloves and headgear. Both are lean and sharply defined, already looking like little men. He blows his whistle. The two boys circle, their soles sliding along ceramic tile, trading well-aimed shots. Both know exactly what they are doing. But it's clear Yunielky is intimidated. He's very game, but his brother's size and older-brotherness is too much; he keeps finding himself trapped or backing up. Between rounds, the 2008 champ goes corner to corner, pouring water down the competitors' throats. At the end of three, Hugo holds up both boys' hands, and the kids and adults crowding the wall unleash a raucous round of applause.

Hugo introduces both boys, and after Yunielky he adds, "He's an artist, too." When I arch an eyebrow, Hugo sends Yunielky back to the center of the floor. I don't know what to expect. Yunielky holds a Coke bottle full of water. He is wearing green-and-white shorts. He's still breathing heavily. Then he begins to sing.

His voice is strong. Yunielky begins a simple Mexican tune about a girl with a blue backpack that he's fallen for. He has a square handsome face, and as he struggles with fatigue and this new demand on his lungs, a thick vein springs to the surface of his neck, bulging. The room has gone church silent. He keeps on: The girl with the blue backpack doesn't notice him and now he can't sleep, can't eat, can't read, can't write, and what should be a bubble-gum ditty about puppy love has transformed into an odd test of endurance. Yunielky isn't going to stop. All I want is to see your eyes, he sings in perfect time and pitch, but the voice is not boyish. It rises and rises, louder toward the finish, a harsh tenor speaking of dust, heat, manhood coming. I'm taken aback. I came to talk boxing but now, at the most unexpected moment, I go cold and speechless. This is it: the pure thing, the essence. Now I have seen *duende* twice.

Hugo stands to one side, away from the other EIDE workers. He shakes his head. Abruptly, under his breath, he says, "I've created so much glory for Cuban boxing, and look what they have me doing . . . up here in a sugar-mill town. . . ." Then he is surrounded by parents and officials. We all head for the door. In the dirt street a new red tractor rumbles past, trailed by two white oxen dragging a boy riding a tire. Hugo says goodbye. Victor thanks him for his grace in hard times. "Hard?" Hugo says. "You don't know how hard things are in Cuba. I might not be here when you come back. But if there's anything you can do for the kids, do it."

It's late. We hurtle down the dirt road, bounce onto the highway to Guantanamo and the start of our long rush back to Havana. We pass a line of soldiers, green head-to-toe, hiking single-file at roadside. Victor salutes, and without breaking stride one man places a hand in the crotch of his arm, clenches his fist, and drives it skyward in the universal gesture of "Up yours." I can't say I blame him. Victor laughs, I laugh. The men march on.

I take the wheel outside Santiago, and Victor soon realizes he has made a costly error. I am a horrible driver under the best conditions, aggressive and inept, but a dark Cuban highway exaggerates both my declining eyesight and a tendency to react out loud. Victor is hoping to relax, maybe even sleep. But the road is full of ghosts tonight—walkers stepping onto the pavement to wave down a ride, bikes veering into my path when they hear the car gaining—and every time Victor shuts his eyes, he's jerked awake by my abrupt "What the . . . ?" or a shuddering slam on the brake. He bolts upright expecting a wreck, a pothole, his own bloody death. But there's never anything to see, of course, nothing there except me peering over the wheel and the fading scent of gringo panic.

After an hour Victor can't take it anymore, and he demands a switch. We roll into Las Tunas and stop at a restaurant of surprising charm. The waiter hands us a two-page menu and says he only has two choices: spaghetti or beef. We take the beef. We also order beer, and notice that Havana's crackdown is Las Tunas' gain. Each table is full of old men and young girls in Day-Glo, except the one occupied by five *jineteras*. A half-dozen Italians stroll in, and within minutes a new dance begins. One, face wrinkled and rounded like a chimp, buys a rose and hands it to a giant black girl in braids. The girls jump to their feet, the other Italians grab stray chairs and commandeer the biggest table. Everyone pairs up. The air fills with the flirty nonconversation of strangers on the make.

The chimp is the last to sit, but there's no chair there: His ass hits the cement, his feet address the ceiling, the girls and all his friends explode in a cackling uproar. He scrambles to his seat hoping a speedy recovery will convince everyone his humiliation never happened, but that's all they can talk about. They've had this bonding moment, unscripted and good for an easy laugh. He sits and smiles, hiding his teeth.

The beef comes, grisly and unchewable. I wonder about the girl who'll end up fucking him. The chimp will never forgive her now.

Chapter 15

If the Cuban people are hungry, they will throw Castro out.

—Dwight D. Eisenhower, January 1960

Half an hour outside of Camaguey, we pick up our first hitch-hiker. It is 11:15 Thursday morning, December 17, but this winter sun knows neither time nor season. It beats down like a bully, assaulting the travelers clustered on the roadside skirts of the sugar-mill town of Florida, so we hump it off the highway and stop, idling. A young woman comes running, thin arms stiffened by two gym bags seemingly brimming with lead. She wrestles them into the back, clambers in, and my nose instantly fills with an overpowering odor, rich and sour. I wonder if this is just her, and as she tells us she's headed to Havana I wonder if I can endure five hundred kilometers of stench. Her name is Margarita. She is a schoolteacher, and she is going to Havana to sell eighty-one pounds of cheese. She has a thick blond mustache, thick black hair, a thick wall of defiance caked over her face. The smell of cheese dissipates with the wind.

Margarita had been standing on the highway for four hours, waiting for a car to stop. She does this twice a month: buys fifteen blocks of cheese from a farmer for 10 pesos apiece, calls in sick to school, gets up at 5:40 in the morning, takes a bus seven kilometers to the highway, settles there to wait. If a ride comes, she takes a day—maybe two—to get to Havana, sells the cheese for 18 pesos a block, then finds a ride back to Florida. If everything goes perfectly, she completes the whole process in two days. Sometimes it takes a week. Sometimes she comes to the highway, waits five hours without a ride, and goes home again; sometimes she can go days without a car stopping. For this, Margarita clears 120 pesos in pure profit—$5.21.

She has been running cheese for a year. She is twenty-two years old, the youngest of five, and lives at home with her father, a truck driver. She went to a technical school in Camaguey and has been teaching three years; her salary is 148 pesos a month. The highest-paid teacher makes 162 pesos. She is very pretty, with huge brown eyes. No, she says, she has never once been mistreated by any of the strangers who pick her up. Only once has she even heard of such a thing; Cuba is notoriously harsh on sexual offenders.

We spin past Ciego de Avila, and a Fidel billboard: "Socialism or Death: We Will Win!" Margarita starts talking about all the *extranjeros*, how they come in and think they can just buy people like rice. "I don't like foreigners," she says. I consider this a brave declaration, considering how quickly we are getting her to Havana. I decide I like her very much. Victor stops to shoot some cane fields, and a driver from across the road comes over to ask if he can siphon some gas. He sticks a rubber hose into our tank, kneels down on the highway, and sucks until his cheeks cave. Nothing happens.

I take the wheel for a while. I nearly crash, but veer back onto the highway at the last second in a cloud of dirt and curses.

We stop at a Servi for gas. I buy a bar of Cadbury chocolate, wide as a brick and stale. I break off two squares, turn and hand the bar to Margarita. She shakes her head, but I insist. I hold it closer to her face. She takes the chocolate, breaks off a piece, then rewraps the foil around the bar and shoves it in her bag. She places the piece on her tongue, and turns to stare at nothing out the window.

"I never talked to him," Pedro Jova says of defector Rolando Arrojo. "The guy never even called me and they think we talked, and for that I lost my whole future, all my chances. They took away my greatest ambition—managing the national team. You have to understand: To just play organized baseball in Cuba is an honor, to play in the National Series is a great honor, to play on the national team is a dream. But to manage the national team is the greatest honor, accomplishment, expression any Cuban man can have. And I was right there."

The weakened light sifts through window curtains, the balcony door. An occasional car rumbles past in the street below. It is late afternoon now in downtown Santa Clara. Margarita is down with the car, parked on the sidewalk, guarding her cheese.

Victor and I have been here before. Back in March, we'd come looking for Pedro Jova during the days when everyone feared his son, Maikel, had been drowned with Toca and the rest of the baseball rafters at sea. He wasn't here then, but his wife conjured up a portrait of a man already in the clutches of mourning—if not for a death, then for the life he'd had with his only son. Pedro was out walking the streets, she said, mumbling, "Why did he do this to me?" Pedro refused to speak to anyone—not even her—until he heard Maikel's voice again.

We came again just a few days ago, on our way out from Havana to Santiago, buzzing the downstairs bell of this second-floor apartment set on a narrow street in the Villa Clara capital. No one answered. Today was our last shot.

I had to see him. When the panic swept through Cuban baseball like a flood in the summer of 1996, it bred distrust and destroyed careers, stranding men who are still waiting for the water to recede. But no one got hit harder than Pedro Jova. Everyone from Valle to young Yasser Gomez's mother points to him as the prime example of what happens when you run afoul of the regime. When I spoke to then-baseball commissioner Domingo Zabala in late 1995, not long after those four exhibition losses to the United States, he jovially and presciently assured me that everyone, from himself to Linares to then-manager Jorge Fuentes, had a head on the chopping block. If improvement didn't come, they'd all be sacked. When I asked for a list of who might replace Fuentes should that day come, Zabala gave me just one name: Jova.

Many believe him to be the best baseball mind in Cuba. That same year, Pedro had won his third straight National Series championship as manager of Villa Clara. Just forty-one years old, the former longtime national team shortstop had single-handedly built a new powerhouse in Cuban baseball, riding Toca's bat and Arrojo's arm and the day-in, day-out heroics of Victor "El Loco" Mesa to the sport's pinnacle. Everyone else who has been banned at least had his shot at Olympic glory, at a world title, at becoming a Cuban hero. Jova was just about to get his first taste. Instead he became the cartoon straight man, mouth open, ready to bite into a soon-to-be-swiped dessert. "I was the number one candidate," Jova says. "I know I was the man for the job. It was my turn. But then the sanction happened ... and who knows what will happen now?"

It's about 4 P.M., time to head out to the ballpark. But Jova has nowhere to go. When we buzzed, some long minutes passed before his bald head popped over the balcony. He waved us upstairs without surprise; we interrupted nothing. A crucifix fashioned out of a palm leaf hangs on the apartment door. He leaves it standing wide open.

Pedro reclines in a chair in his spacious living room. His wife is out. He wears blue sweatpants with C-U-B-A stripped down the side, a white T-shirt, a pair of black-and-white Nikes. His face is seamless and handsome; only the folds on the back of his neck and a weariness behind the eyes give up his age. Pedro is forty-four now. His only son is gone. Old friends don't call anymore. When you mention his name on the street, the inevitable reaction is, "Jova? The guy who got banned?"

Two months after Arrojo defected and Cuba won its Olympic gold medal but hardly dominated, Jova was serving as an assistant coach with the national team during a training session in Mexico. On September 20, 1996, authorities claim, Pedro received a phone call there from Arrojo, then in Costa Rica trying to arrange residency and his upcoming free agency. Pedro denies the call, but it's beside the point: "There's no way they should do this to me because I talked to a player," he says. They did. On July 27, 1997, Jova found himself banned from baseball for life along with five other players and coaches—all members of his Villa Clara team—for, as the official release put it, "communication with traitors to Cuban baseball."

His son Maikel was sixteen then, a star outfielder with the junior national team. He didn't like what happened to his father, a man who'd left the country two dozen times before and never hinted at defecting. He didn't like the idea of waiting years for a chance to play overseas, waiting like his dad for a chance that may never come. Early in March 1998, Maikel boarded the raft with Toca and the rest, and headed into the ocean. For ten days, no one knew whether the rafters were alive or dead. Pedro was rushed three hours west to a Havana hospital with chest pains, then spent a week being treated for hypertension.

"It was very tough for me," Pedro says. "It still is."

The rafters eventually turned up safe on March 22, and were sent to a Nassau detention center. Just a few days after that, I read in *Granma* that Pedro's ban had been lifted. Jova smiles when I say this.

"I didn't hear it had been lifted until May," he says. "And they didn't tell me. I read it later in the newspaper." To this day, he doesn't know why he has been reinstated. "No explanation," he says. "Nothing."

The authorities busted Pedro down to coaching twelve-year-olds, then after a time he began handling older teenagers. His son, and the rest of the ballplayers, were returned to Cuba on May 21. When he first saw him again, Pedro asked Maikel if he would try again to escape. Maikel swore he never would set foot in another boat. "But in my heart I knew he was going to try," Pedro says.

Maikel disappeared again on August 5 with another group, and for eight days no one knew whether they had survived. Pedro sat on his balcony, in his garage, quiet and thinking. His boy had such a powerful arm, a better glove, than he ever had. Pedro takes credit for that; he took Maikel with him everywhere when he managed Villa Clara, and the young boy would work out with the players as if he belonged. Yet Maikel always got nervous when his father, his teacher, watched him play. So Pedro would hide far up in a corner of the stands where his son couldn't see, and view him just as a father and be proud. Maikel, he was sure, would be a great player one day. "It just filled me with joy to watch him," Pedro says. Pedro waited for the news. Finally, on August 13, he heard on American radio station that Maikel had turned up safe in Nicaragua.

Relief became loss. "There's a tremendous void now," Pedro says. "It's never going to be filled."

A telephone, wires exposed, occupies one corner of the living room. The two speak often. Pedro tells Maikel to watch his weight, work hard, and remember what he has sacrificed. Because he was first banned for talking to Arrojo, I ask if he's worried that the regime might ban him again for speaking to this latest traitor to Cuban baseball. "They can't stop it," Pedro says. "If they're going to ban me again, fine. There's no way they can stop me from talking to my son."

So far, he has suffered no reprisals for that. In fact, Pedro has been promoted. He now works for INDER in Villa Clara as one of three men charged with monitoring National Series player hotels, umpires, on-field behavior, and stadium conditions. As he sits, one leg folded over another, I notice that his left sneaker has a gaping gray hole in the sole. I ask Pedro about the state of the Cuban game. He has no doubt more ballplayers will be like Maikel, put their lives at stake and gamble with the sea.

"A lot more, because now they all know there's money to be made," he says. "El Duque, Ordoñez, Francisco Santiesteban—those players weren't even the greatest here, and they're so rich. That opened the eyes not only of the best guys left behind, but the rest, too.

"Somewhere in the system, they have to come up with the support. The Cuban player is so talented. But some players are making 50 pesos, some 75, some 100 a month. The average is 160. What can you do with that? And then you have family? Even the superstars are making just 250 pesos: What can you do with that?"

I ask about Valle's anxiety, his complaint that there aren't enough jobs to reward every retiring star. "The system is worn out," Pedro says. "There has to be more recognition for what these guys have done. There's no room for all of them. What are they going to do? I'm very proud of what I've done with the sport, but I don't know about the future. I know I'll be back in baseball, but for how long? I could get hurt again. I spent thirty years in baseball and I was chopped out overnight. In this country, you can get hurt anytime. Anything can happen."

He envies his son. That is clear. Sooner or later, Maikel will be playing ball in the States, with a chance to be great and make a living—"something I never had." But Pedro doesn't want there to be any misunderstanding. The core of who he is hasn't been touched. He carries himself within an immense calm, the eye of his own hurricane, and in his quiet he commands a fierce dignity. Occasionally his eyes lose focus, as if he has stepped out of the conversation to go see about something better. "I feel very strong, very rich about myself as a man," Pedro says. "But I feel pretty empty about what I've gotten out of my life."

Yet Pedro believes—no, hopes—the system might play fair. He believes that by next year he'll be back in the National Series, perhaps as a coach. Perhaps, in time, he'll even be back managing Villa Clara. I think of Jose Ramon Cabrera, banned and dead and unredeemed, and I ask if he believes the regime will ever give him a chance to manage the national team.

"That's going to be tougher," Pedro Jova says. "That'd be like admitting a mistake."

Outside Villa Clara, Victor pulls over to take a picture of a Fidel billboard, awash in the prime tender light of dusk. I take the wheel again. Margarita says, "You're going to let him drive?"

I come upon Havana from behind, taking a series of impossibly dark highways until she directs me into the dim, crumbly neighborhood of Managua. Time for the cheese exchange. A couple pushes a baby carriage with a small, religious statue propped inside. "The feast of St. Lazaro," Victor says. "If the saint wants to go for a walk, you take him for a walk."

I turn down an alley behind a three-story home with high fences and a pack of yapping dogs. A shirtless man with a beer belly wanders out, her regular connection. He owns a pizza parlor nearby. But this time there's a problem. Margarita has never come with this much cheese before, and he doesn't have the money. The two disappear into his garage with the gym bags, and loud voices snap back and forth from inside. She emerges a half-hour later, empty-handed. Now she'll have to come back in the morning. She trusts him. He has never cheated her before.

Margarita gets out at a corner, glad to be rid of us, and I head toward Parque Central for a phone. We'd called Little Daddy a few days ago from Santiago in the vague hope that he could track down Vinent in Havana before he left, but I'm not expecting much. I'm sure the boxer has started back to Santiago, that I've just missed him again. We walk into the lobby of the Plaza, me to go to the bathroom and Victor to make the call.

When I come out, Victor says, "Little Daddy has got Vinent. He says he found him an hour after we called, and that Vinent put off his trip back to see us. He was kind of crazy. He kept asking me why we didn't call back. He kept saying, 'I've been holding onto this guy for two days!' We've got to go see him now."

The glow of a twelve-inch television spills out onto the pavement, fluttering and providing the block with its only source of light. Our Toyota leans off the sidewalk; kids swarm around it like curious pigeons to seed, then move on. Little Daddy is laughing. We stand next to a ground-floor apartment in the stricken black neighborhood of Jesus-Maria. It is 9:30 P.M., and now around the corner come two men, the first no more than five-foot-eight and clad in blue jeans, a white Gucci T-shirt, and a denim jacket, the second huge and looming: yet another lightweight-heavyweight tandem. The first steps forward, and the glow reveals his face: the same face I saw in a photo at Los Olmos, as somber and unyielding as an Easter Island monument. Hector Vinent shakes hands, scans my features. This is, I realize, my Stanley-and-Livingstone moment, but I have nothing pithy to say.

I tell him I've waiting to meet him for a long time, that I've spoken with Casamayor and Garbey in the States, that I'd like to talk with him soon. Vinent nods, and says he'll do it only if we don't involve INDER. He stands on the balls of his feet, leans in, and as we talk I wonder whether he has ever taken a backward step. He keeps shifting his eyes from me to Little Daddy to Victor, measuring us for trust. He is a man in trouble. He has too much energy. He stuffs his hands in the pockets of his jeans, bobs his head slightly, vibrates with the air of someone trying very hard to keep himself contained. He nods again. Tomorrow, he says. The two men turn, dissolve into Jesus-Maria, vanish.

An hour later, Valle sits on a high stool at the tiny bar on his front porch in Guanabo. His face has gone puffy, his eyes gleam red. "I cry a lot today," he says. "My sister's operation was very bad." I put a hand on his shoulder, but he smiles weakly and says, "No, but tomorrow's my birthday. Don't worry, be happy man!"

Valle will be thirty-six. To prove he's not down, he stands up and begins doing windup imitations: Maddux, John Smoltz, San Diego's Trevor Hoffman, and his piece de resistance: El Duque. He yanks the invisible hat low over his forehead, wipes his hand on his face, peers in with a comical imitation of Orlando Hernandez's most befuddled squint. Valle jerks his left leg up high like a crane, dips his chin down behind it, and whips his right arm around in a three-quarter sidearm—the very same windup that helped the New York Yankees win a World Series. Victor and I shout out our recognition—Perfect! That's him!—and Valle grins over his little success. El Duque may be gone, but Cuba does have the next best thing. Valle is always happy to entertain.

Heading for Havana the next morning, I'm in the passenger seat wondering if Vinent will show when I glance at a group of five men hovering at roadside. I stare, squint as we buzz past, try to be sure at 120 kilometers an hour: There, glasses glinting, dressed from head to toe in white, is Charles Hill. The rest of the men wear the shorts and sandals and energized expressions of obvious tourists, but Hill gazes calmly at the sky. I can't tell if they're waiting for a bus, hitchhiking, stretching their legs. It doesn't matter. We're late. And in the six seconds it takes to sight, recognize, and register the whole tableau, we are already long gone.

The Friday, December 18 edition of *Granma*—"Ahh," Valle said when it landed in his yard, just eight pages bound tight in a rubber band, "the *Washington Post*"—informs me that Omar Luis, in a pitching duel against fellow national teamer Ormary Romero, fired a masterpiece last night to shut out Santiago at Moncada Stadium, 3-0, and even his record at 4-4. He allowed just five hits over nine innings, struck out eight men on the road against a hot team—all in all, a sparkling return to form. I wish I'd been there to see it. But I've got an appointment to keep.

For 350 years men have stood here, on the ramparts of Havana's famed El Morro fortress, and studied the horizon, casting their eyes across the Florida Straits to find the enemy. First came the Spanish to conquer the Indians in the fifteenth century, then French pirates in the sixteenth, then the British to tunnel under these walls and take Havana in the eighteenth, then the Spanish again until they surrendered in the nineteenth, then the Americans. Now, as the twentieth century limps through its final year, Cuba's battle is mostly with itself: Who stays? Who goes? Who gets pushed? Who jumps? Hector Vinent huddles in a tiny cul-de-sac where the guns of the fortress once stood, his back to the sea. On the broad and sloping shelf behind his head lie a few dozen shattered nutshells, bleached now, victims of a high fall from the beak of a gull intent on the meat inside. Gray waves pound the rocks below. He is firm in this one resolve. He will not get on a raft.

"Never," he says. "No way. I don't want to risk my life. Nothing is worth that."

So maybe it will have to be smugglers, coming by speedboat. Or maybe . . . or maybe. He mulls the options. Everything is in play. In the winter of 1998, Vinent is only one step short of where El Duque was in the winter of 1997. He has been banned from the national team and banished to Santiago, and if he isn't ready to take that last desperate step, Vinent is very close.

"I've got no money, no clothes, no food," he says. "I can't offer anything to my baby. They're squeezing me bad."

We met at 11 A.M. on the edge of Parque Central: Little Daddy, Vinent's heavyweight friend, Victor, me. I bought Vinent lunch at a paladar, and afterward he said he wanted to talk alone. State Security, he said, is "still chasing me, watching me." He hunched in the middle of the Toyota's backseat, and directed us out past the billboard on the Malecon reading, "We Don't Want Slaveowners Here," to the tunnel under Havana Bay, out again into the rich cool 1 P.M. sunshine. He pointed us up the drive to El Morro, and his timing couldn't have been better. The old fort and lighthouse is Havana's

Eiffel Tower, but the midmorning tour buses have come, spilled their tourists, and gone. The place is deserted.

Vinent is twenty-five. He began fighting at Los Olmos at thirteen, and quickly impressed coaches with his patience, his coolness and wits. He liked to win big. Their commonalities are obvious, but one vital difference between Duque and Vinent is that Duque was an unknown quantity when he defected; he had performed brilliantly in Cuba but not on the world stage. But Vinent has established himself as one of the era's great amateur athletes. At eighteen, he won his first Olympic gold medal as a light welterweight in Barcelona, blitzing the field by an embarrassing combined score of 91-13 and winning the final 11-1. After 1992, he dominated the division, winning the world title at Tampere, Finland, in 1993 and Berlin in 1995, and repeatedly making his closest rival, a fine Turk named Nurhan Suleymanoglu, look inept. When challenged by Fernando Vargas—one of today's most talented pros—with an early deficit and a bloody lip in a 1995 match in Macon, Georgia, Vinent worked himself, the computer scoring system, and the clock to frightening perfection, battling back in the final thirty seconds to win by a point. Vargas immediately moved out of the weight class. Vinent went on to win another gold in Atlanta, hammering his opponents 81-27 along the way and beating the demoralized Suleymanoglu 23-1, and then punishing Germany's Oktay Urkal in the final, 20-13.

"Vinent's very sharp, has a good pro style," Al Mitchell, Team USA's boxing coach at the 1996 Olympics, told me later. "Lupe Suazo was our number one fighter and he could fight, but when he got in the ring with Vinent you could see he was way behind him, a C-class fighter versus an A-class fighter. Vinent is excellent. He circles, makes you make mistakes and then makes you pay. He's smart." Jesse Ravelo, a trainer for the same U.S. team, went into the

'96 games believing Ariel Hernandez was the best pound-for-pound fighter in the world. But now, he said, "Vinent would be a better pro. He'd be a helluva pro. He's a little different than most Cuban boxers: Most like to work the computer scoring, hit and go. But he's very aggressive."

Hernandez outweighs Vinent by twenty-six pounds, but hates sparring with him. "If I get too close, he'll kill me," Ariel told me the week before. "He's superb tactically, and he loves to fight. When he's well-prepared, there's nobody in the world who can beat him."

But in Atlanta, just as Vinent was cementing his place atop the sport, the forces that would bring him down began to swirl. His best friends on the national team, Casamayor and Garbey, defected on the eve of the Atlanta games, and from there, he says, "things got very ugly for me." Rumors circulated that Vinent had introduced the two fighters to their defection connection, perhaps had even orchestrated the whole thing, and was even then somehow arranging to have heavyweight Alexis Rubalcaba jump during the Olympics. Vinent found himself under constant surveillance by Cuban security in Atlanta. He denies having anything to do with Casamayor or Garbey, but he certainly knew about their plans. I ask why he didn't defect himself then.

"I got scared," Vinent says. "I didn't think I could be a champion over there in the States, and I didn't want my mother and my family to suffer for it." Someone, he says, told the Cuban authorities they were going to send a boat to pry Vinent out of Cuba, "and since then, they've really come down on me. I have no life."

He didn't help his cause. Vinent struggled for years to make weight—one friend saw his meal card at the end of a five-day tournament in the mid-nineties; it had been stamped just once—and Vinent returned home determined to move up to welterweight. He was warned against this by boxing officials, but Vinent put on the pounds anyway. He was sanctioned for disobedience. "That was fair," he says. But then in June 1997, Vinent says, he was abruptly told he'd been removed from the national team, banned from La Finca and sent to Santiago.

"They didn't tell me why," he says. "They just told me they were taking me off the national team until I changed my conduct. I asked, 'Why are you doing this to me? I haven't gone anywhere. Do you think I'm going to go?' But they just said it was because of my 'conduct.' They think I have a conduct problem because they think I'm going to run any chance I get. They don't know I'm going to run, but they think it. That's my 'conduct' problem."

The '97 World Championships in Budapest came and went, then the '98 Playa Giron national championships in Sancti Spiritus, then the '98 Goodwill Games. No Vinent. By June he had dropped out of the world rankings entirely, disappeared. "I feel abandoned," Vinent says. "I've got nothing. Zero. Anything I get, I get on the streets. There's no future in this country. There's no future for me now while I'm considered a good boxer. Imagine what it's going to be like when I'm retired."

He has only one choice. Vinent must do what he has always done. He must dominate in the ring. He must fight his way back into the regime's good graces, change his life with his fists or not at all. So he has been training diligently in Santiago at welterweight, and he plans on taking part in the '99 Playa Giron championships next month. He will fight for the city of Santiago, not as a member of the national team, and be so impressive that the regime has no choice but to reinstate him.

"I'll win it," Vinent says. "I have to."

He sits on the stone with his hands folded in his lap, the brass buttons on his denim jacket winking in the sun. Vinent has a two-year-old daughter. He wonders often about the pro game. He has become convinced that his earlier fear was unjustified; the success of other defectors in the United States, plus the mediocre pro fights he's seen on TV, have boosted his confidence. "A lot of people just fight, but I'm more than that," Vinent says. "I'm a boxer." His eyes are the usual Cuban cocktail of spidery veins and yellowed whites, and his face has begun to harden into the typical mask of stony resignation. His skin has gone pale from dryness, flaking; he looks like a man sprinkled with ashes. One set of eyelashes curls oddly to the lid.

A blue-and-white freighter chugs a few miles off the coast. I write it all down, everything I see, hoping in my questions and furious scribbling to cover up how shaken I am. I can't decide which is more awe-inspiring—Vinent's confidence or his desperation—and, truth be told, I had made no provision for either. By the end, my search for Vinent had become a kind of game, a way to show myself that I could prevail over both the regime and the plodding inefficiencies of Cuban life; I'd been so caught up in the chase I hadn't much thought about what he might actually say if I found him. But now it's clear: Here's another man pushed too far, farther than anyone I've met on the island, for Vinent risks plenty by telling what he tells me and he doesn't care. He is sure he will win, and in that surety he gives the Cuban sports machine an odd and high compliment. For Vinent has one weapon—the knowledge and confidence that years of coaching and nurturing gave him. His skill is one of the system's indisputably great achievements. It is so great that Vinent believes he can use it to beat the system itself.

The national team will take a European tour after Playa Giron, and then there's the '99 Pan Am Games this summer in Winnipeg.

Vinent thinks about little else: He is sure that all his answers lie in winning Playa Giron. "That's all I've got," Vinent says. The whole world will be watching, he is sure. The Cuban people will be asking questions. "If it doesn't happen, it's going to be the lowest point in my life," Vinent says, then he repeats himself, softer now. "I have to win. I have to."

And if he doesn't? Or worse: If he does win and still doesn't gain a spot on the national team?

"If they don't call me up after January, I'm going to go to the president of INDER and say, 'Why are you making me eat dirt? Why are you doing this to me? How much longer am I going to have to pay for something I've never done?'"

He is in an impossible place. As it was with El Duque, the regime's suspicions could well push Vinent into someday making them all come true. Cornered by an ingeniously paranoid circle of logic—because we fear you'll defect, we'll make your life miserable so you'll defect and confirm our fear—he figures he has this one chance to reset his life. And if his fists and the president of INDER and the grumbling of the Cuban people don't prevail and give him a place on the national team, Vinent plans to take his case all the way to the top. "If it doesn't work out then," he says, "I'm going to have to talk to Fidel."

Victor takes Vinent away to snap some photographs: Vinent on the battlements, Vinent in a doorway, Vinent with his face in his hands, knuckles chipped and shiny. I go wandering over the walls, past all the old cannon, cold and rusted. A motor scooter purrs near the guard shack. The sound of laughing rides over the grass, followed by a middle-aged couple on vacation. They glance at me, then duck into a doorway and kiss. The man pulls out a camera. A perfect picture to show the friends back home.

Victor and Vinent come walking up toward the car. To the west, I can see the city's knobby skyline swinging along the Malecon. Victor says, "He wants to ask you something."

I look at Vinent. He's studying the ground. He doesn't seem like he could hurt anyone. He says he'll be returning to Santiago this weekend on the overnight train.

"Please," he says. "Could you give me some money?"

POSTSCRIPT

The last days present the usual mix: elation, bureaucratic posturing, terror. Manuel Zayas calls a meeting for Saturday evening, and over a beer in the lobby of the Plaza he demands to know how we could do what we have done. He does not smile. His face tightens. It has come to his attention that we never registered, paid $60, and took photos for press cards—a simple act with grave consequences. His superiors are furious again. We probably will never again be allowed in Cuba. Olga will certainly be sanctioned and may well lose her job. This has never happened to me before, he says. You went all over the island and nobody knew where to find you. "You have penetrated an invulnerable system," he says. Then he shakes hands and leaves.

The drive out on the Via Blanca to Guanabo begins with recriminations (How could we forget the press cards?), skates to nervousness (What will they do to Olga?), and finally fury (How can they blame Olga? Who cares about press cards?). Victor plants the Toyota in the fast lane and keeps it whining at 130 kilometers per, but we're not paying attention and we're jabbering about the regime and Zayas and there, suddenly, thirty yards off but bearing down fast, a lone headlight rockets right toward our faces. There's just enough time to yell. Victor wrenches the steering wheel to the right, and the motorcycle blasts by. The rider doesn't flinch, doesn't deviate an inch, as if determined to carve some straight line in the wrong lane all the way to Havana, daring the world to take him on in the ultimate game of chicken. "Papi, did you see that?" Victor shouts. "He didn't even care. That guy was coming right for our windshield, and he just didn't give a fuck."

We shake it off, shower, head back. Ana Quirot has invited us out for dinner. We roll up forty minutes late, expecting a large group, but only Ana Fidelia and her masseuse stand waiting in the lobby. Ana Fidelia is wearing a tight, black velvet catsuit. She directs us through the tunnel under Havana Bay and up to El Morro for the second time in two days, then down past La Cabana, the notorious fortress where Batista once tortured enemies and Che set up headquarters. I wonder if Vinent has started back to Santiago.

We leave the Toyota with a valet, stroll past a perfectly decorated Christmas tree and into an expensive, open-air restaurant called La Divina Pastora. It is a gorgeous night, breezy and cool. We order the seafood plate. The huge black form of a tanker enters the bay's narrow throat, glides past. The food is delicious. A four-piece band serenades us with old songs as we slice the fish. Word passes from seat to seat, people turn to look; I'd forgotten how reverently Ana Quirot is regarded now. Men come to the table dripping admiration and pity, ask for autographs, ask whether she'll run in Sydney. Ana Fidelia smiles and thanks them and doesn't answer.

The night spins on. We stop in a club called the Winking Cat, where the doorman is the only one who doesn't recognize Ana Quirot and the manager grovels and we leave. We stop in a bright new bar off the Melia Cohiba called Cafe Habana, where a lovingly restored jalopy and old news photos and a black-and-white cutout of Hemingway allow tourists to experience an antiseptic taste of life in Cuba before the last forty years kicked into gear. I'm taken aback, and not only by the nightclub's spot-on appropriation of Hard Rock Cafe slickness. I'd always considered nostalgia an American luxury, but it makes absolutely no sense in a place where the old days are condemned as criminal. Besides, if anyone wants an idea of Havana in the 1920s, 1940s, or 1950s, all he need do is walk out to the theme park that extends through every street, park, and building, out across a nation where the plumbing is a relic and horse-drawn carriages roll and hookers can bring you back those lush Mafia days in a few breathy minutes. Cubaland is always open for business.

We hit one final spot, a piano bar upstairs in the Melia Cobiba. Mojitos flow. The room is awash in shadows and dim light. Ana Fidelia dances and laughs with her thick husky voice, and in that catsuit and some carefully applied makeup her scars disappear. An old guarachera sits on a stool, ankles swollen, and sings of love above the pounding music. Then it is 4 A.M., and we stagger into the night air, down the driveway, and across to the Malecon. Victor and I light up cigars, and we all stare into the blackness over the Florida Straits toward Miami. Ana Fidelia asks for my cigar and takes a long, sure drag, and as I watch I remember: the face of Cuba. Her eyes gleam. She blows smoke out over the waves.

I don't move. Now Ana Quirot leans in and kisses me, but before I can figure out if she's being romantic, polite, friendly, or merely thankful for a nice evening, a packed blue Lada comes careening down the sidewalk, shattering the calm. The passengers shout out abuse, we all shrink against the sea wall. The car skids over where we stood and shudders to a stop. I take it as a sign: time to head home. We hurry away, pile into the car in silence. In her dark lobby, Ana Fidelia presses the button and presses the button and waits. The elevator doesn't come. The spell is broken. She'll have to walk up.

I hibernate on Sunday in the rooftop restaurant at the Plaza, staring out over the city. A man takes off his shirt and does twenty pushups on top of the building next door. Four Germans occupy one table and pore over guidebooks. A Japanese girl writes postcards. I order an awful cup of coffee. The bar TV shows the Cuban national basketball team playing a game at Sports City. No score.

The next morning, we pack up and head for the airport. Monday's issue of *Trabajadores* reveals that all is now right in the Cuban world: The United States is being condemned for its attack on Iraq, the American Congress has decided to impeach the American president, Industriales is back in first place and Metro has sunk back into the cellar. A pitcher from the town of Granma named Ernesto Guevara threw masterfully yesterday to lift his record to 9-2: Che wins again. We pass the Havana Psychiatric Hospital, where Duque and Cabrera toiled after their banishments. A nicely tended baseball field sits out back. A slogan in white runs across the blue outfield wall: "Mental Rehabilitation Through Sports."

I spend much of the flight to Nassau—and the ensuing months—thinking about both those tourists at the Plaza and that wall, for one represents contact with capitalist values and money and the other control, and despite all predictions the regime continues to keep the two deftly balanced. The crackdown on dissent gains intensity through the spring of 1999; in February, Cuba's National Assembly enacts a harsh, all-encompassing new law designed to quell street crime, free speech, and government opposition, and in March four famous dissidents endure a show trial that draws a barrage of international condemnation. Victor makes two more visits to Havana for photographs, and on the second he is interrogated by State Security at the airport for forty-eight hours without food or water and then expelled from the country. Victor is never told the nature of his offense, but during one session glimpses a photo of us with Hector Vinent at El Morro.

Manuel Zayas was right. I won't be going back to Cuba anytime soon. So I become like half of Miami, frustrated and scrambling for the slightest scrap of news.

I hear that Vinent never fought in January's national championships. A week before the tournament, he was arrested for beating up a policeman in Santiago.

I hear that Felix Savon got beat in the championships, 4-2, by Odianiel Solis, ending his thirteen-year reign as Cuban champion.

I hear that Lazaro Valle had decided to return to pitching. Then I hear that he has been officially retired.

Then I hear he is pitching again.

I hear that Ana Quirot is pregnant.

I hear about the stop-and-go negotiations between the U.S. government and Cuba over a proposed exhibition baseball game, of course, and I watch on March 28 when the Baltimore Orioles travel to Havana for the first visit by a major league team in forty years. It is a great contest, and though unused to wooden bats the Cubans force extra innings and lose 3-2 in the eleventh. Cuban reliever Jose Contreras proves a revelation by throwing eight shutout innings and smothering slugger Albert Belle, and fans walk away overjoyed that Cuba played with the big leaguers right to the end. But the victory belongs mostly to Fidel.

The night before, Castro hosted a four-hour dinner for assorted American owners and baseball officials, and didn't shy from testing himself against the sport's brightest minds. "We talked about player development in the Dominican Republic," Sandy Alderson, an executive vice president of major league baseball, told the *New York Times*. "He's very knowledgeable. He's very big on details." After striding across the field and giving his team a pregame pep talk, Castro moved into a seat next to baseball commissioner Bud Selig. Some exiles speculate that Castro then suffered a humiliation—he had to stand respectfully during the American national anthem as

Selig bellowed the lyrics—but that assumes the power of symbol over fact. And on that day, after eight years of deprivation and defections, Fidel's sports machine—his system—again proved itself strong enough to go toe-to-toe with the number one power in the world. The U.S. government hopes such games will foster contact with the Cuban people, but only those deemed fit by the regime were allowed to attend. Fidel stood indeed for the "Star-Spangled Banner," and it was no humiliation. This is his fortieth year in power; for those who want him dead, that alone is a wrenching loss. He remains Cuba's winning pitcher.

For me, though, the game is over. Castro's country is a place best seen as a tourist, for from the distance of a decent hotel room it is easy to succumb to its charms. Go for the old cars or girls or rum, or a Cold War thrill, or a night at Kid Chocolate on a balmy winter evening, and you can convince yourself that any number of illusions are real. You can enjoy the passionate fans and the frenetic play, admire the skill, revel in the Cuban athlete's palpable joy, and allow yourself the luxury of wondering if this is the way sports were meant to be. But I'm no good for that anymore. I've talked to too many men and women not to understand that the regime will, at the slightest sign of independence, grind even its greatest lives into powder. I left Cuba in December knowing too much and, worse, knowing that there are plenty who love a romanticized vision of Cuba too dearly to listen.

After landing at the Nassau airport, Victor and I headed for customs unsure what to expect. Such are the vagaries of U.S. border guards: Sometimes they wave you through, sometimes they wonder for twenty minutes why you spent so many days in Castro's Cuba. This time, though, Victor and I got something we'd never experienced. "Cuba, eh?" said the U.S. customs officer, gray and bespectacled and bristling with energy. "Oh, yeah, what about that literacy rate before the revolution? And childhood hunger and infant mortality? . . . Oh, yeah, sure, it was far better in the good old days, wasn't it?"

I blinked at the sudden onslaught of sarcasm. It took a moment to regain my bearings. The U.S. customs official rolled his eyes and muttered on about the embargo, about American policy, and I realized that we had come upon a sheep in wolf's clothing, a U.S. government official subversively deriding his government's policy against the enemy. "Oh, no, no, no, I shouldn't say this," he said with a laugh, stamping our passports with little more than a glance. He went on to rip the Cuban exiles in Miami who left their country "because they didn't want to get in line for food," said that Noam Chomsky had it right thirty years ago and rattled on about kids starving in Guatemala while children in Cuba at least get basic nutrition. He told us how much he admires Fidel for his "big balls."

I looked around and wondered if this was some bizarre setup, but the U.S. customs officer was in no particular hurry; in fact, he was just getting warmed up. "Forty years we've been doing this to Cuba and they've survived," he said happily. "It's over! We lost!" Then he recited the regime's gains in education and health care and sports—"Oh, those ballplayers are not very good there, are they? Ha!"—and ended with a giggling flourish as he stood to take his break. "Viva la Revolucion!" he said.

I asked the U.S. customs officer if he'd ever been to Cuba himself. No, he said, I never have. But I'd really love to go sometime, yes, I'd love to go.

ACKNOWLEDGMENTS

Writing a book may be a solitary pursuit, but this project simply couldn't have happened without the great and gracious help of people on both sides of the Florida Straits. First and foremost, my profound thanks go to Mitchell Kaplan, the owner of Books and Books in Miami. I am only one of many writers for whom Mitchell has provided unselfish and unflagging support over the years, but no one feels more indebted than I. Without him, this book would never have happened.

At *Sports Illustrated,* managing editor Bill Colson and executive editor Peter Carry not only assigned the stories that helped provide much of the texture and background for the book, but also patiently allowed me the time to write and edit it.

At the Ecco Press, Daniel Halpern and Judy Capodanno provided invaluable editing, counsel, and enthusiasm.

The manuscript benefited hugely from the careful reading and advice of Bruce Schoenfeld, Don Van Natta Jr., Lizette Alvarez, Nancy Cooney, and Rafael Garcia-Navarro. I thank them all for such a generous squandering of their talents.

Cuba is a rare place, provoking an unmatched passion in those it touches. Many times, the sharing of this passion was the only force sustaining this project, and for their unwitting help I thank Steve

Fainaru, Linda Robertson, Bill Frakes, and, above all, Victor Baldizon. Victor, of course, took the photos that I am honored to have placed next to my text, but his devotion, fearlessness, insight, and caring for the people of Cuba became an incomparable touch-stone. It is the writer's lament that no words can do justice to a well-conceived photograph, and I am humbled by the truth that I can't even approach what Victor accomplishes with one snap of the shut-ter. I am proud to call him my friend.

My rudimentary Spanish carried me through many conversa-tions, but without the translating help of Victor, Chris Hunt, Angel Reyes, Keyvan Heydari, Dan Le Batard, Omar Minaya, and countless others in the States and on the island, I would've been lost. My thanks to all. Any mistakes of interpretation or nuance are mine alone.

I thank Evan Kanew for his insight into Cuban boxing and one nugget of a tip that proved to be gold. I thank Alvaro Saralegui for his company, his humor, and his kindness in accepting one clumsily proffered beer. I thank Rene Guim for his perspective. I thank liter-ary agent Steve Delsohn for his advice and expertise.

I thank Benito Bueno for his strength and spirit. He is one of the great men. Others still in Cuba know how important they have been; I leave them nameless only because they have requested it.

I thank my mother, Marilyn Price, for teaching me the art of the interview. I thank my father, George Price, for teaching me that pol-itics, culture, and sports matter. I thank my wife, Fran Brennan, for her loving endurance and unerring guidance through it all. I thank my son, Jack, my inspiration.

Most of all, though, I thank those across Cuba who treated me with a grace and generosity that I have found nowhere else in the world. The nature of this project dictated many tense moments, but the regime's disapproval never undermined the respectful treatment I received from the officials at Cubadeportes and INDER. Athletes fiercely aligned to the system, like Ana Quirot, Jose Ibar, and Victor Mesa, never allowed their beliefs to override their greater sense of hospitality, and for that I am grateful.

Lastly, I am forever indebted to the courage of people like Lazaro Valle, Pedro Jova, and Hector Vinent, who deemed it vital to speak honestly of their experiences under the most intense pressure. At century's end, my hope is that all three will soon come back to pitch, manage, and box. When and where that will be, only they should have the right to decide.